A WORLD WITHOUT ISLAM

GRAHAM E. FULLER

Little, Brown and Company

NEW YORK   BOSTON   LONDON

Little, Brown and Company
Hachette Book Group
237 Park Avenue, New York, NY 10017
www.hachettebookgroup.com

First Edition: August 2010

Little, Brown and Company is a division of Hachette Book Group, Inc.
The Little, Brown name and logo are trademarks of
Hachette Book Group, Inc.

Library of Congress Cataloging-in-Publication Data
Fuller, Graham E.
    A world without Islam / Graham E. Fuller.
      p. cm.
    Includes bibliographical references and index.
    HC ISBN 978-0-316-04119-5
    Int'l ed. ISBN 978-0-316-07288-5
    1. Islam—History.   2. Islam—Relations.   3. East and West.
4. Islamic civilization.   1. Title.
    BP50.F85 2010
    297.09—dc22   2009054078

10 9 8 7 6 5 4 3 2 1

RRD-IN

Book design by Fearn Cutler de Vicq

Printed in the United States of America

A
WORLD
WITHOUT
ISLAM

To my wife, Prue; to our remaining children,
Samantha and Melissa, and their families; and to my siblings,
David, Meredith, and Faith, and their families: they have watched
me struggle and be shaped by the fascinations, joys, complications,
and frustrations of working with and in the Muslim world,
and have provided consistent encouragement

And to those many good friends—
Muslim, Christian, and Jewish—who have touched my life
in so many ways in the course of working,
and living, in this field

———

Contents

CONTENTS

A
WORLD
WITHOUT
ISLAM

Introduction

Imagine, if you will, a world without Islam. Nearly impossible, it would seem, when images and references to Islam dominate our headlines, airwaves, computer screens, and political debates. We are inundated with terms such as *jihad, fatwa, madrasa,* Taliban, Wahhabi, *mullah,* martyr, *mujahideen,* Islamic radicals, and Shari'a law. Islam would seem to lie at the very center of the American struggle against terrorism and the long commitment to several overseas wars launched with the "Global War on Terror."

Indeed, Islam seems to offer an instant and uncomplicated analytical touchstone for most affairs in the Middle East, by which to make sense of today's convulsive world. By referring to Islam, we can reduce things to a polarized struggle between "Western values" and the "Muslim world." For some neoconservatives, "Islamofascism" is now, in fact, our chief sworn foe in a looming World War IV or "Long War"—a titanic ideological struggle that conveniently focuses on religion and seems to ignore myriad other factors that have contributed to a long-building East-West confrontation.

This book will argue the case from the opposite direction. If there had never been an Islam, if a Prophet Muhammad had never emerged from the deserts of Arabia, if there had been no saga of the spread of Islam across vast parts of the Middle East, Asia, and Africa, wouldn't the relationship between the West and the Middle East today be entirely different? No, I argue, it might actually be quite similar to what we see today.

As counterintuitive as this argument might seem at first glance, a powerful case can be made for the existence of deeply rooted geopolitical tensions between the Middle East and the West that go very far back into history indeed, predating Islam, even pre-dating Christianity. A multitude of other factors have powerfully influenced the evolution of East-West relations over a very long time: economic interests, geopolitical interests, power struggles between regional empires, ethnic struggles, nationalisms, even severe clashes within Christianity itself—all of which provide ample ground for East-West rivalries and confrontations that really have little if anything to do with Islam.

Indulge me a bit, then, as we look at the course of events between the West and the Middle East over time that provide powerful alternative explanations for the roots of today's conflict, which we often conveniently simply ascribe to "Islam." It doesn't require special knowledge of the Middle East to grasp that ties between the West—especially the United States—and the Middle East are presently dangerously skewed. What is going on? Why is the Middle East the way it is? Or the West the way it is? Without Islam, wouldn't we be spared many of the current challenges before us? Wouldn't the Middle East be more peaceful? How different might the character of East-West relations be? Without Islam, surely the international order would present a very different picture than it does today, or would it? The balance of this book aims to suggest some alternative answers to these questions.

INTRODUCTION

———

THE WEST, and especially the United States, has shown no serious or sustained interest in the Middle East until the last half century. We tend to be comfortably ignorant of the history of Western interventionism in the region over centuries — or even over a millennium. We are only superficially aware of Middle Eastern critiques of Western policies that touch on oil, finances, political intervention, Western-sponsored coups, Western support for pro-Western dictators, and carte blanche American support for Israel in the complex Palestinian problem — which, after all, had its roots not in Islam, but in Western persecution and butchery of European Jews. European powers have also exported their local quarrels and parleyed them into two world wars that were fought out partly on Middle Eastern soil, as was much of the Cold War as well. All this suggests that many other causative factors are at work that have at least as much explanatory power for the current turmoil as does "Islam."

It is not simply a matter of "blaming the West," as some readers might rush to suggest here. I argue that deeper geopolitical factors have created numerous confrontational factors between the East and the West that predate Islam, continued with Islam and around Islam, and may be inherent in the territorial imperatives and geopolitical outlook of *any* states that occupy those areas, regardless of religion.

It would, of course, be silly to suggest that Islam has had no role whatsoever in coloring elements of this East-West confrontation. Islam represents a powerful and deep culture that has exercised huge impact upon the whole Middle East and beyond. But in terms of *East-West relations*, I argue that it has primarily served as flag or banner for other, deeper kinds of rivalries and confrontations taking place.

If nothing else, I hope this examination will cause readers to rethink the nature of East-West conflict and how Americans, in particular, regard their own foreign policies. Such a process of self-examination comes hard to superpowers; they suffer from their own particular kind of isolation and myopia: possession of great power suggests a security and certitude, an ability to ignore situations that smaller states find threatening or dangerous and that they cannot afford to get wrong. International politics is not unlike the jungle: smaller and weaker animals require acute intelligence, sensitive antennae, and nimbleness of footing to assure their own self-preservation; the strong — such as elephants — need pay less attention to ambient conditions and can often do as they wish, and others will get out of the way.

Power also brings a certain arrogance: the belief that we can control the situation, we are in charge, we can persuade or intimidate with ease — or so we think. Indeed, one senior official in the Bush administration, when asked about looming realities of the wars in the Middle East, stated without a pause, "We create our own realities." The course of events of the past decade reveals how sadly true that has been.

The problem lies in the optic we employ. Washington — perhaps as many global powers have done in the past — uses what I might call the "immaculate conception" theory of crises abroad. That is, we believe we are essentially out there, just minding our own business, trying to help make the world right, only to be endlessly faced with a series of spontaneous, nasty challenges from abroad to which we must react. There is not the slightest consideration that perhaps US policies themselves may have at least contributed to a series of unfolding events. This presents a huge paradox: how can America on the one hand pride itself on being the world's sole global superpower, with over seven hundred military bases abroad and the Pentagon's huge global footprint, and yet, on the other hand, be oblivious to and unacknowledging of the magnitude of its own role—for better or for worse—as the dominant force charting the course of world events? This Alice-in-Wonderland delusion affects not just policy makers, but even the glut of think tanks that abound in Washington. In what may otherwise often be intelligent analysis of a foreign situation, the focus of each study is invariably the *other* country, the *other* culture, the negative intentions of *other* players; the impact of US actions and perceptions are quite absent from the equation. It is hard to point to serious analysis from mainstream publications or think tanks that address the role of the United States itself in helping create current problems or crises, through policies of omission or commission. We're not even talking about blame here; we're addressing the logical and self-evident fact that the actions of the world's sole global superpower have huge consequences in the unfolding of international politics. They require examination.

There is a further irony here: How can a nation like the US, which expresses such powerful outpourings of patriotism and ubiquitous unfurling of the flag on all occasions, seem quite obtuse to the existence of nationalism and patriotism in other countries? Washington never fared very well in the Cold War in understanding the motives and emotions of the nonaligned world; it dismissed or even suppressed inconvenient local nationalist aspirations, thereby ending up pushing a large grouping of countries toward greater sympathy with the Soviet Union. This was a kind of strategic blindness that viewed other nations' interests and preferences as something that needed to be hemmed in, or isolated. We have been obtuse toward nationalism and identity issues in the Middle East and have lumped it all into the basket of "Islam."

When we do not like a foreign adversary, we tend to denigrate them in strong, sometimes nearly apocalyptic terms. One less desirable aspect of democracy is that it seems to require serious demonization of the enemy if the nation and public opinion are to be galvanized sufficiently to pay a serious price in blood or treasure at war. And the message as to why we are in confrontation or at war must be simplified enough to fit on a bumper sticker.

In today's world, "Islam" has become that bumper sticker for America, the default cause of many of our problems in the Muslim world. In the past we have gone in to do battle with anarchists, Nazis, Fascists, communists—today it is "radical Islam." I put this term in quotation marks not because it does not exist, but because it is a broad and complex phenomenon that comes in various shapes and sizes and requires a wide array of differing responses. The term does not begin to present an accurate or useful description of the kinds of problems we face in dealing with the Muslim world. In even more simpleminded analyses, we sometimes hear that the problem is not "radical Islam" but really perhaps even Islam itself. Why do "they" hate us, why are they violent, why do they "hate democracy," why do they not accept America's nostrums and values, why do they engage in guerrilla war or terrorism, why do they resist American policies, why will they not accept America's best-laid plans for their futures—Islam seems to supply a ready answer.

———

ACTUALLY, in many senses there is no "Muslim world" at all, but rather many Muslim worlds, or many Muslim countries and different kinds of Muslims. Nonetheless it is important to acknowledge that under assault and siege from the West in both real and imagined ways, the Muslim world has come together to an unusual degree over past decades. Indeed, US policies over this time have probably done more to forge a common-minded *umma*—the collective international community of Muslims—than any other factor since the time of the Prophet Muhammad.

History did not begin with 9/11. Our dealings with the Middle East go back a long way. The attack on 9/11 was a violent, extremist, and outrageous act, but it was also almost a culmination of a preceding chain of events over many years. If we choose to see history beginning at 9/11 — whereby we suddenly become the sole justifiably aggrieved party, now authorized to bring vigilante justice to the world — then we will continue to do what we have been doing all along, with disastrous consequences evident to all.

———

IT IS, OF COURSE, ABSURD, in a sense, to speak of a "world without Islam." We cannot rewrite history, nor can we truly guess what would have happened in history if certain other things had not happened. In other words, once you get into theoretical, "what if" types of arguments, they open the floodgates to endless speculation. Indeed, a great many interesting books have been written on precisely these "what if" speculations: What if 9/11 had not taken place? What if the Archduke Ferdinand had not been assassinated in Sarajevo in 1914? What if Lenin had never been sent back to Russia by the Germans in a sealed railroad car on the eve of the Russian Revolution, and if the Bolshevik Revolution had never taken place? Or what if the Confederacy had won the Civil War? Would our world be dramatically different than today, or would it have ended up reasonably similar in the long run?

Such questions are inherently unanswerable. But the point of the exercise is to employ imagination to illuminate history from an alternative angle, to permit new contours and features to suddenly appear before our eyes that had previously remained unnoticed. Maybe the odds were only 51 percent that an event would turn out the way that it did. That suggests that there are 49 percent of other factors at work that did not, in the end, happen to dominate. But they were there all along and possibly still remain below the surface, exerting considerable, even if not decisive, influence on later events and may again in the future. I remember my stint as Vice Chair of the National Intelligence Council at the CIA in the 1980s in charge of long-range strategic forecasting; we occasionally employed one type of brief intellectual exercise among many that could often be analytically illuminating: to posit an important future event—however unlikely we felt it might be—and then briefly write the scenario in some detail as to how it came to pass. Assume that Saudi Arabia undergoes a radical Islamist revolution—how might it have come about, in quite specific scenarios? Assume that the Communist Party in China collapses—how might it happen and what would the process look like on a daily basis? What hidden forces, little tracked today, might rise to the fore? The purpose of such exercises is to lend flesh and substance to otherwise unthinkable or unlikely series of events; they serve to sharpen the analytical antennae to indicators of such possible events in the off chance that the "unthinkable" might come about. They represent exercises in political and social imagination, just one tool among many.

In the same spirit, this book looks at key events in the history of the Middle East and attempts to identify what forces were at work that might have had little to do with Islam, events that could have occurred in roughly similar ways without Islam. This book, in effect, shines a spotlight upon events from a completely different angle, illuminating features we perhaps did not note before. Even if you disagree with some of the assumptions and explanations, the chances are that you will not look at events in the Muslim world in quite the same way again. Other factors at work suddenly become sharper and cause us to consider them anew in our own analyses.

Inevitably many readers will offer alternative paths to the ones I have chosen—that's fine. I'm aware of having to make choices myself. Indeed, I could write a rebuttal to some of the arguments presented here, but that is not the point. The point is to reconsider our facile assumptions that Islam is what the Middle East is all about—the source of the problem and the solution—and instead attend to other deeper and systemic types of problems and issues that exist, making the Middle East what it is in the face of the West.

One point I wish to make very clear: the purpose of this book is not at all to denigrate or dismiss the role of Islam in world history. Islam has had great impact upon the world, as one of the greatest and most powerful continuous civilizations in history. No other civilization has lasted as long over such a broad expanse of the world as Islam. I have immense regard for Islamic culture, arts, sciences, philosophy, and civilization, and for Muslims as people. The world would be a much more impoverished place in the absence of Islamic civilization.

Nor do I ignore the fact that Islam has created a powerful and distinct edifice — the "Muslim world" — linking large numbers of diverse peoples, states, cultures, and climes in ways that might not otherwise be the case. This is hugely important for the peoples of that region. But the focus of interest in this book is specifically how *the relations between the West and the Middle East* would be if there were no Islam. I do not examine how the whole of the Muslim world might be different if there had been no Islam. Or what the West would have lost in the absence of Islamic culture. We look at the continuing trajectory of East-West relations. And to the extent that those relations have severely deteriorated, I argue that Islam is not the primal or even secondary causal factor — for that we have to look elsewhere. The minute we do look elsewhere, we are struck by the huge variety of alternative forces affecting the nature of East-West relations.

I want to make some additional points as well. First, the West has a tendency to view Islam as somewhat exotic and strange, distinct and alien from our Western perspectives. Here I try to place Islam in the context of other world religions, especially Judaism and Christianity. To an astonishing degree, Islam comes directly out of a long tradition of Middle East religious thought, including multiple heresies, fitting in as an integral piece of the whole religious picture. Indeed, Islam came to fit in comfortably with large numbers of preexisting forces.

Another key theme is the relationship among religion, power, and the state. I argue that the close affiliation of religion and the state over most of *Western* history has affected Christianity and Christian history *vastly more than it has affected Islam and the Islamic world*. The theme of heresy becomes very important here. I look at how heresies—religious views not accepted by authority—are often major *vehicles* for political opposition to the state at the mass level. Thus, when we look at issues of religious dispute, how much are we really talking about *power* relationships?

I also try to point out how the evolution of Islam moved along tracks often similar or parallel to the evolution of Christianity— although hardly in all respects; this observation suggests that most religions follow certain inevitable trajectories when it comes to authenticating scripture, maintaining theological orthodoxy, dealing with accretions or corruptions of the faith, and the like. Here again, Islam is not special but fits into the general course of religious developments in theological terms; this in turn suggests that it is not religion per se that creates distinctions so much as *state use* of religion, and that furthermore, the foundation of distinct religious communities may hinge little upon theology and a great deal on *secular* rivalry.

The book devotes major attention to the tensions and differences between Eastern Orthodox Christianity and Western or Roman Catholic Christianity. If Islam had not dislodged Christian rule across most of the Middle East, the entire region today would most likely still be under Eastern Orthodox Christianity. And relations between Orthodoxy and Catholicism have ranged between suspicious and toxic for nearly two millennia despite many shared classical traditions. So there are excellent grounds for imagining that Orthodox Christianity today could have served as a religious and ideological springboard for crystallizing the grievances of the Middle East against the West—witness the evolving history of Eastern Orthodoxy in its current center of gravity, Moscow.

This theme continues on into an examination of the Crusades: was it a religious or a geopolitical event? Furthermore, while popularly conceived as a struggle between Christianity and Islam, it was in reality an important *three*-way political struggle among Eastern Christianity, Western Christianity, and Islam.

I devote a chapter to the Christian Reformation that finds striking parallels between the logic of events in Christian Europe and in the emergence of Islamic "fundamentalism" under differing conditions later. The role of politics in both cases seems to dominate theological issues; theology again primarily serves as a vehicle to mobilize action. And we note how loss of state or church control over theology has led to major radicalism in both Christian and Muslim traditions.

We find some striking resemblances among issues in conflict between Orthodoxy and Catholicism on the one hand and between Christianity and Islam on the other. These issues include historical grievances, differing views on the role of the church and religion in society, on the forging of public and private values, the relationship between the state and the church/mosque, and the debate over the meaning and implications of "secularism" in the contemporary world. Power and bad blood again seem to supersede theological issues that often appear relatively trivial in themselves.

The book then launches into an examination of the theme of the political scientist Samuel Huntington in his reference to the "bloody borders of Islam," expounded in his well-known article and book, *The Clash of Civilizations*. What are we really talking about here? I look into what are fascinating relationships between Islam and four other major civilizations with which it has been in long-term close contact: Western Europe, Orthodox Russia, Hindu India, and Confucian China. In each of these cases, complex and shifting accommodations were reached between them; cross-pollination resulted. These relationships present a far subtler picture of how Muslims actually manage their relationships with other cultures and religions than is commonly portrayed in more lurid and simplistic confrontation scenarios.

Some readers may take issue with the fact that the book focuses more on the grievances of Muslims against the West than on the many grievances others might have *against Muslims*. That is indeed the case. In the first instance, Muslim perspectives and historical grievances against the West are not so well known in the West. I could write at length—indeed many thousands of others have already written—about outrages that Muslims have perpetrated against Christians, Hindus, or Jews at one time or another in history: everyone has heartrending stories to tell. Muslims have equally terrible tales to tell as well about what others have done to them. This book makes no attempt to provide a balance in a tally of blood-libels on one side or the other; it is rather an attempt to put these events in perspective—especially along the civilizational "fault lines" where Islam meets and joins with other major civilizations. Once again, we see how the role of Islam is usually less important than ethnic confrontations, which may or may not be augmented by religious differences on either side.

The last part of the book examines some modern aspirations of the Muslim world, beginning with a look at the history of the Muslim struggle against colonial power. We see how relatively *recently*, in fact, the Middle East's struggle against Western imperialism developed and how anti-imperial thinking remains a deep theme in the Middle East's view of the world today. I note similarities with the anti-imperial rhetoric and experience of several other cultures today, including China, to demonstrate how much of a piece with other Asian cultures Muslim thinking is on imperialist interventionism from the West.

I also look at the most urgent of contemporary topics—*jihad*, resistance, war, and terrorism. These are the issues that seize the media and confront the general public most vividly; they are the source of immense legitimate concern, as well as the subject of fear-mongering, exaggeration, and misinformation. Are these at bottom religious or geopolitical issues? And finally, in the concluding chapter, I return to specific policy concerns and offer some brief, unvarnished points on how policies and perspectives must change sharply if we are ever going to get out of the present morass that has been so costly to everyone.

In some ways, then, this book is at least as much about *other* civilizations neighboring Islam—Byzantine, Russian, Western Christian, Indian, Chinese—as it is about Islam. Central to my argument is how comfortably Islam fits in so many ways into the broader cultural assumptions, aspirations, and world outlook of these other major cultures. There are certain near-universal suspicions and fears of Muslim societies toward the West today that are actually shared widely by many other cultures of the developing world, even if they don't always agree on the cultural details. In other words, many of the values and political views attributed to the Muslim world today that so worry the West also exist in a "world without Islam."

This book is an *argument,* not a narrative. I seek to illuminate certain specific trends and forces that are often ignored or buried in more traditional historical accounts. Through the vehicle of this hypothetical argument, I hope to present a new perspective on how and *why* things have developed in the Middle East, beyond Islamic factors. In the end, I hope the reader will think about Islam as a much more complex and integral part of a common human, political, and religious experience in the world. If there is a "problem with Islam," it is a problem with us as well.

I refer to "Islam" repeatedly in the book, including in this introduction; but of course in one sense there is no "Islam"—there are many Islams. Or, put another way, there is one Islam, but many different ways *Muslims* live and interpret it that differ greatly from country to country, age to age, issue to issue, person to person. In fact, Islam is what Muslims *think* Islam is, as well as what they *want* it to be. And they differ, as do adherents of other faiths.

To generalize about such a huge and dynamic phenomenon as Islam is to pin it as a butterfly in a collection box to preserve it, to be consulted and examined as a specimen for all time. There are really thousands of butterflies out there, and the species is evolving and changing even as we seek to grasp it. Ironically, it is the most fanatic and rigid of Muslims, on the one hand, and their most zealous enemies in the West, on the other, who both seek to freeze Islam into one single immutable phenomenon, the better to promote it or denigrate it.

In the end, I hope to persuade the reader that the present crisis of East-West relations, or between the West and "Islam," has really very little to do with religion and everything to do with political and cultural frictions, interests, rivalries, and clashes. This conclusion matters a lot: it has everything to do with how we end up treating the problem of Western-Muslim confrontations today. Are we in fact headed toward a titanic and implacable clash of civilizations, a new Hundred Years' War or World War IV, as some have suggested? A small group of Muslims, Christians, and Jews actually like such a stark narrative of existential struggle. But if we conclude that religion is *not* the central issue at work in present tensions, then we have a much better chance at dealing with and even resolving those issues, however more complex they may be. In that sense, we are hopefully working toward building a solid foundation for the three great Abrahamic faiths—Judaism, Christianity, and Islam—that share more than they dispute. It is the *states* that dispute.

———

SADLY, WHEN RELIGION BECOMES linked with political forces, it tends to lose its soul—its spiritual dimension. Yet in so many places, religion is regularly invoked in numerous bloody struggles for territory, sovereignty, political control, political agenda, and existential preservation of the community. This applies to most religions: Christianity, Islam, Judaism, Buddhism, Hinduism, Shintoism, and many others, including traditional aboriginal faiths.

We are living at a point of time in the West when rational, secular thinking seems to largely dismiss the phenomenon of religion as an archaic force that inhibits the social order at best, or as the source of hatreds, violent conflict, and war at worst. Many in the West have been dismayed by the "return of religion," when it appears to be more powerful and sometimes more dangerous than ever. There is some truth to this observation. Yet the real issue is not the danger of religion per se, but of dogmatic thinking. The true horrors of the twentieth century have almost *nothing* to do with religions: two world wars, Franco, Mussolini, Hitler, Lenin, Stalin, Mao, Pol Pot, Rwanda—the deaths of hundreds of millions of people, all involving secular, even atheist regimes that seized upon dogmatic ideas and brutally implemented them at all cost.

Finally, I'm not really writing about religion as *faith* at all, but about "organized religion" as a supreme vehicle for many other facets of human aspirations, including politics, fears, drives, prejudices, dreams, and bitterness. I would not for a second claim that these concerns are all that religion is about. But as we watch the agonies of the twenty-first century unfold, we should be quite realistic about the complex burden of issues that contemporary religion carries; most of what passes for "religious issues" are not truly about religion at all, however much it is publicly invoked. And that goes as much for America as it does for Cairo, Tel Aviv, Mumbai, or Colombo. Religion speaks with many voices; it serves many ends, fully as noble and ignoble as humans themselves can be. In that spirit, then, let's take a look at a world without Islam. How different will it be in terms of our relations with the Middle East? What other forces do we find at work?

PART ONE

HERESY AND POWER

CHAPTER ONE

Islam and the Abrahamic Faiths

God neither begets, nor is He begotten.

—Qur'an 112:3

There was a time, of course, when there really was no Islam—up until the early seventh century CE, when the Prophet Muhammad received his revelations from God and announced them to the world. But in one sense, it would be erroneous to view the establishment of Islam as a momentous turning point in the Middle East. In political terms, it may indeed have been a watershed, but in religious or cultural terms, it is also easy to view the emergence of Islam as yet one more strand, one more turn on the path of what is a continuum—the ongoing evolution of Middle Eastern monotheistic thought. We hear the term "Abrahamic faiths" used more frequently today to reflect an awareness of this triple monotheistic heritage that includes the prophet Abraham and embraces three religions: Judaism, Christianity, and Islam. These religions are all closely linked, whatever political differences may have arisen among them over time. This is indeed the point: politics and power struggles have often magnified theological differences for political ends, rather than stressing common heritage. Politics rule; enduring points of geopolitical tension in the region that *precede* Islam tend to persist even after Islam. We're looking for continuities. It would be quite off the mark to view Islam as something alien to the religious tradition of the Middle East. Islam absorbed, represents, and perpetuates many of the region's deeper drives and cultures.

A map of religions of the Middle East before Islam reveals a world dominated by Christianity in its Eastern Orthodox forms; it shares some space with basically monotheistic Zoroastrianism in Persia (under the Sassanid Empire), with small pockets of Jews in a few urban areas, while Buddhism and Hinduism dominated the Indian subcontinent. Europe itself was of course part Christian, part pagan. In religious terms, then, Islam was a latecomer and in fact the *last new religion in history* ever able to hold sway over state structures. But Islam would make up for lost time in spreading quickly to assume dominant position over the huge areas formerly under Christian and Zoroastrian control in the Middle East. Without Islam, Eastern Orthodox Christianity would likely have remained the dominant faith of the Middle East down to today, with the possible exception of Zoroastrianism in Iran.

While the expansion of Islam and its ongoing conquest of large parts of the known world had huge *political* impact like any conquest does, in *theological* terms it exerted far less impact upon local populations in its early decades. Islam actually grew out of the existing religious environment of the Middle East in a relatively natural and organic way. In fact, what is surprising is how, in theological terms, Islam fitted in quite comfortably with the existing religious milieu.

Nor is the birth of Islam some remote event off in a distant and isolated desert, an exotic cultural plant alien to the roots of Western culture. The ideas of Islam flow directly out of a broader Eastern Mediterranean and Middle Eastern cultural milieu that had long witnessed intense religious interchange, cross-pollination, and debate. Probably no other region of the world has seen as many diverse religions and sects trek across its landscapes as has

the Middle East. As Islam emerges, we witness a reprise of many of the same old themes and concerns that were part of the earlier evolution of Judaism and Christianity. After witnessing the religious and doctrinal strife of the first six centuries of Christianity (which we'll look at shortly), our encounter with Islam does not surprise us; the arguments and beliefs propagated by Islam weighed in on quite familiar debates: What is the nature of the One God? Who was the message of Judaism for—the Jews as the Chosen People, or for all peoples? Was Jesus literally the Son of God, or simply a divinely inspired human being? We will shortly examine the fascinating nature of many of these debates and note how some religious doctrines triumphed with the backing of political power, while others with less political backing came to be denounced as heresies.

Above all, we will see how intimately linked all these doctrinal struggles were to the politics of the great empires. Power invariably attracts religion, and religion attracts power. Theology is secondary. Furthermore, the enduring forces of culture, time, tradition, history, and beliefs are powerful; they possess great ability to bend new events into well-trodden channels. Islam, for all its new and incredible civilizational brilliance, was very much a product of its larger environment.

Arabia

Even Arabia itself was not an isolated place but rather linked to the grand regional swirl of religious thought and ferment. Yemen, in the southwest corner of the Arabian peninsula, was the center of one of the oldest civilizations in the Middle East and perhaps the original home of all Semitic peoples. Semitic tribes migrated from there in the earliest of times up into Mesopotamia, conquering Sumeria in BCE and transforming it into a Semitic culture. A rich spice and textile trade ran all along the Red Sea coast to

Egypt, the Levant, and the Mediterranean, where Yemenis were in regular contact with the Phoenicians in the earliest days. The Queen of Sheba purportedly resided in Yemen and was in contact with the Christian kingdom of Axum in Ethiopia. Christians and Jews had large communities in Yemen. The Persians even moved in for a period.

Farther north, up along the Red Sea coast (Hijaz), lay the city of Mecca, one of the most important cities of Arabia, with a history going back some four thousand years. There is little historical mention of Mecca in ancient histories up to the time of the Prophet Muhammad, at least in external sources. Yet it had become a major commercial entrepôt along the Red Sea trade route to Syria. Major Jewish communities existed in several key cities of the Hijaz, especially Medina. The Christian lands of the Byzantine Empire lay just to the north, with major centers in what is today's Syria and Jordan.

Arabia had long nourished its own traditional religions consisting of local or tribal gods similar to those known to other Semitic peoples, including earlier Jews. Much worship was centered in the Ka'ba in Mecca, which was a repository for some 360 gods, reportedly including statues of Jesus and Mary. The shrines lent Mecca considerable economic and political power: it had managed to establish control over a huge tribal confederation with the aim of overseeing the complex intertribal politics of the peninsula and limiting disruptive tribal warfare. As a result, the city maintained a treaty relationship with Byzantium to facilitate trade through the region. Mecca's prosperity was the direct source of new political and social tensions as well, since the old tribal structures and kinship support systems were breaking down under the growth of a rising capitalist market economy; old social values were fading, creating a vacuum for new ones.

Such was the lay of the land in geopolitical and theological terms, when in 610 CE the revelations received by the young Mec-

can merchant Muhammad added a new chapter to the ongoing development of monotheistic ideas. Muhammad had been orphaned as a boy and had been working for his uncle. At the age of forty, at a time when he had been suffering from periods of psychological restlessness, Muhammad reported a remarkable experience during a sojourn in the mountains: he had been visited on several occasions by the angel Gabriel, who instructed him to recite words brought from God. He was told to preach the message that God is One and to carry it to the regional tribes and to the corrupt society of pagan and polytheistic Mecca. Muhammad proceeded to promote that message and to inveigh against the harsh and unjust social order and the idolatrous presence of these idols of polytheism in the Ka'ba—the very symbol of Meccan authority and trade. Jesus and the moneylenders come immediately to mind, but Muhammad had a political vision as well.

More important, Muhammad early on identified himself as standing in the same line of prophets as others of the Old Testament, going back to the first Prophets, Adam (in Islam) and Abraham. Indeed, the Qur'an, the book containing these accumulated revelations, identified these figures as the "first Muslims"—even though they had not, of course, designated themselves as Muslims at the time—simply because they were the first humans known to experience and acknowledge the Oneness and power of God. Muhammad insisted that he, too, was nothing more than the messenger (*Rasul*) or prophet (*Nabi*) of God, and had no divine nature. Indeed, to those in the region, his message was hardly dramatically new, but simply a sharpened reaffirmation of the eternal message of the Oneness of God, in new form. Muhammad also propounded a clear and direct theology, stripped of the abstruse and conflicting theories about the nature of Jesus that had fractured theological centers across the lands of Eastern Christianity for six centuries. He emphasized the need to return to God's prescriptions for a moral community.

The prescriptions for embracing Islam are simple: the new recruit needs only to profess with pure heart the *shahada,* or statement of witness: *Lā ilaha illa al-Lāh, wa Muhammadun rasūlu l-Lāh*—"There is no god but God, and Muhammad is the Messenger of God." All Muslims are expected to fulfill the five pillars, or duties, of a Muslim: to profess the *shahada*, pray five times a day, observe the fast during the month of Ramadan, make the pilgrimage (*hajj*) to Mecca once in a lifetime, and pay alms, or tithe (*zakat*).

The requirements of faith entail a belief in the One God, an acceptance of all the Prophets of God (including Moses, Jesus, and Muhammad), a belief in the Angels, a belief in the key holy books sent by God—which include the Old and New Testaments and the Qur'an—a belief in the Day of Judgment and Resurrection, and belief in Destiny, or Fate. The theological underpinnings of the new faith facilitated easy transmission, explanation, and acceptance.

Muhammad was the first *self-professed* "Muslim," that is, one professing *Islam,* or submission to God's design. He perceived the need to clarify and sharpen the message of the One God and to clear up the errors and misbeliefs that had crept into human interpretation of the earlier Jewish and Christian messages. But the line of revelation was one and the same.

Traditional Muslim scholars, of course, reject any causality in the emergence of Islam that is not divine; in other words, no acknowledgment of possible external, regional, or nondivine sources and influences upon the revelations received by the Prophet. That's fair enough within the framework of their own theological commitments. But the environment in which Muhammad lived would, of course, also exert influence over his mind, thinking, and personality; it would affect his receptivity to the message and the manner in which his revelations were understood and applied by himself and his followers. So it is also fair enough for others to examine possible and plausible external influences upon the experience and interpretation of revelation, paralleling the experience and revelations of other prophets and religious figures in history.

At this time in the Arabian Peninsula, then, most of the basic new Qur'anic precepts were familiar concepts, starting with the Jewish belief that denied Jesus as the Messiah and saw him only as a faith healer. Also familiar were the range of Christian "heresies" that had spread across the Middle East, speculating about every aspect of Jesus's nature. Indeed, the strict monotheism of the Qur'an was closer in many respects to the views of the very earliest Christians in the Middle East than they were to the theologically strained doctrinal compromises of the Eastern Orthodox Church in later years. Variations on the basic themes of monotheism permeated all cultures of the region.

Muhammad is the first prophet of a major religion to have lived in the full light of history. Information about his life and actions abound, both in the Qur'an and even more so in the accounts of his life from contemporaries of the Prophet who recorded these events and sayings (the *Hadith* or *Sunna*). But even then, Islam faced the same problems encountered by nearly all religions, including Christianity: how accurate were the accounts of contemporaries about the Prophet's life and sayings? These sayings and actions had been transmitted orally; in Islam, it would be over one hundred years before they were collected in written form, analyzed, and systematically assessed. The task parallels the Christian problem of collecting all the accounts of Jesus's life to determine which Gospels, for example, were "reliable" and which were not; this is a subject still rife with speculation and debate and has yet to be laid to rest.

And while the Hadith are not literally sacred in Islam in the sense that the Qur'an is — *directly* derived from God through revelation — they often provide a more important source for later

Islamic legislation than the Qur'an itself; the Hadith simply provide much more material dealing with specific, concrete situations arising in the development of the early Islamic community that were never touched upon in the Qur'an. The Hadith also supply an important guide to indicate how the Prophet himself understood and situationally applied the revelations that he had received. An analogy would be to those Christians who ask today "What would Jesus do?"

Even then, there are small groups within Islam who argue that only the Qur'an—due to its divine source—should be the source of understanding of Islam, given the complex and varying natures of various Hadith, the differing degrees of their reliability, and sometimes even the self-serving nature of authorities adopting certain Hadith over others. It is interesting to note the clear parallels here with the *sola Scriptura* (scripture alone) basis of the Reformation movements that overthrew vast amounts of church history and its accretions, council rulings, and so on, in favor of establishing theological understanding on the basis of scripture alone.

The practical obstacles to applying the new revelations to a new Islamic political and religious community were daunting, particularly in the face of early militant opposition from the Meccan elite that felt its power, wealth, and position threatened by Muhammad's message. His life endangered, the Prophet and his followers fled to the city of Medina, where he established the first Muslim community and, by invitation, presided over warring elements within the city in order to bring a peaceful new order. This is referred to as the Constitution of Medina, in which the rights, responsibilities, and relationships among the various tribes and religious groups within the city—Jews, Christians, and Muslims—were spelled out in a document of clarification and reconciliation. Meanwhile, this Muslim community in Medina continued to be militarily and politically threatened by Meccan forces hostile to Islam over many years, until Mecca finally gave up its opposition and the Prophet returned triumphantly in a bloodless victory in 630 CE. This long period of tensions, hostility, war, shifting alliances, and betrayals is reflected in some of the darker and more warlike passages of the Qur'an, with its concern for Muslim unity in the face of enemies seeking subversion of the fledgling community. The darkness and anger of many of these passages resemble similar periods of the struggle of the Israelites to counter hostile Semitic tribes, where the Old Testament calls for the ruthless extirpation of all the enemies of the Jews who stood in their way of achieving a state in Israel; reconciliation and peace are not in the spirit of those troubled periods in either religion.

The problem of the reliability of the Hadith had major political implications as Islam developed, spread, and became involved in empire-building. As with the Christian Church, how much might later Muslim secular or religious authorities seek to retroactively influence, control, or interpret the message of Islam? Unlike Christianity, Islam was fortunately spared debate over the possible divinity of the Prophet—neither he nor others ever claimed it. Islam has, in fact, seen far fewer heresies and divisions on the basis of scriptural interpretation than Christianity has, perhaps in part due to the lean lines of its theological vision. Nonetheless, even until today questions of interpretation of the Qur'an and the Hadith remain central to the ongoing evolution of Islam.

As Islam spread, it encountered new languages, geographies, cultures, and historical experiences. Like other religions, it adapted itself to local conditions to facilitate acceptance and conversion to the new faith. But in the eyes of later reformers, some of these accommodations and accretions were viewed as non-Islamic, as innovation (*bida'*), requiring theological purging and a return to orthodoxy. These issues will form the foundation of Islamic renewal and fundamentalism. Such accretions were also a key issue for early Protestant reformers such as Martin Luther.

—

FRICTIONS AMONG RELIGIONS and their followers are rarely based on specific theological differences but rather on their *political and social implications*. Let's examine the gist of some of the actual theological differences that do exist in the three-way relationship among Judaism, Christianity, and Islam. How much do these theological differences really matter in the politics of the ancient and medieval Middle East? When we look more closely, we note a constant repetition of certain basic arguments about the nature of monotheism that pervade the region and the culture. We note that Islam, rather than transforming the area theologically, ended up adopting a posture of balance between the other two faiths, reinforcing a kind of theological continuity. Popular modern theories that Islam represents some kind of disruptive cultural and theological force alien to Judeo-Christian belief, or that it laid a groundwork for later anti-Western feeling, is to utterly remove it from its cultural and historical contexts. Islam, in fact, represents and extends some of the deepest cultural, philosophical, and religious trends of the Middle East, including quite guarded attitudes toward the West. Islam did not create these trends; take Islam away and the trends still remain. Let's look at how these three religions regarded each other.

The Jewish Perspective on Christianity and Islam

Judaism's critique of Christianity clearly influenced a number of later Christian heresies — and the theology of Islam, as well. First, and perhaps the single most sensitive issue for the entire Middle East, was the all-important issue of the nature of the Messiah: while Christians believed that Jesus *was* the Messiah whose coming was foretold in the Old Testament, Jews rejected Jesus as being that Messiah. In the eyes of some Christians, Jews are the worst heretics of all, because they actually deny what was supposedly foretold in their own scriptures — the coming of the Messiah. Jewish scholars largely reject that argument, claiming that it is quite clear that Jesus was not that Messiah prophesied in the Old Testament. They claim that the true Messiah needed to fulfill a number of specific messianic prophesies in order to be recognized as the Messiah: he had to be born of the male line of King David (Jesus was purportedly begotten by God); he must fulfill the Law of the Torah (Jesus clearly did not do so and indeed sought to change the Law). The true Messiah would also usher in an era of world peace when hatred and oppression will cease to exist — which did not happen. The Old Testament expected the Messiah to fulfill these revelations immediately and not after a "Second Coming," to which there is no reference in the Old Testament. Jews also did not accept the idea that mankind can be saved through the sacrifice of Jesus, or by anyone else, but only through righteous living, as prescribed by Jewish Law.

Judaism furthermore castigates Jesus as having taken Jewish monotheism and corrupted it, dividing Jews against themselves and weakening Judaism. The great medieval Jewish philosopher and theologian Maimonides, who lived in Muslim Spain, minced no words:

> The first one to have adopted this plan [to wipe out any trace of the Jewish nation] was Jesus the Nazarene, may his bones be ground to dust…He impelled people to believe that he was a prophet sent by God to clarify perplexities in the Torah, and that he was the Messiah that was predicted by each and every seer. He interpreted the Torah and its precepts in such a fashion as to lead to their total annulment, to the abolition of all its commandments and to the violation of its prohibitions. The sages, of blessed memory, having become aware of his plans before his reputation spread among our people, meted out fitting punishment to him.

Thus, from a Jewish perspective, these arguments refute the Christian argument that Jews willfully rejected the Messiah prophesied for them in the Old Testament; these critiques suggest that it was abundantly clear to Jewish scholars that Jesus did not meet the qualifications of the Messiah prophesied for them.

Islam actually strikes middle ground on this issue by acknowledging Jesus as a great Prophet of God, who did commit miracles and was indeed born of the Virgin Mary. The nineteenth chapter of the Qur'an is entitled "Mary" [*Miriam* in Arabic]; she is mentioned more often than any other woman in the Qur'an—more often than in the New Testament itself; she is the most revered female figure in Islam.

However, according to Islam, Jesus was not God himself, nor the literal Son of God, but rather a divinely inspired human prophet. God is strictly One. And for Muslims, any denial of Jesus as a great prophet violates the beliefs of Islam itself; Muslims, for example, regularly declare works of art that are insulting to Jesus to be blasphemous. The Qur'an refers variously to Jesus as "the Word of God," as "the Spirit of God," and as a "Sign of God." There are no disparaging remarks about Jesus in the Qur'an. Thus, in a world without Islam, the much harsher Jewish critique of Jesus, as expressed in Judaism, still stands.

Judaism likewise does not accept Muhammad as a prophet. Nonetheless, the relationship between Islam and Judaism is striking, far closer in spirit than that between either of those faiths and Christianity. Both Judaism and Islam are fiercely monotheistic, and both proclaim the unity of God several times in daily prayers. Both Jews and Arabs are Semitic peoples who have long shared much common space, common history, and speak languages that are closely related. Both Islam and Judaism are strongly law-based; personal salvation is attained through personal fulfillment of the law in life. Both have community law courts for the adjudication of many issues in accordance with religious law. Judaism insisted that God could not be portrayed or personified, and that he did not possess human form. Islam firmly follows that same precept that God is not anthropomorphic. Thus to both Jews and Muslims, Christian art is shocking, if not blasphemous, with its unconstrained, direct, and detailed portrayal of God in various styles—usually as an old white man with a white beard in white robes—and with the proliferation of paintings of Jesus in a huge variety of diverse physiognomies and cultural affiliations.

Both Judaism and Islam share many regulations about the ritual of foods, slaughter of animals, prohibition of pork, and ritual cleanliness—indeed, Islam derived them mostly from Judaism but vastly simplified the complex Jewish Kosher laws. Oriental Jews (Sephardim) have been influenced in their practice of their religion through long centuries of living together with Muslims. And while in the bloody history of humanity Jews, too, have suffered at various points while living in Muslim societies, Jewish scholars would be near unanimous in agreeing that Jewish communities and culture have fared far better over the centuries under Islam than under Christianity. The creation of the state of Israel in 1948, establishing a homeland for the Jews after the horrific experience of the Holocaust in Europe—but coming at terrible expense to the Palestinians—represents a dramatic and sad turning point in what is now a tense and angry relationship between Jews and Muslims. Indeed, that strained relationship is now entirely geopolitical, fought over questions of territory and relationships with the new Israeli state.

The Islamic Perspective on Judaism and Christianity

As the last of the three Abrahamic faiths, Islam is able to look back on the evolution of the earlier two. According to the Qur'an, Jews made several critical errors in receiving the message: Jews saw themselves as God's uniquely Chosen People, they perceived

33

the One God to be the God of the Jews, they perceived the message of Judaism to be for the Jews. No, said the Qur'an, God has no chosen people: "On those who believe and work deeds of righteousness, will [God] Most Gracious bestow love" (Qur'an 19:96). This, of course, was the message of St. Paul as well in definitively breaking with Judaism—that Jesus's message about God is not for Jews but for all mankind. Thus Islam propounds a revisionist view of its Jewish predecessor and probably was influenced by Paul's vision of Jesus's message that he proclaimed to be universal.

Yet Islam and Judaism share a common critique of Christianity; both see the idea of any "son" of God as blasphemous to the concept of the One God, who does not beget and cannot be subdivided. The concept of a Trinity smacks of polytheism, which is equally anathema to both Jews and Muslims. According to Islam, Jesus did not die on the cross but was taken up to heaven by God. And it will be *Jesus,* not Muhammad, who will return at the day of judgment to quell the anti-Christ, punish the enemies of Islam, and bring justice.

Yet, historical evolution has a way of changing the way humans perceive religion over time; this reality helps explain differences among the faiths. Muslims often acknowledge this reality, even if in a slightly self-serving way. More than once, Muslims have told me, "All three religions are from God, but they were received at different times in the evolution of human history. Human understanding of God has advanced each time. In modern technical terms, we can look at Judaism as something like Word 2.0, a software that worked perfectly well in its time, works even now if you wish. But Christianity came along as, say, a Word 5.0, considerably upgrading the sophistication of the 'software'—the understanding of God's message. And then six hundred years later, Islam brought out the equivalent of a Word 8.0, the most sophisticated understanding of God and his message of all. Each 'version' works, is acceptable, but advances are made over time."

34

We are hardly bound to accept this definition of religious evolution offered in some popular Muslim thinking, but the same concept of evolution of religious understanding occupies a major place among theologians, even if the Microsoft analogies are grating. Karen Armstrong, in her book *History of God*, identifies clear landmarks in the ongoing evolution of human understanding of the divine over time.

Nonetheless, with their own popular hi-tech analogy, Muslims open the door to a logical follow-up question that is truly heretical in Islam: is there no possibility, then, of a still later revelation, a Word 9.0? For Muslims, the Prophet Muhammad brought the final and perfect revelation that cannot be improved upon; there will be no more legitimate prophets. Muhammad is thus the "seal of the Prophets." This belief has put Islam in the curious position of being quite tolerant in looking back into religious history, but intolerant in looking forward to any possible post-Muhammad religious teachings that involve new revelation; this is the source of the intense strain Islam has with the later Ahmadi, Sikh, or Baha'i religions, which have some foundation in Islam but which in effect "update" Islam in the preaching of still later prophets. These three movements are thus vigorously condemned by Muslim clerics, and their followers have been subject to persecution in several Muslim states.

Jewish and Christian Views of Islam

Finally, we have the retrospective views of Judaism and Christianity looking back upon Islam, the newcomer religion among them—and the view is much less charitable. In contrast to Islam's acceptance of huge parts of the Old and New Testaments, both Judaism and Christianity reject Muhammad even as a prophet of God. Not surprisingly, they also repudiate the idea that the Old Testament and New Testament messages can in any way be "updated" by Muhammad. Muhammad is treated in much Christian literature over the ages as a heretic, even a devil, including being cast into one of the lowest circles of Hell in Dante's *Inferno*. (For that matter, Catholicism historically also viewed Protestantism as heretical and the work of the devil, and the feelings were mutual.)

———

THUS, THE RELATIONSHIPS among all three of the Abrahamic faiths are complex and striking: they parallel each other in many respects, contradict each other in yet others. Nonetheless, Islam represents a powerful new phase in the *continuity* of the monotheistic tradition in the Middle East. Islam was born of, and coexisted with, Christianity and Judaism in the same region. While Islam indeed established a new political order, we are not talking about a brand-new religion, new gods, or new perceptions of morality. If there had been no Islam, the world would have been less rich culturally and intellectually, but the *cultural and theological* groundwork of thinking in the Middle East might not have been vastly different.

———

NEARLY ALL RELIGIONS DEVELOP out of earlier religions and doctrines. Buddhism developed out of Hindu religion, culture, and philosophy even though it is not viewed by Hindus as a heresy. Sikhism developed out of both Hinduism and Islam. Baha'ism developed out of Christianity and Islam. In one sense, heresy can become a creative act of evolutionary religious thinking as future generations struggle to sharpen, clarify, and reinterpret those earlier religious impulses and understandings, often in keeping with their contemporary cultural surroundings.

Ironically, it is striking that it is the fine-grained details and culturally specific characteristics within each of these religions that are viewed by their followers as *most essential* to their faith;

these details can even prompt violent action against others. So when seemingly small theological differences can stir up hatred, violence, and war, it is a sure sign that a great deal more is going on than mere theological dispute. It is like a furious marital blowup in the kitchen over whether the pasta is overcooked: the anger is very real, but outside observers instantly grasp that something more is going on here beyond whether the pasta is *al dente*.

So in the case of the Middle East and its religions, it is not the theology that really represents the source of conflict. Other things are obviously at stake: identities, communities, states, politics, power, regional nationalisms. Religion serves as a handy tag, constitutes an important element of identity in which the specific theology is really only incidental. In fact, we are rarely Christians, Muslims, or Jews by choice; we are born into one of these traditions whose richness of community we accept; it is not about balancing or choosing among alternative theological arguments offered to us. Jewish communities have been a powerful cultural force over history, but not because of the specific ritual details of Judaism. Those could vary, and do. It is really the *cultural identity and glue of theology*—any theology—that sustains a community on an ethnic or a religious basis. The same goes for the diversity of Christian sects. The religion helps establish communities; communities can drift into conflict or even war over community security, resources, leadership, and turf.

In our modern era, the world has made some modest but serious steps toward religious reconciliation and ecumenism, even acknowledgments of shared commonalities. For example, our regular use of the term "Judeo-Christian" is quite recent, coming to prominence only at the start of the twentieth century. It was designed to acknowledge certain religious commonalities ignored in periods of anti-Jewish discrimination during most of the history of Christianity—even though, in theological terms, the differences between Christianity and Judaism are the greatest among the three faiths. And in the past twenty or thirty years, we now see the term "Abrahamic faiths" beginning to achieve some currency, bringing Islam into the fold of commonality. Theologies have not changed much; human desire to overcome the differences has.

Religion, State, Power, and Heresy

Religion is an exceptionally powerful human force. It deals with gut issues such as the meaning of life, death, war, moral behavior, community, and sexuality. It acts on the individual human psyche, psychology, and behavior. Its impact is rarely limited to the individual alone, but acts upon an entire community of believers who take part in community acts of worship. At the same time, religion helps define and strengthen the community of like-minded believers.

Given the extraordinary power of this force, can we be surprised that seats of worldly power should seek to harness the force of religion to their own ends? Such is a key focus of this book: the relationships among religion, power, and the state. The state ultimately seeks to adopt and take over the religion, making it the "state religion." Once tied to the state, the religion's doctrines and theology then become linked to state prestige, power, and control. The religion can be Judaism, Christianity, or Islam; it doesn't really matter. Because at that point, disagreement on doctrine ceases to be merely a theological exercise and, rather, takes on serious political implications. Those who part company with the state-dominated ideology are branded as heretics — indeed, such differences can become tantamount to treason.

But what is heresy actually? The word evokes images of robed Inquisitors, instruments of torture, tearful recantations, martyrs, and burnings at the stake. And so it has often been in history. But in fact, heresy often gets a bad rap. In reality, it seems closely linked to a creative process in the history and evolution of ideas.

The origin of the word "heresy" is innocent enough; in Greek, it originally simply meant "choice," a conscious decision to follow a particular path of ideas. In Christianity, it began to denote divergence from orthodox teaching. And orthodoxy, of course, originally meant no more than "correct opinion." But who is to say what opinion is "correct" or "right"? This is the nub of the problem: the quality of heresy actually lies in the eye of the beholder. And the determination of what is "right opinion" eventually emerges almost strictly as a *prerogative of power.*

Heresies have existed from the dawn of the most basic religious cults, when individuals who stood up and critiqued community teachings about the gods and spirits were blamed for catastrophes that subsequently befell the community. Victims get sacrificed on altars, virgins are tossed into flaming volcanoes to placate the gods. The fulminations of Old Testament prophets focus on how Jewish iniquity has brought suffering to the Jewish people and how God will visit further punishments upon the community for flouting His commandments. Jonah gets tossed into the sea. Jesus preaches the imminence of the end of a sinful world.

Preservation of orthodoxy seems to emerge as a supreme and contentious problem for all three monotheistic faiths, far more so than for other major world religions such as Hinduism, Buddhism, Daoism, or Confucianism. This may be partly due to the fact that the monotheistic religions are "revealed," that is, they are believed to have existed eternally and *preexist* the exact moment of revelation to their prophets. There is less room for flexibility on doctrine.

I remember discussions in India over a decade ago when I was researching material for a book on the issue of Islam versus the West. Several Hindu scholars told me, "Your proposition is flawed from the start. The real fault line is not between Islam and the West at all, but between Hinduism as *polytheism,* and all the *monotheistic* religions of the West—Judaism, Christianity, and Islam."

In the Hindu view, the monotheistic faiths, with their commitment to the One God and his revealed nature, are thus inherently more narrow-minded and intolerant.

We are all familiar with the use and abuse of religion by states or power groups in warfare, politics, or struggle for other ends in history. It would, of course, be simpleminded to reduce the entire phenomenon of religion to no more than a pretext for power and conflict; nonetheless the exploitation of religion for secular ends is a constant in political and social history. Religious institutions therefore end up spending a great deal of time striving to preserve orthodoxy. In this sense, then, orthodoxy comes to represent the *right to define and control ideas that affect power.*

Let's not just blame religion; "orthodoxies" reign in all fields of human endeavor, including history, philosophy, and even science. You find orthodoxy wherever dogmatic certitude replaces skepticism, inquiry, and debate, and where that certitude is then buttressed by power. Recall how in the Marxist, atheist Soviet Union, communist orthodoxy was vigorously enforced by Stalin across a broad range of intellectual fields including history, the arts, and the sciences; ideological heretics in many different fields often met their fate with a bullet in the back of the skull in the dungeons of the KGB. Orthodoxy and ideology were all there to serve and preserve the welfare of Communist Party rule. Political parties, too, especially ideological ones, rise and fall on their ability to articulate beliefs that attract and organize followers, and the parties seek to impose ideological consensus on its members. In the absence of consensus, the party falls apart. The struggle of political parties to maintain ideological purity differs little from the state's handling of religious doctrine—except that religious organizations hold the trump of appealing to a Higher Power.

Heresy lies at the *junction of belief and power.* When religions become institutionalized, they face the problem of "ownership" and control of doctrine. Belief counts for nothing if anybody is free to believe whatever he or she wants, or to craft a do-it-yourself kind of personal faith. Finding God for oneself in the texts was indeed the ultimate rationale of the Protestant Reformation—an event that split Christianity wide open into fissiparating shards of small religious communities. Fundamentalist *salafi* or Wahhabi doctrine is also revolutionary in calling for the individual to interpret scripture directly, not through some intermediary to God.

Power, then, is the final trap, the ultimate corrupter: the closer religion becomes linked with state power, the further it drifts away from the realm of intellect and spirit and into the realm of the political—with direct implications for state power and authority. The state cannot then be indifferent to theology. When the state's official beliefs and doctrines are challenged, the state's authority itself is challenged—and the state does not look kindly upon it.

It's a self-serving cycle. Theological doctrine comes to serve the state's interests. The state then recruits clerics who bestow their theological imprimatur upon the state's self-serving interpretations. Both Islam and Christianity, with their long linkage to various state powers over history, continue to face this challenge to this day. In fact, church and state in Christianity have been far *more* closely tied over most of Christian history than was ever the case in Islam, where clerical power almost never exercised political rule—until the Islamic Republic of Iran today. Meanwhile, Judaism, lacking the instruments of state power for most of its history, was a bit more able to avoid this path, although now that Judaism has become linked with the power and politics of the modern Israeli state, it, too, is no longer exempt.

Conversely, when religion becomes *independent* of the state, something important happens: the state actually loses much stake in the preservation of religious orthodoxy. But even then, we are still not home free. Even personal religious beliefs can still affect the state very much if certain doctrines and views affect the public's *perception* of the state. Thus, some evangelical movements in the United States directly impact the public's view of the government; how fundamentalist movements in Islam view the state can directly threaten the legitimacy of the most secular authoritarian regimes.

None of this is at all meant to suggest that religion is nothing more than a cynical façade for power struggle. It can be that. But human ability to bend religion to political or commercial ends should not diminish the profound spiritual power that personal belief can have in shaping one's personal life, philosophy, and conduct, and hence the behavior of society at large.

Even tolerance can be elusive. Hinduism seems to have remarkably avoided most of the compromising problems of power and orthodoxy. Indeed the concept of orthodoxy and heresy is almost entirely absent in Hinduism, since it embraces all religious ideas within its bosom, each one representing partial insights and glimpses of elements of truth as parts of a vast, fundamental, ineffable, ultimately never fully knowable Truth of the Divine. But none of this tolerant polytheistic character of Hinduism suggests that a Hindu-dominated state, or followers of Hinduism, is not equally capable of discrimination, persecution, and brutal violence toward people of other religions; the world has sadly witnessed in recent times the use of violence under militant Hindu leaders of Hindutva (Hindu nationalism) against Muslim, Sikh, and Christian communities.

All of this has everything to do with politics and nationalism and little to do with religious doctrine per se. Note here that *against outsiders* Hinduism, too, can readily be translated into an intolerant and narrow religious nationalism; this parallels what happens with Islamic fundamentalism when it operates as an "Islamic nationalist" movement against Western incursion. While philosophically highly pacifist, even Buddhism, when combined with ethnicity in ethnic struggles such as with the Sinhalese in Sri Lanka against the Hindu Tamils, quickly loses its ethical considerations of pacifism, even on the part of Buddhist monks, when it comes to fighting in the name of the Buddhist Sinhalese community. Theology seems to count for little.

And can we forget that God in Islam has ninety-nine revered names: the Merciful, the Compassionate, the Loyal, the Avenger, the Comforter, the Victor, the Savior, and so forth—all different facets, faces, of the same God? Nobody would claim that Islam is polytheistic, but it clearly recognizes multiple faces of the Divine.

Tolerance, Inclusivity, and Exclusivity

It appears the world can be divided into two distinct psychological mind-sets. There are those who seek *exclusivity*, who seek to draw boundaries between themselves and others, who wish to see their own beliefs as unique, quite distinct from what others believe, views in which they themselves are right and the others wrong. On the other side, there are those whose goal it is to search out common ground among beliefs, shared points of overlapping inclusivity and commonality. This happens even among believers in the same faith. As one wise man put it: "They drew a square and left me out; I drew a circle and included them."

But what personal psychological element is it that impels some adherents of a religion to a search for narrowness and exclusivity, others to seek embrace and inclusivity? This dichotomy comes up endlessly in discussions in the West about the relationship with Islam. When I lecture on commonalities within the Abrahamic faiths, I sometimes encounter objections. I note, for instance, that for Muslims *Allah* does not refer to a different God any more than *Dios* is a "different" God for Spaniards, *Dieu* for the French, *Bog* for Russians, or *Tanrı* for the Turks. Indeed, Arab Christians refer in Arabic to their God as *Allah*. These are all just different words in different languages for the same concept—the One God. But a few Western Christians will object: "Allah is not my God. My

God brought forth Jesus as his only begotten Son, the salvation of mankind and my intercessor. That is not the God of Islam." In one sense, this is absolutely true. Some Jews, too, will object that "the Christian God is not my God because he begat a Son, a concept alien to Judaism. Furthermore, according to the Old Testament, Jesus clearly is not the Messiah that Christians consider him to be." And this is true as well. And some narrow-minded Muslims will describe Christians and Jews in exclusionary terms as "nonbelievers" in Islam, rather than as "People of the Book" as stated in the Qur'an.

Perhaps those who feel their own culture and community are threatened will drift toward drawing sharp borders, toward exclusionary belief in an effort to protect their cultural heritage under threat. In which case, we are really talking about elements of personal and social psychology, not theology at all.

We see, then, how Islam is very much of a piece with the evolution of religious and theological thinking in general and can be located at a midway point between the theological polarities of Judaism and Christianity. Islam did not come as a theological shock to the region. But it did serve the interests of geopolitical powers of the region just as Christianity did. Thus, most of our story will involve the interplay of states with religions; at that point the power and goals of the state dominate any independent role of religion. This reality sets an important stage for a key argument of this book: that most of the history of the West's relations with the Middle East is really about the geopolitics of empires and states and not much about religion itself—regardless of the slogans, banners, and ideological fervor invoked at the popular level to support the state. Take Islam out of the equation, and there's a very good chance you'd still find the Middle East at loggerheads with the West.

CHAPTER TWO

Power, Heresy, and
the Evolution of Christianity

Religion may in most of its forms be defined as the belief
that the gods are on the side of the Government.
—Bertrand Russell

The fourth century was fateful for Christianity: it marks the
period in which Christianity came to be embraced by the
Roman/Byzantine Empire; doctrine was now to fall directly
under state control. We will note how politics affects theology
directly. Religion and heresy become the chief instruments, the
banner, and rallying point of diverse cities, regions, groups, and
ambitious patriarchs in the internal political struggles of the
Roman/Byzantine Empire. The groundwork is being laid for the
further development of regional conflict in the Middle East, even
within Christianity. The Middle East will be moving eventually
into a three-way struggle among Rome, Constantinople, and
Islam, but for the moment we will observe how power and heresy
affected the geopolitics of the area even before Islam existed,
including rising antipathy between East and West, that is, between
Constantinople and Rome. Islam will soon adopt and share this
geopolitical distrust and wariness toward the West. It may come
with the territory.

The issue of heresy came up almost immediately after the life,
mission, and death of Jesus, when divisions sprang up among his

followers over how to interpret those dramatic events, thereby lay-
ing the groundwork for the development of later heresies. Over
time, the state and competing political powers were inexorably
drawn into the definition and management of theology and heresy, impacting directly upon the state's own policies as well. Who
was promoting one or another theological principle mattered as
much as the principle being promoted.

Politics was involved from the start, beginning with the execution of Jesus. Most of the Jewish religious leadership in Jerusalem
had viewed Jesus as a false prophet, the movement heretical, and
had called for Jesus's death. The state—the local authorities of
the Roman Empire—finally bowed to the leaders of the Jewish
community in putting him to death. On the part of Rome, this
was a *political* decision, not a theological one. One can readily
argue that for the leaders of the Jewish Sanhedrin itself, it was also
a political act to eliminate Jesus because of the threat he posed to
their authority in the community.

Right away, the potentiality of heresy was present. What would
the linkage be, if any, between Judaism and the new faith? Naturally, virtually all of the early followers of Jesus were Jewish and
thought of themselves as Jewish Christians. Yet if Christianity was
really a sect of Judaism, did new pagan converts to Christianity
have to accept Judaism before they entered Christianity? For most
Christian theologians today, it was Paul, not Jesus, who really
established Christianity as a distinct new religion quite separate
from Judaism; after Paul, one no longer had to be a Jew in order
to be a Christian. And it was Paul who broke new theological
ground in establishing faith as the essential component of salvation, rather than personal fulfillment in one's life of Jewish Law.
The new direction of the church under Paul created the most
shattering schism in the history of Judaism. The new Christian
faith would lay claim to being a universal religion, open to all, in
which ethnic or religious origin had no role to play. There was no

longer a Chosen People; all could become "chosen" by choosing Christianity. Faith, not Law, was the road to salvation.

So, from early on, diverse views on Jesus emerged as the early Christian community sought to make sense of his life, mission, and teachings. At the heart of these early controversies in Christianity lay the issue of *Christology:* what is the true nature of Jesus Christ? These arguments would inevitably affect Islam.

- Was Jesus man, or was he God, or both?
- Was he truly biologically conceived and born of a virgin, or had he always existed prior to birth? If he had always existed, had he existed as long as God had existed?
- Is Jesus coequal to God, or *is* he God?
- Did God come first, and then create Jesus? If so, does that not make Jesus "number two" to God?
- Is God one, or truly a dual personality combining Jesus and God? Or a triple personality combining the Holy Spirit?
- If Christ is both man and God, which is the more important element: the element of man, or God? Can God actually come down to earth and live as a human being, be killed, die on the cross?
- What happened to Jesus after he died and rose again from the dead? Does he still exist independently or did he fuse with God? Or has he always had a separate existence?

These questions and many others roiled the church and later the Roman Empire, incited rebellions, created new sects, sparked civil and military conflict, and divided earthly power. They remain without consensus and still roil the ranks of Christianity.

For the first three centuries, of course, Christianity had no official legal status. It was still only a movement, rejected and periodically persecuted by the Roman state; Christians sometimes

refused to pay even basic lip service to the state religion of Rome—
a loose and flexible affair involving brief obeisance to the few symbols of imperial power, even as one went about one's own personal
religious practice. But refusal to acknowledge even this minimal-
ist state religion alongside one's own personal religion was taken
as an act of rejection of the state, an act of rebellion.

Meanwhile, competing views of Jesus coexisted for long periods of time, until the church began systematically to reject numerous alternate visions of Jesus, seeking to extirpate them and forge
unity around a single "orthodox" view. The ultimate formal adoption of Christianity by Roman imperial power in Constantinople
only hastened the process of enforcing, with new muscle, the una-
nimity of Christian creed.

For the state, theology is too important to be left to the theologians. Theological decisions could not be limited to the obscure
proceedings of theologians sitting solemnly in council, but rather
included a constellation of competing authorities—believers,
diverse theologians, politicians, and ultimately the Emperor—all
vying to determine the true message of Christianity in line with
their own interests. They had one all-important goal: to ensure
that church and state maintained sole monopoly over doctrine. To
challenge monopoly over interpretation was to challenge church
and state power itself. In the zeal of the new faith, the nature of
Jesus was publicly debated among Jewish and Gentile communities around the ancient world—particularly in the Levant, Anatolia, Greece, and Egypt. There are tales of popular debates
within barbershops and taverns in Constantinople about the
nature of Jesus. Hellenized Jews, who made up a large proportion
of the Jewish community, were at the center of such debate. The
issues of Christ's nature would not go away, but would resurface
again and again in later heresies, even in the emergence of Islam
itself.

With the official adoption of Christianity by the Roman/

Byzantine state, the state moved to bring under control all inter-pretations and schools of thought that existed in the empire, to establish a degree of orthodoxy and define "right opinions." Par-tisans of differing views were brought to reconciliation, overruled, or suppressed. Not surprisingly, the power and influence of par-ticular dissenting officials inevitably affected the calculus of state decisions. How would the state identify, organize, rationalize, codify, collate, integrate, reconcile, and ultimately impose the manifold religious ideas swirling in the public space since Jesus's time? The first step was to convoke a series of ecumenical councils to hash out and codify the formal nature of the faith. When the Emperor Constantine I convened the Council of Nicaea in 325 CE to hammer out the basic principles of Christian theology in the Nicene Creed, the Council thought it had crafted the decisive statement on Christian faith for all time.

Yet it was not so: more Councils had to be held, more changes had to be made. One of the first tasks of the official church was decision on scripture. Among the many writings about Jesus, his apostles, and the early Christian movement, which ones would be consecrated as the heart of Christian doctrine? And which *versions* of which books, when there were often several? Acceptance of one book and rejection of another had direct consequences, generat-ing clear winners and losers; certain books were considered "inside" books and canonized; others were rejected as noncanon-ical, or "outside" books. Criteria for acceptance into the canon varied widely: some books were considered to have been written too late to speak authoritatively of Jesus's life. Or Rome weighed in to support and promote certain of its popular texts that were not especially popular or well-known in the Greek-speaking world of Constantinople. Some books were popular within certain spe-cific communities, others were not; some accounts were consid-ered unreliable, yet others considered so far outside of standard church teachings as to be downright heretical. Some books were seen as possessing historical value in documenting the early movement but could not be considered as scripture.

And what is "scripture" in the end? It is the body of texts adopted by recognized authority as authentic, thus canonized and later regarded as "sacred." The quality of the sacred in the end is determined by a judgment call on the part of quite interested parties. As a result, numerous important Christian texts were rejected by the authorities on one or another of these grounds. Yet the authenticity of these texts, even though rejected from the canon, included documents of vital importance to understanding Christianity, impressive works such as the Gospel of Thomas, the Dead Sea Scrolls, the Apocryphal Acts of the Apostles, and others. (Islam would undergo much the same process in sorting out the authenticity of thousands of Hadith relating to the reported sayings and doings of the Prophet in his lifetime—and they, too, are still under debate and examination today.)

It was not just texts that ended up losers. So were certain bodies of ideas and beliefs; whole communities that embraced them were excluded as the church authorities, acting with state sanction, passed judgment. Old and cherished ideas die hard. And to the various ecumenical councils that were convened, who would be invited? Who would be heard? How would decisions be made? Church leaders and communities whose views were not accepted were required to renounce their views or be pronounced heretical.

The power of the state became evermore intrusive in the process of the authentication, spread, and imposition of religion. Although much of the process of conversion to Christianity took place peacefully through evangelization, it was often buttressed by state takeovers of earlier "pagan" shrines, temples, and institutions from the pre-Christian era, and the banning of their rites and practices. In later years, some conversions were not peaceful at all; take the conquest and conversion of the Saxons by Charlemagne in the extremely violent thirty-year Saxon Wars beginning in 732. Here "conversion" was basically an ideological justification for the expansion of Charlemagne's Frankish Carolingian Empire. Capital punishment was imposed on those Saxons who continued to practice rites of their traditional gods; the campaigns were so violent that some Frankish bishops feared the long-term consequences of such bloody conversions by the sword.

The backing of the state, with all its coercive and persuasive power, greatly facilitated the evangelical process; the advisability of appearing loyal to state doctrine made such conversions easy and politic. The church employed different techniques to discredit and eliminate paganism. It would often demonize the pagan gods, declaring them devils or witches worshipped at one's peril. In other cases, the church compromised with local pagan practices, accepting some of the native pagan gods, to be rendered into instant "saints" so that they could remain as a comforting presence in the new Christian environment, albeit diminished in importance. Sacred pagan sites were often retooled into sites for local "saints." These practices were widely conducted among the barbarian tribes of Europe and into modern times in the Roman Church's conversion of native populations of Latin America and Africa. Islam faced almost precisely this same problem as it spread east and west, north and south, encountering earlier faiths, cults, and saints, many of whom were at least informally maintained, now in Islamic guise, by new converts to Islam.

The cult of the Virgin Mary represented another expansion of the realm of the divine as it moved to include evermore figures in the church's pantheon. Mary's official adoration took place some four hundred years after Jesus, and against considerable opposition. It was not until the sixth century that the veneration of Mary took on broad public dimensions in the Eastern Church, and only later still in the Western. (The religious scholar Karen Armstrong even suggests that the adoption of the Virgin Mary into the Catholic pantheon was an unconscious compensation for the abolition of the vital presence of female deities in so many early eastern religions, under the sternly patriarchal monotheism of Judaism and, much later, Protestant Christianity.) The book *When God Was a Woman,* by Merlin Stone, reflects this transition from societies that were often matriarchal, with worship of female deities, to patriarchal, which tended to associate women as a source of temptation and sin. All three Abrahamic faiths picked up on the idea.

Responsibility for most of these early political decisions on theology and doctrine fell to Constantinople rather than to Rome. Rome may have been the capital of the Roman Empire, but by the time of the legalization of Christianity, the Eternal City had fallen onto hard times, an uncomfortable place reeling from regular barbarian invasions and occupations. Meanwhile, the new city of Constantinople had been chosen as the alternative, and increasingly dominant, capital of the Roman Empire, where the Roman emperor would now reside almost exclusively. It was the Eastern Roman Empire that took the decision to formally adopt Christianity. The huge Eastern Empire, or Byzantium, would maintain the full trappings of an imperial state for another thousand years, even as Rome dwindled to geopolitical insignificance as an imperial power. It was Constantinople that took on most of the early task of determining orthodoxy, identifying the corpus of canonized texts and deciding which were heretical. It was also the Eastern Roman (Byzantine) Empire that ultimately spread Christianity throughout most of the Middle East, the Mediterranean world, up into the Balkans, and through much of the Slavic world. The empire at its high point had conquered the lands encompassing most of North Africa, Egypt, the Levant, Syria, and most of what is today's Iraq and Asia Minor (Anatolia). Christianity's only rival at all in the region was Zoroastrianism in Persia—until the emergence of Islam.

A Smorgasbord of Heresies

A fascinating panoply of Christian ideas emerged over time in the Eastern Mediterranean, most of which later came to be marked as heresies. These heresies matter. They tell us a lot about the dynamics at work in the power politics of the Byzantine Empire. They reveal much about the religious culture and mind-set of the time — even setting the stage for many of the theological views of Islam. An understanding of dynamics of heresy shows us again and again how religion acts as the vehicle, and not the cause, of conflicts, splits, and confrontations based on other quite worldly interests and rivalries. What better way to promote one's ambitions than to cloak them in religious and godly garb?

One of the earliest and most persistent heresies was *Marcionism*. According to the Christian scholar G. R. S. Mead, Marcion (110–160 CE) was a rich shipowner in Sinope, on the Black Sea coast of today's Turkey. Marcion followed in his father's footsteps to become bishop of Sinope. He reportedly made major contributions of his own money to the church and visited Rome as a known figure to promulgate his vision around 140 CE — approximately 160 years before the empire legalized Christianity. Even then, the church was hostile to Marcion's message, excommunicated him in 144 CE, and returned all the funds he had contributed.

Marcion's error in the eyes of the church was to become more Pauline than St. Paul himself. Paul had, of course, posited that Jesus had preached an entirely new religious vision, quite distinct from Judaism. Marcion, as a consecrated bishop of the church in the second century and a recognized leader in Asia Minor, declared the *entire* Old Testament to be irrelevant to Christian doctrine. He drew up elaborate tables of the characteristics of the Hebrew God as described in the Old Testament, alongside the qualities of God preached by Jesus. Marcion concluded that the characteristics of jealousy, wrath, violence, and vengeance of the Hebrew God were incompatible with the God of love and forgiveness as preached by Jesus, and that therefore the Hebrew God was not the true God, not the God of Christianity at all, but a lesser deity whose power was transcended by the power of the God of Jesus. Marcion even rejected most of the Apostles as unreliable witnesses, declaring only Paul to have clearly understood the nature of Christ's message; he concluded that it was fruitless and unnecessary to try to reconcile Judaism with Christianity.

Despite his being declared a heretic, Marcion's community was strong, and he established large numbers of churches that rivaled Rome for centuries in Italy, Egypt, Palestine, Arabia, Syria, Asia Minor, and Persia. The Marcionite Church was the second most influential and important movement among early Christian communities after the official church itself.

Elements of Marcion's message have persisted to today, in the form of groups and organizations that propagate his views. The remarkable longevity of Marcion's thinking lies in the fundamental theological dilemma that he posed: how can the parochial Semitic tribalism and violence of much of the Old Testament, with its often wrathful, arbitrary, and fickle God, be reconciled with the God of the New Testament, along with Jesus's message of love? And so the question remains: is there continuity, or a sharp break, between Judaism and Christianity? If there *is* continuity, then Christianity is clearly heretical from the perspective of Judaism; if there was a complete break from Judaism, then Christianity cannot be perceived as a Jewish heresy but rather as an independent body of faith in which the relevance of the Old Testament to Jesus's teachings is questionable. These questions do not go away. They also represent an early version of an argument, still regularly encountered today, that rejects the idea of any "common God" of the three Abrahamic faiths, and declares the Gods to be different. But Marcionism, in any case, represented a major challenge to Christian state authority in Byzantium.

After the legalization of Christianity in the empire in 313 CE, the next major and long-lasting heresy to arise was that of *Arianism*. Once again, the nature of Christ lies at its center. Arius (c. 250–336 CE) was a prominent theologian who was born in Libya, educated in Antioch (today's Turkey), where he absorbed a great many of his ideas, then lived and taught in Alexandria, Egypt, one of the major (rival) centers and patriarchates of early Christianity. He preached that Jesus had been *created* by the Father, just as the Holy Spirit had been, and that both were therefore subordinate to God the Father, who was the "true" God, the Creator. Jesus thus had a beginning, but God never did. God is self-existent, whereas the Son is not, who therefore cannot himself be God. Jesus thus becomes a lesser being.

Such a belief sharply undermined the orthodox position of the church that God the Father, God the Son, and God the Holy Spirit have always existed and all continue to exist simultaneously as coequals. The Arian doctrine was denounced and declared as heretical in the Nicene Creed negotiated at the Council of Nicaea in 325 CE. But the movement maintained great power and attracted even the sympathy of the Emperor Constantine's successor. Arianism became deeply established among the Germanic tribes of Europe and across the Middle East, especially Alexandria, where there was strong predisposition to accept this kind of thinking about Jesus as a "secondary" being and not on a par with God the Father. The doctrine became the vehicle for an Alexandrian bid for influence. The persistence of this Arian view reflects discomfort with the complex concept of the Trinity and of the position of Jesus himself as on a par with God; in short, there is an abiding sympathy for elements of a purer monotheism that does not dilute the One God—the essence of Jewish belief and of Muslim doctrine to come. It is also the theology of the modern Unitarian Church.

Despite being officially declared heretical and anathema, some heresies actually succeeded in breaking away and permanently establishing themselves. Indeed, debate over Christ's true nature could never, and has never, been fully laid to rest in any kind of Christian consensus.

While Arianism rejected granting Jesus "equal status" with God, another major heresy, *Monophysitism,* tilted the pendulum in the opposite direction, maintaining that Jesus did have some human qualities but that he was *essentially divine* in nature. This contravened the church's teaching that Christ was *both* fully human and fully divine. Monophysite teaching was branded heresy at the Fourth Council of Chalcedon in 451 CE, a major watershed that led to the first serious and permanent rupture in the body of the church—and the permanent breakaway of what are today called the Oriental Orthodox or Monophysite churches. Significantly Monophysite views were particularly strongly embraced in Syria, the Levant, and Egypt, all centers that resisted the power and authority of Constantinople, and also in other more distant places such as Armenia and Ethiopia.

Still other variations on the theme of Jesus's nature created other heresies. *Ebionism* was a first-century Jewish-Christian sect that revealed the pervasive influence of Judaism: it regarded Jesus as a prophet rather than divine, in rejection of Paul's vision (and directly parallel to Islam's vision of Jesus today).

Eutychianism argued that while Jesus possessed some human elements, the divine elements were dominant. Much of the controversy over this issue therefore related to Mary: Was she the Mother of Jesus as *God?* Or Mother only of Jesus in his *human* aspect? Her title in Greek differed accordingly.

Typically, theological dispute over these issues was bolstered, or even sparked, by geopolitical interests: Eutychianism was closely linked to a quest by the city of Alexandria in 433 CE to confirm its status as the second most important Christian city after Constantinople, a position that was equally sought by its rival Antioch, which promoted a more orthodox view of Jesus.

Docetism argued that Jesus's body was a physical illusion and that he only seemed to die; he was, in reality, a pure spirit who could not die. This belief was also linked to the notion that material in the world was inherently evil, and thus God or His Son could not be material. Islam, believing that Jesus was only a physical being and not a divinity, shares the view that Jesus only seemed to die on the cross, but was saved by God and taken to heaven.

Pelagianism derived from an obscure monk who may have been from the British Isles. He denied the central church teaching of "original sin"—the belief that mankind was inherently sinful from the original sin of Adam and Eve. The problem with the denial of original sin is that it undercuts the need for salvation solely through faith, as taught by the church. The view was thus declared heretical in 416 CE. Islam, too, denies the validity of original sin and of mankind's inherent sinfulness.

Monotheletism unsuccessfully sought to forge a tortured compromise between competing churches in Alexandria and Constantinople over whether Jesus's acts represented one single divine spirit or the cooperation of both human and divine wills. While seemingly abstruse, this doctrine had almost a purely political basis in seeking to heal the splits in the Eastern Church brought about by the Monophysite heresy. In the end, however, this compromise formulation was rejected. Politics trumped theology.

The details of these heresies are astonishing for what they reveal about the broad range of complex, detailed, and legalistic interpretations of the nature of Jesus. And all of this occurred primarily before the emergence of Islam. Islam must obviously be viewed as part of this context of debate over Christology.

Nor could any discussion of heresy be complete without mention of a few modern insights into these controversies. Power may possess the prerogative to determine what is and is not heresy, but heresy doesn't always mean something *new* on the scene. The fascinating work of the German theologian Walter Bauer in the late nineteenth century examined the evolution of early Christian doctrine and reached the conclusion that what we consider today as "heresy" actually often reflects the very earliest Christian understandings of the nature of Jesus. He argued that, in fact, it was the church itself that introduced newer interpretations of theology in later centuries, established new orthodoxies, sometimes altering the original Christian beliefs and even the texts themselves. These interpretations were driven by the later institutional and political imperatives of the church to declare earlier understandings to be "heretical." These views have recently been further propounded by the influential scholar Bart Ehrman, chairman of the Department of Religious Studies at the University of North Carolina at Chapel Hill.

Indeed, we still find considerable flexibility in the theological interpretations of a few smaller branches of the Abrahamic faiths. For example, doctrines of *continuous revelation* of God's word characterize the approach of Quakers, the Church of Jesus Christ of the Latter-day Saints (Mormons), Pentecostal, and Charismatic Christians, as well as the Baha'i. According to these precepts, revelations from God never cease and are available to succeeding generations to receive the word on an individual or communal level. These ideas are gaining broader currency over time. The Baha'i, among others, espouse a doctrine of "progressive revelation," including the ongoing emergence of prophets of God through time to reveal his word; these progressive revelations are designed for a humanity whose own understanding of God deepens and changes. Different historical conditions thus require different revelations in the human quest for greater precision in their understanding of the Divine.

Islam falls into many of these same patterns. The collapse of the first Islamic dynastic caliphate, the Umayyad, in 750 CE was driven by two key issues, among others: it had a power base in the very Arab city of Damascus and was being challenged by the rising power of the Abbasids, who represented the interests of Baghdad and its Iraqi-Persian culture. Furthermore, the Abbasids represented the demand for voice of newer non-Arab Muslim converts, who were excluded from equal power and rights under the Arab Umayyads. These caliphates thus rose and fell on regional and political grounds, not theological ones.

The role of power in religion continues to be recognized to our day. Take the comments of the Shi'ite mufti of Tyre in South Lebanon as recently as June 2009 over the issue of the disputed elections in Iran, in which he came into conflict with the leader of Hizballah. Sayyid Ali Amin said that the Lebanese Shi'ite Hizballah movement was attempting to stop discussion of the thesis of clerical rule in Iran, because challenging this ideology would undermine Hizballah's own power in Lebanon. "This is the biggest proof that [clerical rule] is not part of religious beliefs, but it is a power and political ideology," he said.

Furious debate over theological issues in the end is essentially a debate about underlying political interests of the state. By the time Islam came along, it was no longer the theology that mattered to the region but the shift in power and territorial control to a new rival state institution. It was politics as usual in the Middle East. Frictions among state, power, ideology, and heresy would continue to interact for centuries to come.

But the really critical factor for our present argument is the fast-rising tension between the Christian Byzantine Empire and the *Western* Church. As we will see in the next chapter, Islam, as a new geopolitical force, inherited not only much of the anti-Westernism of cities within the Eastern Empire in rebellion against Constantinople but also some of the latent anti-Rome views that grew over time within the Byzantine Empire itself.

While Byzantium drew its deepest identity from the belief that it was perpetuating the true tradition of the Roman Empire, it increasingly came to view the Western Church as a geopolitical rival whose power was ultimately as threatening to Byzantine power and identity as Islam itself. The Middle East was thus quite capable, without Islam, of developing aversion to the West.

CHAPTER THREE

Byzantium versus Rome: Warring Christian Polarities

If Islam had never appeared on the stage of history, there is no
doubt what religion would dominate the Middle East today—
it would still be Eastern Orthodox Christianity. There has been
no other credible religious challenger. And a still-dominant
Orthodox Church would likely have maintained deep suspicions
toward the West until now. If Eastern Orthodoxy had preserved
its dominance across the Mediterranean and the Middle East, it
would very likely have been the standard-bearer today for accumulated Eastern anger over the many centuries of grievances and
clashes with the West. We will see this theme build over the next
few chapters, providing an important basis for the case that the
Middle East could distrust and fear the West even without Islam.

The existence of these differences between the Eastern (Byzantine) Empire and the Western (Roman) Empire—religious, cultural, geopolitical, historical, artistic, and psychological—caused
scholars such as Samuel Huntington to posit Eastern Orthodoxy as
one of several world civilizations that could "clash" with the West,
with or without Islam. Indeed that hostility in many ways is still
there, even though the church no longer controls the Middle East.

In our Western tradition, we are rather blind to the Eastern Orthodox Church. We see few of these churches around us, and we usually fail to appreciate what an important place the Eastern Church enjoys in Christian and Middle East history. First, it is the earliest and most "native" Christian religion of the Middle East, compared to the Roman Catholic Church, which grew apart from it in rite, theology, politics, and outlook, and at much greater remove from Jerusalem. Furthermore, Orthodoxy still exists in the Muslim Middle East in the form of minority Orthodox communities. It prides itself in being closest in form and spirit to the original church; it began life on the original church lands, and nurtures the belief that it has avoided the doctrinal and institutional corruption that it perceives in the Western Latin Church.

Deep roots of anti-Westernism still exist in the Orthodox Church. What is more striking, many of these anti-Western feelings among the Eastern Orthodox strongly resemble certain Muslim attitudes toward the West as well, suggesting a common geopolitical source of shared views, suspicions, and grievances toward Western influence, intentions, and interventions. We have already noted this tie-in with Islam: how numerous Christian doctrines on the nature of Jesus, later denounced by church authorities as heretical, resemble some Islamic views on Jesus as well. Shared grievances toward Western power on the part of both the Orthodox Church and Islam suggest that civilizational "fault lines" are not simply cultural peculiarities of these *religions;* they also had a lot to do with the nature of the West and its confrontations with the Middle East going back a very long way. Differences of a political, social, and economic nature could often transform seemingly small theological differences into major heresies and rebellions. (The same is true of the Sunni-Shi'ite split within Islam, where initial differences over succession to the Prophet had almost no significant *theological* character, but later grew into deeper communal hostility.)

There's a chicken-and-egg question here: Do theological differences spark political, social, and economic conflicts? Or is it the converse—do existing, concrete political, social, and economic differences come to be *reflected* in theology or ideology? Once a small theological split emerges, it can often end up entrenched in communitarian issues of identity and even community existence. Put another way, people might reasonably differ over smaller theological points relating to Jesus's precise nature. But what impels people to kill and die over them? Other important factors are obviously at work here as well.

———

WE NEED TO GO back to Alexander the Great to witness the opening scene of a more than two-millennia history of East-West geopolitical struggle. Alexander launched the first great thrust of Western power into Asia in 334 BCE, as his forces crossed from Greece into Persian-dominated Anatolia and conquered the powerful Persian Zoroastrian Achaemenid Empire of Iran. These regions formed only a part of the Alexandrine Empire, which came to include Syria, Egypt, and parts of Iraq as well, ultimately reaching the borders of India. This was very much a foreign cultural invasion from the point of view of Asia and left a significant legacy of interaction, culturally often rich but politically hostile. Persia had already been at war off and on with Greece for many centuries. For Asia, Greece was the West, the rival and enemy.

The successor to Alexander's empire, the Seleucids, maintained Greek military and frontier posts at the frontiers of a Semitic- and Persian-speaking world as Greek influence was pushed back. Syria and Anatolia represented the key front lines where these diverse cultures met and contested over many hundreds of years. The Roman Empire eventually superseded Alexander's Hellenistic empires. By the fourth century CE, it had spread to Constantinople and beyond, the region which at first was known as the eastern wing of the Roman Empire. So by the time of the foundation of the Eastern Roman Empire, there is already a significant legacy of some six centuries of East-West political contestation and warfare between Greek/Roman power and Persian or Semitic empires.

But conflict in the region was hardly limited to Greek versus Persian or Semitic cultures. Antagonisms between Rome and Constantinople themselves—within the Roman Empire—go back at least to the second century CE, when rivalries emerged among the five early Christian patriarchs: Rome, Constantinople, Alexandria, Jerusalem, and Antioch. As one by one the latter three patriarchs fell under Islamic rule in the seventh century—maintaining their religious positions, but losing their local secular authority—the struggle came down to a binary struggle for influence and power between Rome and Constantinople. And over time, as differences in theology and rites deepened between the two, Rome continued to insist on its own preeminence while Constantinople felt itself every bit a coequal. Rome's subsequent establishment of a papacy in place of the Rome patriarchate was a further effort to extend its credentials over the "lesser" ranks of patriarchs in the major Christian centers to the East. This issue of preeminence persists even today.

Differences over power were reflected also in growing cultural differences. When we speak of Constantinople, we are essentially speaking of a region of long-standing *Greek* culture. Constantinople was the center of the Greek-speaking world. This cultural difference helped fuel subsequent clashes between Greek and Latin Christianity—Middle Eastern and Western. The Greek roots of Constantinople actually go back a long way; its port was first known to the Greeks as Byzantion in sixth century BCE. Some nine hundred years later, in 330 CE, the city was "refounded" by the Roman Emperor Constantine, who named it after himself; he saw it as a more secure second capital of the vast Roman Empire at a time when Rome itself was already reeling under constant barbarian siege. Two distinct wings of the Roman Empire—an Eastern and a Western—now emerge.

Even the very concept of a meaningful "Western Roman Empire" was becoming increasingly a fiction in this period as civil wars, rival emperors, and constant barbarian assaults continued to rend Rome. With the final collapse of the Roman emperor in Rome, in the face of Germanic invasions in 476 CE, the Western wing of the Roman Empire had come to an end. The Eastern wing in Constantinople now inherited the full mantle of the Roman Empire, complete with all its vast territories in the Balkans, Anatolia, the Eastern Mediterranean, and North Africa.

The emergence of Constantinople as the new seat of the Roman Empire carried fateful cultural consequences. In contrast to the absolute dominance of Latin in the Western Empire, Greek was the lingua franca of all the Eastern Mediterranean, marking the city and the region with a distinct Greek cultural character. One of Constantinople's trump cards was that the New Testament itself had been written in Greek, not Latin. Latin would hang on as the official administrative language of the Eastern Empire for only a few more centuries. The educated class in Constantinople no doubt prided itself on maintaining a knowledge of Latin language and culture and for continuing to bear the standard of Roman civilization. But the languages themselves began to determine their broader cultures: the remnants of a "Latin" Empire in the West, and a powerful "Greek" Empire in the East. In later centuries, these terms took on overtones of mutual contempt: to be called a "Latin" in Constantinople, or a "Greek" in Rome, passed as nothing less than derogatory. Furthermore, no emperor would ever again rule over both Rome and Constantinople. Rome shrank to a fraction of the size of the Eastern capital; the pope was left there in splendid isolation as little more than a symbol, a virtual prisoner of the forces around him, for the next several hundred years.

In the absence of any remaining Western Empire, what then was the nature of this "Roman" capital in Constantinople now to be? Over time, Constantinople developed a sense of special mission — the perpetuation and preservation of the Roman Empire in the East. Constantinople was now the last bastion of Christian civilization and spirituality against the new barbarian conquerors in both the West — against Goths, Franks, Celts, Alans, Huns — and in the East — against pagan Slavs, Zoroastrian Persians, and later Muslim Arabs and Turks. The Eastern Roman Empire was developing its own cultural identity in increasing distinction now from Rome and the West as centers of power.

The War of Names

Names carry psychological weight, bespeak identity. You can still whip up a heated argument among Greeks about what Constantinople and the Eastern Church should be called. The struggle over the very name of the Eastern Empire spoke volumes about East-West tensions.

Constantinople, without the slightest hesitation, continued to refer to itself as the capital of the Roman Empire, despite its roots in a Greek-speaking world. So at what point can we mark the transition of Constantinople from the Eastern Roman Empire into a de facto Greek, or Byzantine, Empire? Actually, such a formal transition never occurred. (In fact, the term "Byzantine" first appeared only in the sixteenth century, when a German historian described the Eastern Empire as "Byzantine.") Constantinople steadfastly considered itself the Roman Empire to the end, and it never wavered from the use of that term, even in the Greek language.

The power of this word "Roman" to describe the Eastern Empire spread far beyond Greek speakers and into the mouths of the Muslim cultures in the region as well. Note how in the main languages of the Middle East — Arabic, Turkish, and Persian —

the Eastern Christian Empire was known as *Rûm* (Rome)—and still is, even today. The word *Rûm* is still associated with anything to do with the Eastern Roman Empire, or with Anatolia (Asia Minor). The Qur'an itself has a chapter called *al-Rûm* that talks about the Byzantine Christians. The first Seljuk Turkish state based in Anatolia, which fought long wars with Constantinople over Anatolian territory in the ninth and tenth centuries, arrogated to itself the title of "Sultanate of Rûm." The very Mediterranean Sea was then called "the Sea of *Rûm*" in Arabic. (For fans of the renowned Sufi poet Rumi, we need only note that the name was the adjectival form for one who lives in *Rûm*, on what was once Eastern Empire soil, in Anatolia.)

But the West would not yield up the term. Despite the widespread use of "Rome" across the Middle East to refer to the Eastern Empire, the West still remained bitterly unwilling to surrender the mantle of the Roman Empire to Constantinople, even though it was undeniable that the Eastern Empire was still flourishing in the East, long after the fall of the Western Empire to barbarian control. The West insisted on referring to the Eastern Empire only as *Imperium Graecorum,* or "Empire of the Greeks," clearly rejecting any title suggestive of the Roman Empire, a term they wanted reserved solely for Western rulers. We see how this struggle over "who is Rome" reemerges vividly on Christmas Day in 800 CE when, at High Mass in Saint Peter's in Rome, Pope Leo III crowned the powerful new Germanic barbarian ruler Charlemagne as *Imperator Romanorum,* the Emperor of the Romans. By invoking this designation, he sought to restore the title to the West, wresting it away from the Greeks in Constantinople who had "usurped" it in this war of names.

In any event, Charlemagne, as the most powerful ruler of the time in the West, ultimately decided against trying to wrest back the title of Emperor of Rome for himself, but he did attempt to arrange a dynastic marriage with the Empress Irene in

Constantinople as one means of recovering the title and uniting the two empires under his authority. In this he did not succeed. It would not be long, however, before a federation of German tribes decided to adopt the grandiloquent title of "Holy Roman Empire" and to deny it to Constantinople and the Eastern Empire. The arrogation of the additional designation of "Holy" added real fuel to the fire; it marked the German federation's claim to the *spiritual* power of the empire as well, even though the federation did not even control the city of Rome. (Hence the legendary essay question for English schoolboys on European history: "The Holy Roman Empire was neither Holy, Roman, nor an empire. Discuss.")

Thus this war of names carries the freight of a deep, ongoing geopolitical struggle over authority, legitimacy, even spirituality. The pope, isolated in Rome, clung to the title and belief that he was the head of Christendom, even though he had originally been only one of five equal bishops of the church in the fourth century. With each passing century, the political gulf between East and West grew. In Constantinople, a sense of Greekness would come to form part of a "national" identity based on language and culture, especially at the popular level.

Passions hardened into prejudices; over time the barbarian-dominated West came to think of Constantinople as little more than the locus of an overgrown, effete, and corrupted Eastern tradition that ultimately was increasingly hard put to defend itself against the encroaching Muslim infidels in the Holy Lands. This dismissive attitude was maintained even in the face of the extraordinary political, military, and cultural accomplishments of Constantinople over a thousand years, as it spread its power across North Africa, the Eastern Mediterranean, the Balkans, and the Fertile Crescent. But Constantinople's power could not last forever, and by 1453 the last segments of the "Greek Empire" had fallen irrevocably to the Muslim Turks.

Still, unlike the short-lived Roman Empire, which had barely made it into the fifth century, the Eastern Roman Empire had enjoyed a magnificent run of another thousand years, into the fifteenth. And even though the empire did fall, the Eastern *Church* itself was far from dead, even then. The Eastern Orthodox Christian Church today remains the second-largest single Christian communion in Christianity after Catholicism.

The Birth of National Churches

In acknowledging the accomplishments of the Byzantine Empire, we would be missing a large part of the picture if we did not look at its massive cultural impact in all those surrounding areas where Orthodox Churches would be permanently established.

One of the single most important legacies of the Eastern Empire, and a key theme of this book, was its creation of national churches in Eastern Europe and the Middle East—churches that to this day remain culturally and emotionally linked to specific language/ethnic groups. The consequences of this historic nationalization of churches haunts us even today in the bloody history following the breakup of Yugoslavia in the 1990s, which pitted Eastern Orthodox Serbs against Roman Catholic Croats.

Apart from contesting names and theologies, the "Greeks" of the East spent centuries in a much more elemental struggle with Rome over territorial influence, especially in the Balkans and parts of the Middle East. In one of the fateful cultural decisions of history, the Eastern Orthodox Church dispatched missionaries in all directions to convert the pagan world and establish new local linguistically based churches—Bulgarian, Serbian, Russian, Macedonian, Coptic, Albanian, Armenian, Romanian, and so on, across and beyond Byzantine lands. These ethnic, or "national," Eastern Churches, with their use of local languages in liturgy, stood in sharp distinction to the supranational and "universal"

Catholic tradition based on scripture and rituals conducted everywhere strictly in Latin. And nearly every one of these "national" Orthodox Churches would come to have some future close relationship with Islam in a checkered coexistence. The Western Church, on the other hand, would rarely experience close proximity to Islam, except in Spain.

The Orthodox Church did not actually have any specific intention of enshrining ethnicity as the foundation of the church; rather, the process evolved naturally. The linking of religion and ethnicity came about as Byzantine missionaries fanned out to pagan peoples, particularly in the Slavic world, to reach them by preaching and translating the Bible into their native languages. The conversion of the Slavs began in the ninth century with the mission of Cyril and Methodius into the Balkans, where they created the first alphabet for Slavic languages.

This missionary work held far greater significance than mere religion: it was a vital strategy in the Eastern Church's rivalry with Rome to convert pagans to Eastern Christianity rather than let them fall to Western Catholicism. Translation of the Bible into the vernacular languages of the peoples on the borders of the empire became a key instrument in their conversion; it brought the Bible to them in their living language and secured their cultural loyalty, especially since the translated Bible was often the first document ever to be written in their languages—such as what is now called Old Church Slavonic, the liturgical language of the Slavic Orthodox world. In response, German Catholic clerics in the region fought unsuccessfully to dissuade the Slavs from adopting the liturgy in a Slavic language. (Astonishingly, at this same period in the West, the Bible still had not been officially translated in full into vernacular languages, nor would it be until the Protestant Reformation five hundred years later. Indeed, the Catholic Church insisted on maintaining Latin as the sole liturgical language until the twentieth century—even though the New Testament had originally been written in Greek.)

A second attractive feature of Eastern Christianity was the relatively greater autonomy that Eastern Churches were offered as opposed to the requirement of rigorous submission to Rome, even on church administrative matters, under Catholicism. The pope, furthermore, insisted on arrogating to himself immense secular powers in ways that the Byzantine patriarch did not. The history of the European Middle Ages is replete with just such massive power struggles between the pope and worldly princes. This reminds us that there is, in fact, a much deeper tradition of religious interference into Western secular politics by the Roman Catholic Church than has ever been the case in Islam and its consistently secular (nonclerical) rulers (until modern Iran).

As the East-West rivalry continued in Eastern Europe, the Serbs, Bulgarians, Romanians, Russians, and the southern half of the Albanian population were ultimately converted to Orthodoxy. But Rome won out in the conversion of the Poles, Czechs, Slovaks, Croats, Slovenians, and Hungarians, who chose Catholicism. This simple choice of religion fatefully cast the die for the entire future political and cultural orientation of these countries that lasts until today. A sharp Latin-Orthodox fault line still runs from the Baltic Sea down through the old Yugoslavia to the Aegean.

Thus, without explicitly intending to do so, Constantinople had fused religion with ethnicity within the Orthodox tradition— a particularly potent combination. Indeed, the richness of the Orthodox Churches lay in their cultural diversity even as they remained part of a broader, powerful Orthodox community united in common spiritual values, belief, and ritual. In sharp contrast, Islam strongly resisted the creation of any "ethnic" Islamic movements or use of local languages to replace Arabic for worship; but Islam also never adopted the highly centralized model of control that Rome did. Rome had a pope, Islam had a caliph, but the latter never remotely maintained the centralized position of religious power that the pope did.

East-West Conflict Deepens

The conflict between Christian Byzantium and the West deepened over the next several centuries before the fall of Constantinople in 1453. The Eastern Church remained consistently dismayed by what it saw as papal arrogation of greater jurisdictional authority over all aspects of the Western Church; the clear implication was that the pope assumed that his jurisdiction should be similarly accepted in the East. For Constantinople, the pope was little more than the "Patriarch of Rome" and never had legitimate claim to universal authority over the entire Christian Church, and never would be allowed to do so.

The struggle for domination thus transformed relatively minor religious issues into volatile symbols of rivalry. Byzantine Emperor Leo III banned the use of religious icons in the church in 717 CE in the famous iconoclasm controversy, in which the Eastern Church came out for a period against all portrayals of humans in religious art (probably reflecting similar views in Judaism and Islam as well). The pope in Rome actually attempted to overthrow Leo III over this issue, and failing, then excommunicated the Eastern patriarch, leading the Eastern Church to excommunicate the pope in return. This serious rift was later patched up, but it was symptomatic of bad blood and worse things to come.

In the tenth century, a vicious geopolitical struggle took place over who would convert the powerful new Bulgarian state to Christianity; Constantinople's victory for Orthodoxy was a bitter blow to Rome.

In 1054, the long-simmering theological and political dispute reached the cataclysmic breaking point in the history of Christianity: Rome and Constantinople stumbled into the incredible act of mutual excommunication, marking the start of the "Great Schism" in the Christian Church. The alleged cause was an unbelievably arcane debate over whether "the Holy Spirit proceeds directly from the Father," as Constantinople professed, or, whether the Holy Spirit "proceeds from the Father and the Son together" as Rome insisted. Clearly an abstruse theological issue had become freighted with the weight of centuries of powerful geopolitical hostility and struggle—a near Cold War. The split has yet to be healed. The Orthodox Church also rejected the "new" Roman concepts of the Immaculate Conception of Mary, and Rome's "invention" of the existence of purgatory—doctrines adopted by Rome many hundreds of years after the time of Jesus.

Yet even this stunning event of mutual East-West excommunication would not match the bitter suspicions and ultimately armed conflict between the two Christian sides during the years of the Crusades (discussed in chapter 5) in which Latin (Catholic) crusaders from Europe pillaged the city of Constantinople itself with incalculable lasting effects. The event was consummated in 1182 by the immensely emotional so-called Massacre of the Latins in Constantinople. Anti-Western sentiments ran deep among the general population, who resented the powerful community of Venetian (Catholic) merchants who virtually ran the economy of Constantinople. In the ensuing rioting, a staggering eighty thousand "Latins" were massacred in the city, driving a further wedge of emotion, blood, and hatred between Rome and Constantinople.

Today, nearly six hundred years after the Ottoman Turks conquered Constantinople, this loss of its crown jewel is still remembered and mourned by the Orthodox world with an intensity not readily appreciated in Europe. Although Europeans viewed the fall of the city to Islam as a significant setback to Christianity, they had little stomach for further crusades and precious little nostalgia or attachment for the old Greek capital of the Eastern Empire. For most Western Christians, Constantinople and its legacy had come to be seen as little more than a corrupt Orthodox backwater and a historic anomaly worthy of scant attention. The poisonous legacy would never be forgotten in the East and would fatefully affect Russia in particular, as we will see in a later chapter. And who in the West today really has much sense or awareness of Eastern Christianity?

But Orthodox Christianity in no way perished with the fall of the Eastern Empire to the Turks; indeed, the patriarch himself remained based in Muslim Istanbul (even today), from where, with Turkish permission, he continued to exercise religious, but not secular, authority over portions of the Orthodox world. Even in collapse, Byzantines maintained such resentment against Rome that they actually came to feel it was better to be defeated by the Muslim Turks than by the Christian Latins. For they knew the church would survive and operate under Muslim rule, as was evident from other Christian areas that had already long fallen to Muslim power, including the Holy Lands; Orthodoxy would continue to exist. But conquest by Rome would mean the Latinization of the church — an abomination — and the end of Orthodoxy forever, a far worse fate. The choice between domination by Muslim or Latin Christian rule thus remained a no-brainer for most Orthodox believers.

Mirrors and Echoes

We have watched a broad range of tensions, hostilities, rivalries, and suspicions unfold between Eastern and Western Christian worlds. Even while frequently cloaked in theological dispute, in most cases the struggle involved worldly issues of rivalry for converts and struggle over territory and institutional power. In the end, it's quite evident that state religion and theological disputes were ultimately instruments to serve the social, political, and even psychological needs of the state.

The scholar Vasilios Makrides notes that "popular protest movements of an overtly religious character often had a different hidden character. In other words, they reflected social and economic dissatisfaction vis-à-vis the policies and influences of Westernization....Anti-Westernism may take the form of an extreme nationalism, which can function as a surrogate for religion too." In the modern era, even issues such as Western-led globalization within the old Orthodox world spark similar fears, echoing earlier geopolitical struggles in which the East lost out to Western power.

These themes apply equally tellingly to the rift between the Muslim world and the West today. If this dynamic of deep East-West rivalry and tension exists even within Christianity, it reflects similar foundations of tensions between the Muslim world and the West. Identities and power are at stake, far more than religion; and issues of gut identity in turn bolster communal differences. As Makrides comments, "Many Orthodox are still fully convinced of their real superiority toward other peoples and of their salvific [redemptive] mission in the world." The same could be said of many Muslims' belief that Islam, too, can one day serve to rescue a morally rudderless and foundering West.

As the gap today between the developed and powerful West and a weaker, lagging East grows, the weaker party naturally casts about for explanations. One tendency has been to blame the West for all the failings of the Orthodox and Muslim worlds. Makrides adds that

> in some cases anti-Westernism represents a convenient means for providing ready-made answers and outlets for various problems of the Orthodox world....This mechanism of alleviating personal responsibility and guilt feelings

by constantly externalizing the main sources of evil (here the West) is a typical phenomenon in the Orthodox East as well as being a form of diverting social dissatisfaction and unrest.

Makrides finally observes that in modern Greece and elsewhere in the Orthodox world, such as Russia, anti-Western political groupings look even to some form of confederation with Turkey based in part on the power of a visceral anti-Western agenda. We will see how pro-Muslim and pro-Turkish feelings, even if not part of mainstream thinking, do exist in contemporary Russia today, reflecting some of these historic reflexes.

We see here, too, the early roots of a process in which Islam and Eastern Orthodoxy ultimately come to share many views on the West. Indeed, if Islam had never emerged in the Middle East and Eastern Orthodoxy had maintained its sway there, how far-fetched would it be to imagine Orthodoxy still carrying single-handedly the torch of anti-Western feeling in the Middle East today?

CHAPTER FOUR

Islam Meets Eastern Christianity

A rab armies, energized by the new social, political, and religious ideas of Islam in the mid-seventh century, quickly advanced north out of Arabia. We witness here a classic encounter of the old and the new. It was the great Byzantine province of Syria that was the scene of the first military encounters between Christianity and Islam. And as we look at the sweep of Arab armies north into Byzantine territory in the Levant, some striking features emerge. First is the hostility so much of the mainly Semitic Fertile Crescent felt toward Western attempts to rule them—and for these regions, the "West" meant not just Rome, but Greek Constantinople as well. We are talking about lands whose histories and cultures are essentially eastern and Semitic—long a part of the contested turf between various Persian empires and Greece. There is little love lost for Greeks or Byzantium here. So we encounter deeply rooted anti-Westernism—meaning resistance to invasion and control from Greece *or* Rome—even before Islam arrives on the scene.

Second, we see again and again how religion provided the rallying cry for this resistance against Rome or Byzantium. These

cities regularly embraced "heresies" as symptomatic of their opposition. It wasn't simply that they were Monophysite and hence
opposed Constantinople. It was partly that they opposed Constantinople and hence were inclined to embrace theologies hostile
to central rule. Thus, Muslim conquest of these great Levantine
cities of the Byzantine Empire was facilitated by long-standing
anti-Byzantine feeling within them.

Finally, these conquests by Muslim forces in one sense seem to
have transformed the religious world, but in reality at the time
they tended more to change control of the *state*. The actual
mechanics of how Arab administration spread provide fascinating insight into how little religion lay at the center of these struggles. Instead, they suggest how much Islam was primarily the
latest banner under which old geopolitical struggles of the Middle
East were perpetuated; the great prize was enjoying the fruits
of rule.

It would be absurd, of course, to entirely exclude the role of
Islam itself from the dynamics of struggle among Middle Eastern
cities, provinces, and rulers. After all, Islam very much represented a fresh spirit on the scene. But the Middle East region, in
effect, was ripe for some kind of new galvanizing force that could
empower fractious local rulers and cities to rise up against the
existing centralized power of Constantinople. Ideology, wherever it exists, is almost invariably pressed into the service of
local geopolitics. In short, we witness the role of anti-Byzantine
impulses facilitating the Islamic conquest in many of the Semitic
regions.

Syria and the Culture of Dissidence

Syria is an excellent case in point, because the region harbored
multiple latent discontents that regularly burst forth over the centuries. The invasion of Muslim armies was merely the latest spark

to help foment rebellion, not only against Constantinople but also against Rome. Syria's long-standing dissident character, embedded in its geopolitical culture, goes a long way toward explaining the endless problems the Byzantine Empire faced in trying to defend these territories against early Islamic conquest.

What conditioned Syria for this rebellious role? Syria is one of those great crossroads of culture where ideology and power regularly come together in history, conferring upon Damascus a vibrant role in the unfolding of Middle Eastern politics. "Syria" in its time, of course, encompassed what are today the modern states of Syria, Jordan, Palestine, Lebanon, Israel, and western Iraq. Throughout history it has contained many diverse forces that stamped it with a distinct and fractious character. From 312 BCE it was the heart of the large Hellenistic Seleucid Empire, successor to part of the empire of Alexander the Great that held sway from Anatolia to India for over 250 years. But it was at least as much part of the East as it was of the West, particularly touched by Persia and cultures to the East. It had been the shaky outpost for the eastward projection of Greek culture against the other powerful Semitic and Persian cultures in the region.

The city of Edessa in northern Syria provides a particularly dramatic example of strong local identities hostile to Western control. Edessa had been a Greek military garrison town for the Eastern Roman Empire. But the dominant Greek language of its rulers gradually came to be displaced by Syriac, a Semitic language akin to Aramaic, and Syriac culture began to undermine the Hellenic outposts. Despite its inclusion within the Eastern Christian Roman Empire, Edessa's sympathies often lay to the east, with Parthian/ Zoroastrian Iran, rather than with the Byzantines.

Nor can we make the case that Edessa was anti-Christian, hence anti-Byzantine. It had actually been the *first* Christian state in the world under the Abgar Dynasty, which was founded by Arab, or Nabatean, tribes in 132 BCE. It was Christian missionaries from

Edessa who carried the word of Nestorian Christianity east into Mesopotamia and Persia, where the Nestorian Church would establish a strong foothold. This region, then, was one of the earliest of Christian communities, but its Syriac-speaking Nestorian Church was clearly Eastern in a cultural sense, lying beyond the sway of the Greek-speaking parts of the empire. In 410 CE, the Nestorian Church made its move: it rejected any affiliation or subordination to Western bishops. And "Western bishops" was a reference not to Rome, but to the Byzantine authorities themselves, whom the Nestorians very much perceived as a Western force. This Nestorian move toward religious independence was an unmistakable political statement even if couched in theological terms.

Not content with embracing one heretical faith, Edessa later fell under the sway of the equally "heretical" and highly monotheistic Christian Monophysite beliefs. This doctrine spread rapidly throughout Syria in later centuries, in spite of fierce opposition from Constantinople that insisted on the two separate and distinct natures of Jesus. Religious doctrine becomes a litmus test of political loyalty. The consistently heretical character of Syrian Christianity reflected its own fiercely independent character. As the German scholar Arthur Vööbus points out, "The earliest extant sources of Syrian Christianity reveal a powerful spirit of self-consciousness for independence. This desire is imprinted on every page of the historical records." In the writings of an early Syrian Christian leader we find *"hatred, for everything bearing a Greek or Roman label....* Autonomy is the hallmark of the early Syrian conception of the church." These events again precede Islam; Islam will easily adopt the regional and anti-Western culture—even anti-Byzantine—of so much of the Fertile Crescent.

And it wasn't just Edessa. Look at what happened in Palmyra, another prominent Syrian city, which actually brought the Roman

Empire to its knees in a major revolt in the mid-third century CE, before the East-West division; Palmyra threatened to reshape the entire structure of power in the Eastern Mediterranean. As a major commercial hub of Syria, it had long been a crossroads of trade between Persia, India, China, and Rome. It, too, had adopted Syriac as its language, reflecting the powerful Semitic culture of Edessa and equally influenced by Persian culture as much as by Rome or Greece. In 269 CE, its legendary Queen Zenobia launched a powerful military campaign against Roman rule. And who was Zenobia? Tellingly, she was descended from nobility in Carthage (today's Tunisia)—another city that famously nurtured historical hatred of its chief Mediterranean rival, Rome, which had laid waste to Carthage several centuries earlier.

Within a few years, the forces of Palmyra had conquered a huge area: all of Syria, Egypt, and half of Anatolia. Indeed, this "Palmyran Empire" for a few years made up the entire eastern third of a Roman Empire that had fallen apart into three distinct regions. Palmyra was poised to succeed the Roman Empire in the East, an event that, if successful, would have perpetuated a Syriac-Semitic Christian rule of the Eastern Mediterranean instead of the Byzantine Greek one. The beautiful Queen Zenobia was finally defeated by Roman forces, reportedly wrapped in golden chains, and sent to Rome, where she was eventually pardoned and became an exotic leading figure in Roman society, even after her empire had long been crushed. But the spirit of revolt across great parts of Syria remained strong—against Rome, and against Constantinople. The Persian Empire took strategic advantage of this dispute within the Byzantine Empire to publicly support the Nestorian Christians and offer them refuge in Persia. Religion *was* the ideology of the period, working in support of conflicting geopolitical interests.

Political, ideological, and theological dissidence against Rome and Greece was thus embodied in the predisposition of Syrian religious culture toward a more monotheistic view of Jesus—as having a single nature (either purely divine or purely human)—and a rejection of Constantinople's complex doctrines of the Trinitarian three-in-one. The simplified Monophysite doctrine soon spread across a vast area: Anatolia, Syria, the Levant, and Egypt, where it enjoyed strong popular support and, of course, lasts to this day.

The drama of the later Monophysite heresy was no less vivid. It had its seat in Alexandria, Egypt, another city that was one of the leading competitors for church power in the Eastern Mediterranean. Alexandria had also thrown its weight behind the proposition of the "one divine nature" of Christ—a simple, direct, accessible doctrine highly popular across Syria, Egypt, and Anatolia. Constantinople repudiated the doctrine at the first Council of Ephesus in 431 CE. But church politics and personalities move in strange ways, and only eighteen years later, at the second Council of Ephesus, a theological about-face took place on political grounds, and the Monophysite doctrine was officially embraced. With each major shift in doctrine, key church figures rose and fell, intensifying the struggle. In the ensuing political turmoil four years later, the church reversed itself yet again at the Council of Chalcedon in 451 CE and now declared the Monophysite doctrine to be heresy again. New winners and losers emerged; key bishops and church leaders were swept from office, affecting the power and influence of the cities in which they were based. Nor was the story over. This time, despite artful efforts at theological rewording to accommodate both sides, large numbers of Monophysites flatly refused to accept Constantinople's ruling. In the end, they broke outright with Constantinople and reestablished their various independent churches to be known as Oriental Orthodox, primarily in the eastern regions of the empire.

As striking as the Council's about-face was on the Monophysite doctrine, the Council of Chalcedon took yet another fateful step vis-à-vis Rome: it declared Constantinople to be the "New Rome," equal to the old original Rome. Indeed, it was to be the "sole Rome" as the paltry remnants of the Roman Empire in the West foundered before barbarian assaults. The concept of a New Rome would never lose its powerful resonance: one thousand years later, with the fall of the Byzantine (Eastern Roman) Empire itself, Moscow would arrogate to itself the title of "Third Rome," suggesting a further extension of the continuing legacy of Christian authority.

These powerful figures—the pope, the Roman emperor of the East, and sundry bishops and patriarchs with their own constituencies and interests—had much more at stake in these fine theological debates than mere theology. The doctrinal struggle over Jesus's nature, for example, also lay at the very foundation of the pope's claim to power. If Jesus was solely Divine in nature, then how could the pope legitimately claim to be the "vicar of Christ"? There can be no vicar of divinity itself—whereas if Christ had a human nature as well, a succession could appropriately follow from Peter down to the church fathers and then to the pope as the vicar of the human Christ.

In effect, we are witnessing here a massive power struggle operating at three different levels: first, between Rome and Constantinople over who was the real Roman Empire and who would lead it; second, a struggle within the Eastern Church over doctrine inside the Eastern Empire; and finally, the struggle of heretical and rebellious Christian forces in the East entirely opposed to the power of Constantinople's *political* writ in the eastern provinces. This was the scene onto which Islam made its appearance—into a severely riven political region with all its various historical, cultural, and political predispositions. Islam would only add to—and inherit—this already complex equation of power and ideology.

Islam Enters Byzantine Territory

How Islam actually expanded says a lot about the complex process of religious conversion and civilizational change. It also tells us something about the nature of religious accommodation and coexistence; here, Samuel Huntington's facile term "bloody borders of Islam" is little more than a caricature of the complex political and social interactions that took place.

After the earlier sagas of rebellion in Edessa and Palmyra against Byzantine power, Damascus was next. Here, too, we already see the first impact of dissenting religious groups facilitating the Muslim conquest of the city in 635 CE—the first major city to fall to Arab Muslim armies.

The city had actually fallen to the Persians some twenty years earlier, assisted by the Jews and Monophysite Christians, who were unhappy with Byzantine discrimination and taxation. The city was recaptured by the Byzantines, only to fall again quickly, this time to the Muslim Arabs. The Arab conquest, too, was facilitated by support from within the city by much the same dissident elements of Nestorian and Monophysite Christians. Above all, Islam's well-known profession of the single, strictly human nature of Jesus could hardly have come as any surprise to Christian populations already steeped in their own debates and heresies over the nature of Jesus; Islam was just one more variation on the many contending arguments. What mattered about Islam was not its theology, but its political power and the type and character of rule to be imposed.

After much debate, the Arab commanders in charge of the siege were persuaded that an offer to Damascus of peaceful surrender was strategically wise if they wished to avoid fierce resistance from other Syrian cities in their advance. Thus, after long confrontations between Arab and Byzantine forces, in 634 CE the city finally agreed to surrender when promised by the Muslim commander Khalid bin Walid that

> when the Muslims enter, they [the people] shall have safety for themselves, their property, their temples and the walls of their city, of which nothing shall be destroyed. They have this guarantee on behalf of Allah, the Messenger of Allah, the Caliph and the Muslims, from whom they shall receive nothing but good so long as they pay the Jizya [poll tax].

Jerusalem was next to fall to Arab forces in 638 CE. The city agreed to surrender if the caliph would personally guarantee its safety. The Caliph 'Umar then entered the city riding on a white camel, accompanied by the city's patriarch, with whom he signed an agreement guaranteeing the city's safety and preservation of Christian rights of worship. Arab sources reported that 'Umar helped clean out the abandoned Jewish Temple Mount and prayed there, later ordering a mosque to be built in the southwest corner.

Conversion and Proselytization

The process of conversion to Islam in these former Byzantine regions of Syria and beyond reveal a great deal about the political and cultural forces at work. As we noted above, it is absurd to think in simplistic terms of "loyal Christians falling to anti-Western Muslim forces," the often-popular Western version of the process. The Christians in these Semitic regions were not particularly loyal or happy with Byzantium and were already quite anti-Western in predisposition. Simple theories of "Islam versus West" dichotomies here simply collapse in the face of the realities. Indeed, Islam at that point had had little direct encounter with Western or Byzantine military power, so there was no preexisting historical anti-Western predisposition, as had developed within many segments of the Byzantine Empire. Other major cities in Syria soon fell to the Muslims, pushing back the empire's borders and beginning in the region a long process of converting to Islam.

Again, popular Western images of Muslim conquest often portray conversions to Islam at sword point. The realities of these processes are quite different; they resemble processes of conversion familiar in most religious cultures when political situations shift dramatically. First, in the very earliest decades, Muslim *political authority* was of course immediately established after military conquest. Muslim Arab armies within thirty years of the Prophet's death had swept west along the Mediterranean coast as far as today's Tunisia, north to the borders of the Caucasus and half of Anatolia, and east to the borders of today's Pakistan. Old regimes fell and were replaced by new Muslim rulers. But the process of actual religious conversion at the individual and social levels was greatly delayed. As the historian of Islam Ira Lapidus points out in his monumental work on Muslim societies, "The conquests, then, were due to military triumphs over militarily weakened powers, and were consolidated in the first decades of Arab rule because local populations were content to accept the new regime." Elements of internal discontent within the Byzantine and Persian empires—Monophysites and Nestorians in Syria, Christians and Jews within Iran—facilitated the overthrow of both empires, city by city, as the Muslims advanced. According to the Boston University professor of medieval Islam Merlin Swartz, most of the Jewish population was discontented with their persecuted status within the Byzantine Empire and welcomed the Muslim armies, whose rule would turn out to facilitate a new flowering of Jewish culture.

Furthermore, contrary to expectation, conversion of the conquered citizenry to Islam was not at all the immediate goal of the Arab conquerors; the extension of Muslim *power and authority* was. We are really talking more about secular change—change of rulers—than of religion itself at the social level. As Lapidus points out, "The Arab conquerors did not require the conversion as much as the subordination of non-Muslim peoples. At the outset, [the Arab conquerors] were hostile to conversions because new Muslims diluted the economic and status advantages of the Arabs."

Indeed, for the new Arab administrators of these regions, there was a positive incentive *not* to extend the special benefits of being Muslim to the population at large. Arab forces had privileges and benefits that the conquered populations did not, while the latter had to pay a tax (*jizya*) levied upon non-Muslims in lieu of service in the army and in return for receiving protection. The minorities were required to recognize Muslim political rule and to refrain from any efforts to convert Muslims to Christianity. As Arnold Toynbee in his magisterial *Study of History* points out:

> In the first place we can discount the tendency—which has been popular in Christendom—to over-estimate the extent of the use of force in the propagation of Islam. The show of adherence to the religion exacted by the Prophet's successors was limited to the performance of a small number of not very onerous external observances. . . . In the conquered provinces of the Roman and Sassanian Empires the alternatives offered were not "Islam or death" but "Islam or a super-tax"—a policy traditionally praised for its enlightenment when pursued long afterwards in England by a Laodicean [religiously disinterested] Queen Elizabeth.

The Arabs did not initially wish to share power. The new Muslim administration maintained life more or less as before, only under new rule—a process familiar to all peoples living in regions where power at the top often changes hands through the fortunes of war, without necessarily changing life below. In fact, few conversions took place at all. As Lapidus states:

The second principle of 'Umar's settlement was that the conquered populations should be as little disturbed as possible. This meant that the Arab-Muslims did not, contrary to reputation, attempt to convert people to Islam. Muhammad had set the precedent of permitting Jews and Christians in Arabia to keep their religions, if they paid tribute....

At the time of the conquest, Islam was meant to be a religion of the Arabs, a mark of caste unity and superiority. The Arabs had little missionary zeal. When conversions did occur, they were an embarrassment because they created status problems and led to claims for financial privileges.

It's noteworthy that at this point the early Arab conquerors were still strongly ethnically oriented and perceived Islam to be an *Arab* religion of which they were the privileged recipients; this outlook reflected Arab awareness of Moses' revelations about a religion that was to be special for the Jewish people. Islam was now perceived as the prized privilege of the Arabs. But it was this privileged Arab position, and the second-class citizenship status of even *non-Arab converts* to Islam, that began to rankle severely; these tensions eventually led to the overthrow of the very Arab-oriented Umayyad caliphate by the more multiethnic Abbasids in 750 CE. And this privileged position for Arabs within Islam was, of course, directly contrary to the final address of the Prophet himself:

O people! Verily your Lord is one and your father is one. All of you belong to one ancestry of Adam and Adam was created out of clay. There is no superiority for an Arab over a non-Arab and for a non-Arab over an Arab; nor for white over the black nor for the black over the white except in piety. Verily the noblest among you is he who is the most pious.

The history of Islam represents a gradual shift away from an ethnic perception of the process of conquest and conversion and toward a more idealized process of the universalization of Islam. Still, the problem of self-asserted "Arab superiority" within Islam, while weakening, has still not completely disappeared at the popular level among many Arabs. It stems from the fact that Islam emerged from Arabia; that the Qur'an, the very words of God, was revealed in Arabic; that the Prophet was an Arab; and from the unparalleled richness of the Arabic rhetoric and language in the Qur'an, and the stunning success of the early Arab conquests. But a key function of the pilgrimage, or *hajj*, as an institution is to bring together Muslims from all over the world, multiple languages and races, in one place to worship. Modern communications have also hugely increased the awareness among all Muslims of the major contributions of non-Arab Muslims to the totality of Islamic culture at the expense of ethnic identity.

How did conversions actually proceed? All conversion processes are complex; they involve personal considerations as well as religious ones. Lapidus perceives two distinct phenomena under way in this process. The conversion of the *animists and polytheists* of the desert areas lay in the attraction of a vision of becoming part of a greater and richer civilization for which there were multiple incentives to join. This process stood in marked distinction to the urban or agrarian monotheistic populations for whom "Islam was substituted for a Byzantine or Sassanian *political* identity and for a Christian, Jewish or Zoroastrian *religious* affiliation....The old elites and the administrative machinery of the Byzantine and Sassanian empires were incorporated into the new regime."

Thus, an extraordinary transformation took place over vast areas in less than a century. As Lapidus states:

> The Arabs were changed from a clan or tribal people
> into an "urban" people, mingled with non-Arab peoples,

abandoned military affairs, took on civilian occupations, and lost their monopoly on Islam. Correspondingly, non-Arab peoples entered the military and government services, converted to Islam, adopted the Arabic language, and claimed a place in the government of the empire in which they were initially subjects.

In addition, minorities who had resented Byzantine, Sassanid, and other rule believed their situation would improve under Muslim rule; time and experience under the new Muslim caliphate mainly confirmed those hopes. Certainly fear of the conquerors might impel some to conversion, but so would a desire to curry favor with the new authorities for personal gain. Those who had long been minorities began to perceive greater benefit in joining the religion of the majority and becoming part of a mainstream culture, enjoying patronage and new social mobility. Others would even choose to join the Islamic campaigns of military conquest for adventure and riches.

But even this conversion process was not as rapid as is popularly conceived. Research by the Columbia University scholar Richard Bulliet on the rates of conversion of non-Arabs to Islam shows just how slow the process was in the first Islamic century. Under the Umayyad caliphate, only 10 percent of the populations that were conquered actually converted to Islam, compared to the more multinational Abbasid caliphate, where the conversion rate went from 40 percent to nearly 100 percent by the end of the eleventh century.

Nor were all communities converted. The very existence of large Christian communities of many denominations across the Middle East, as well as many Jewish communities, showed that "People of the Book" could opt not to convert, and continue to worship as Christians and Jews, agree to pay the poll tax, and thereby avoid military service and receive the protection of the state. Under the Ottoman Empire a millennium later, the over-whelming majority of the empire's subjects in the Balkans indeed remained Christian and the rhythms of their lives and religious worship did not change significantly.

In effect, then, the conversion process was very gradual and did not entail huge or sudden changes in the life of the region, even as a rich new international Islamic culture slowly emerged. Religion mattered far less than political, social, and economic change. We witness major elements of continuity in the political and social, even geopolitical, character of the Middle East as Islam gradually moves in and takes over. Simplistic "Islam versus the West" or "versus Christianity" polarity makes no sense.

Islam changed the political environment but was also changed *by* the environment. As the Abbasid Empire took in ever more diverse ethnic populations, cultures, and languages from Spain to Central and South Asia, it inevitably developed a more cosmo-politan outlook, drawing on the talents of the newly conquered populations. Nestorian and Syriac theologians, philosophers, and thinkers helped form the intellectual foundations of the Abbasid Empire. The Nestorian patriarch living inside the boundaries of the new Muslim Empire came to possess great power and influ-ence within Abbasid governance. A process of intellectual ferment was under way that would lift Islamic civilization to the highest level anywhere in the world at the time and for centuries to come.

We see an important process of fusion here as Islamic culture gradually absorbed ambient cultures, traditions, languages, arts, histories, and experiences, making Islam part of the region rather than merely an Arabian import imposed on the area. It is this deep integration of Islamic culture into the most ancient region of civilizations in the world that suggests in many ways a continuum of large numbers of values, attitudes, and attributes. The Middle East was not transformed by Islam into something brand-new, but rather subtly but importantly took on one more rich new layer of culture on top of a deeply rooted and established earlier mosaic.

Thus, these patterns of integration of Islam and Islamic culture into other cultural traditions are a vital part of our perception and understanding of the argument that the powerful geopolitical and cultural continuities of the region abide. Had Islam not emerged onto the scene, most of these forces would have remained and evolved, just as they did with the new layer of Islamic culture on top of them. Much of the same geopolitical forces and tensions were perpetuated. There is no doubt, though, that Islam was able to unify these regions under common civilizational patterns that proved exceptionally durable to the present day, regardless of shifting political borders within Islam.

We have witnessed, too, how various Christian heresies served as ideological vehicles for local resistance against the power of Rome or Constantinople; it should not be surprising, then, to see these same problems of heresy were perpetuated under Islam as well. Take North Africa. As Arab Sunni armies swept along the North African coast establishing Arab power, the dominant Berber populations, with their own distinct language, culture, and traditions, saw this spread of Arab power as primarily an *ethnic and political* threat. As a result, once the structures of new Muslim rule were established, the Berbers tended to turn to Shi'ism and Kharijite (a radical Islamic school of thought) ideas; these nonmainstream Islamic theologies served as a form of protest against dominant mainstream Arab Sunni power. Berber nationalism, in effect, finds a vehicle in heterodox Islam.

Staying Power

It is one thing to note the speed of Muslim conquest — a tribute to military and strategic skills. But it is another to note the remarkable staying power of Islam across such broad regions, cultures, and peoples for the rest of history. There's no way we can explain this away by attributing it merely to Muslim military power over the centuries. Why did Syria, for example, not revert back to Christianity, or some other earlier form of faith, after later Arab power weakened? Why did Iran not revert back to its ancient Zoroastrianism as soon as the Abbasid Islamic Empire weakened and collapsed before the Mongols? If Islam had sat uncomfortably upon these diverse populations, might we not have expected that at some point over the next fourteen hundred years they would have risen against Islamic authority to reclaim an earlier faith and culture?

When Mongol armies in the thirteenth century shattered Islamic power across most of the East, how was Islamic civilization able to arise again from the ashes? The resilience of Islam as a community, culture, religion, and political order seems impressive, even at its lowest points. The cohesion of Muslim societies through all kinds of events on down into the modern period—including European colonialism, world wars, and a Cold War—continue to suggest a kind of civilizational glue that cushions it against external challenge, even as Muslim civilization came to lag behind the Western power and technology in the modern period. Islam has thus served to help hold the region together, united in a common high civilization of Islamic culture. But the attitudes toward the West, Rome, even Constantinople, had deep roots that preceded Islam and continued on into Islam.

The directness of the message of Islam seems to have spoken to the populations that came to accept it. Its theological clarity and simplicity, compared to the intellectually complex—even arcane—theologies of Christianity, hammered out in endless church politico-religious councils, seemed to work in its favor. The religious appeal of Islam and its rapid spread may have been why many Christian powers feared Islam and demonized it early on.

And while all rulers are quite capable of harshness of governance, the Islamic formula for rule seemed to have worked better than those of its opponents in most cases, judging by its longevity of governance. The sword can prevail early on, but other more positive skills of governance are required thereafter. Witness the fall of multiple mighty empires.

With its new political and religious dominance of the Middle East, Islam seemed to fit in relatively comfortably with previous systems of religious thought and belief, a fusion of older and newer ideas. It is hard to argue that Islam represented some kind of new and aggressive force that suddenly changed the character of Middle Eastern geopolitics or established some kind of new precedent of anti-Western impulses. Traditional cultures, attitudes, and geopolitics persisted, but now under an Islamic patina. If Islam had never existed, would the old patterns of Semitic pushback against Greek and Roman Byzantine culture not have continued?

CHAPTER FIVE

The Great Crusades
(1095–1272)

W estern crusaders brimming with Christian fervor, banners unfurled, marching east under the pope's edict in the twelfth century to liberate the Holy Lands from the infidel Muslims — such scenes make up part of the great saga of Western history. It's all about Islam against the West, right? For many fundamentalists — Christian or Muslim — the Crusades mark the beginning of just such a clash of civilizations. But on closer examination, the story assumes more complex lines. Are we really talking about a clash of civilizations here, another phase in an "eternal conflict" between Islam and the West? Or are perhaps other, more complicated things going on? This chapter will argue that religion was really the backdrop, the popular narrative, the justification of what was a powerful geopolitical move by the West in sending its armies east. Could there even have been Crusades in the absence of Islam in the Holy Land? Let's look at the deeper structure of events. The answer might be surprising.

In a way, what historical event could be more about religion than the Crusades? Historians note a general growth of piety in eleventh-century Europe, which the church was quick to take advantage of. The venture even assumed an apocalyptic note, as many believed that the reestablishment of a Christian state in Jerusalem might usher in the End of Time—always a popular theme. And for the first time in Europe, new awareness emerged of the existence of a "Christendom," as preachers began to inform the public about a heathen "Other" in the Middle East—a theme less familiar in earlier, darker, and more isolated periods of European history.

The church encouraged men to enlist as "soldiers of the church" to fight for expansion of Christian lands; chronicles recount the solemn ceremonies of enlistment, whereby each warrior swears an oath to complete the journey to Jerusalem and receives a cross from a papal representative recognizing his status as a soldier of the church. Enlistees were granted exemptions from civil jurisdictions during the period of service. Judgment Day concerns, too, were on the minds of many—particularly how to achieve remission of sins. Was it enough simply to go off on a Crusade? And if one went, would only those sins committed up to the point of departure be remitted, or would all sins be remitted forever after? Did one actually have to die to achieve such remission? And after Jerusalem had been rescued, would the priceless door for easy remission of sins then close again?

These were troubling questions for crusader recruits, perhaps analogous to discussions today among some Muslim fundamentalists as to what constitutes "dying as a martyr." Properly speaking, of course, martyrdom refers strictly to death in defense or propagation of the faith. But if one undertakes a suicide mission against the enemy—and the Qur'an forbids suicide—does such a death via self-inflicted martyrdom constitute true martyrdom?

Pope Urban II's Call

The argument for the religious character of the Crusades could not be better evoked than in the address of Pope Urban II to the public at the Council of Clermont in 1095; this is a remarkable early Western document invoking Christianity in a struggle against the infidel Muslim East. There are no exact accounts of precisely what Urban said, only summaries from various leaders in attendance who offered their own differing versions. But it's the rhetoric that matters: we see roots of a later "civilizational struggle" that eventually affects both Christians and Muslims. Some of the flavor of the pope's remarks can be gleaned from a few selected paragraphs from just one of several observers, Fulcher of Chartres, reportedly quoting Pope Urban on fear of Muslim invasions into the West:

> For, as the most of you have heard, the Turks and Arabs have attacked [the Holy Places] and have conquered the territory...as far west as the shore of the Mediterranean and the Hellespont....They have killed and captured many, and have destroyed the churches and devastated the empire. If you permit them to continue thus for awhile with impunity, the faithful of God will be much more widely attacked by them. On this account I, or rather the Lord, beseech you as Christ's heralds to publish this everywhere and to persuade all people of whatever rank, foot-soldiers and knights, poor and rich, to carry aid promptly to those Christians and to destroy that vile race from the lands of our friends. I say this to those who are present, it is meant also for those who are absent. Moreover, Christ commands it.
>
> O what a disgrace if such a despised and base race, which worships demons, should conquer a people which has the faith of omnipotent God and is made glorious with the name of Christ!
>
> Let those who for a long time have been robbers, now become knights. Let those who have been fighting against

their brothers and relatives now fight in a proper way against the barbarians.

One striking feature of the various accounts of Urban's speech is the apparent absence of the word "Muslim" or "Islam" anywhere. References are to "heathen," "nonbelievers," "Turks," and "Arabs" who are oppressing "our Christian brothers" and the Holy Land. Christian authorities did not acknowledge these people even to be Muslims—albeit despised. The enemy is viewed strictly in ethnic terms or as infidels or as oppressors of Christians. Any other religion must of course be heathen.

Massacre of Jews

In his call for a Crusade at the Council of Clermont, Pope Urban II regularly referred to "nonbelievers" as the enemy. Yet, this could imply either Muslim or Jew. Anti-Semitism was already a familiar phenomenon in Europe, where Jews were routinely considered "Christ-killers." As a result, before even departing Europe on their mission, crusader bands scoured many areas of Germany, particularly the Rhineland, where Jews were given a choice between conversion to Christianity or death. On this occasion, some twelve thousand Jews were killed and a number of Jewish communities engaged in mass suicide.

The pope's call thus ennobled violence for a sacred cause and painted a picture of rewards in heaven for the killing of all non-Christians. Even more astonishing, while the pope never included Eastern Orthodox Christians in the ranks of nonbelievers, at the popular level, many European Christians very much thought of Greek Christians as nonbelievers as well, particularly after the "Latin Massacre" in Constantinople in 1182, nearly a century after the First Crusade.

In any event, the wildly popular response to the first papal call brought forth few knights but hordes of common people who volunteered for the trek, including large numbers who lacked fighting skills and were ignorant of the actual military tasks ahead of them. Large numbers of women and some children set off as well. These bands were often little more than undisciplined rabble subject to scant control beyond their own apocalyptic visions of salvation and an urge to escape the miseries of everyday life at home. Their behavior en route indeed revealed their character. This "People's Crusade" found itself engaged in local confrontations with other Christians even as they marched down through Christian lands in the Balkans. Coming only decades after the Great Schism between Rome and Byzantium of 1054, Eastern Orthodox Christians were held in low esteem. The Byzantine Emperor in Constantinople recognized the potentially dangerous nature of this uncontrolled rabble from afar: as they approached the city, he was anxious to move them quickly on past the city and into the Turkish-controlled parts of Anatolia. Most of the people's armies actually never even made it to Jerusalem, dying of disease and hardship, or perishing at the hands of the Turks in Anatolia.

Those who did make it to the Holy Land were largely ignorant, culturally and geographically lost, sometimes starving, and capable of great violence during the conquest of Eastern cities, often killing most inhabitants, destroying mosques, and pillaging the cities. They also engaged in several well-documented cases of cannibalism, according to Western crusaders themselves:

> Radulph of Caen, an eyewitness to events at Ma'arra in 1098, wrote, "In Ma'arra our troops boiled pagan adults in cooking-pots; they impaled children on spits and devoured them grilled."

The chronicler Albert of Aix seemed to rank Muslims lower than dogs when he wrote, "Not only did our troops not shrink from eating dead Turks and Saracens; they also ate dogs!"

The People's Crusade actually represented the first major military confrontation of the European West with Middle East, apart from Spain far to the west, which experienced eight hundred years of often-contested Arab rule. The Crusades also marked a historic major invasion of the Middle East by the European West—with lasting impact. Tales of crusader barbarity were seared into Muslim folk memory thereafter.

In later Crusades, more experienced knights responded to the call to go to Jerusalem. But these same professional military forces now posed as great a threat to Byzantium as they did to Muslims: these Western troops were operating on Byzantine soil but outside Byzantine control. Byzantine fears were soon to be richly realized in the Fourth Crusade.

When the troops of the First Crusade finally reached Jerusalem in 1099, reconquest was a brutal affair, in extraordinary contrast to the manner in which Jerusalem fell to disciplined Arab forces some five hundred years earlier. In 637 CE, we recall the second Caliph 'Umar had personally entered the city after a siege of many months; Arab troop discipline was maintained and the city was not pillaged, in accordance with a treaty 'Umar had signed with the patriarch of Jerusalem at the time of surrender. In reference to the Christians, that treaty had stated that

> their churches are not to be taken, nor are they to be destroyed, nor are they to be degraded or belittled, neither are their crosses or their money, and they are not to be forced to change their religion, nor is any one of them to be harmed.

Jewish sources furthermore report that 'Umar was shocked at the condition of the ruins of the Jewish temple, which had been turned into a garbage heap under the Romans; since the site was sacred for Muslims as well, 'Umar personally helped clean the site by hand along with his men. Jews were allowed to practice Judaism in the city for the first time since their expulsion by the Romans some five hundred years earlier.

But the capture of Jerusalem by the first crusader forces in 1099 was quite a different story. Jews, who feared the arrival of Christian rule, fought on the Muslim side in defense of the city, but to no avail. After a long and costly siege, the crusaders broke into the city on 15 July and in a twenty-four-hour period murdered virtually every single inhabitant—men, women, and children, Muslim, Jew, and most Eastern Orthodox Christians—probably around sixty thousand people. This included thousands of Jews taking refuge in their synagogue, and many thousands more Muslims in the al-Aqsa mosque. *The Catholic Encyclopedia* reports tersely: "the Christians entered Jerusalem from all sides and slew its inhabitants regardless of age or sex."

Fulcher of Chartres, a crusader who participated in the conquest, wrote: "Indeed, if you had been there you would have seen our feet coloured to our ankles with the blood of the slain. But what more shall I relate? None of them were left alive; neither women nor children were spared."

There are numerous other accounts of immense cruelties inflicted by the crusaders on Muslim towns and populations on the way to Jerusalem. It would, of course, be foolish to suggest that cruelty and killing were all one-sided. Warfare in all ages is brutal. The point of reporting a few of these selected accounts here is not to suggest that the crusaders were evil and Muslims mere innocent victims. But European forces were in fact invading the heartland of the Middle East. This was the first of what was going to be a long history of Western armed intervention into the

Middle East over many centuries to come. The bloody-minded-ness of the crusaders themselves is scarcely known in any Western popular tales of crusader chivalry. Furthermore, there is a strik-ing contrast of religious and legal aspects between the Muslim conquest of Jerusalem in 637 and the Christian conquest of Jeru-salem in 1099. Muslims were *required* by the tenets of Islam to respect the place of Christians and Jews in Muslim society and largely did so (although there were, of course, other cases where they did not observe Islamic strictures); yet Christians were in no way required by Christian doctrine to protect the place of Jews and Muslims in Christian society and largely did not. And finally, the West needs to be aware of the Muslim mirror-vision of the crusader tales; their own alternative narratives of these events still influence Muslim culture today.

Second Crusade

If the First Crusade was known as the People's Crusade, the Sec-ond was distinguished by the participation of several European kings as it sought to expand the conquests of the First. But the military results were deeply disappointing: the Seljuk Turks defeated most of the royal hosts in Asia Minor, before they even reached the Holy Land. As with the First Crusade, the further transit of diverse new groups of Western military forces through Byzantine lands heightened Byzantine fears about crusader inten-tions. The emperor once again sought to delay Western entry onto Byzantine lands and then hustled them as quickly as possible across the Bosphorus and on their way south through Turkish-held territory. Crusader forces coming from Sicily, in the mean-time, plundered several Greek cities on the way, confirming Byzantine fears about their real intent.

In the end, the crusaders failed to take Damascus, a major goal, and the Second Crusade had little to show for itself. Bernard of Clairvaux declared it was the sins of the crusaders that had brought about their failure. Worst of all for the crusaders, by 1180 the Muslim commander of the area, Saladin (Salah al-Din), had unified Muslim forces in the region and recaptured Jerusalem from the crusaders.

Third Crusade

The shocking recapture of Jerusalem by Muslims now galvanized Europe into a third Crusade. Saladin's recapture paralleled the events of the first Muslim capture of the city in 637 CE under the Caliph 'Umar: few of its Christian civilian inhabitants were harmed after Muslim troops entered Jerusalem this time as well, and most of the churches were left untouched, although ransom money was demanded from the crusaders. The Third Crusade was also notable for the participation of several more key royal figures, including England's Richard the Lionheart and France's Philip II. Ongoing Byzantine suspicions were reinforced when Richard, en route to the Holy Land, captured Cyprus from the Byzantine Empire. European integrity and sense of humanitarianism were further compromised when Richard, during the siege of Acre, promised the safety of all its Muslim citizens if it capitulated; yet upon its surrender, he massacred them all. After failing to capture Jerusalem, Richard reached agreement with Saladin on terms for maintaining an ongoing Christian pilgrimage to the city.

Fourth Crusade

The ongoing suspicions between the "Latins" and the "Greeks" during the first three Crusades were now to reach a crescendo. The Fourth Crusade entailed a series of events that still live in infamy in Greek minds to this day. In total disregard of the mission to recapture Jerusalem for Christianity, in 1204 the crusaders diverted their attentions away from Jerusalem and instead proceeded to attack, sack, pillage, occupy, and rule Constantinople itself in the name of the Roman Church for many years. This indeed was a "civilizational" cataclysm, the final psychological breaking point between the two great churches and Christian cultures of East and West, with incalculable repercussions that still echo today.

Pope Innocent III had not in fact approved any attack on Constantinople. But Latin clerics closer to the scene were driven by other motivations, including cupidity and the quest for power, and sought to override the pope's view. The prominent contemporary Greek historian Spiros Vryonis describes the crusader attack on Constantinople in the following terms:

> The Latin soldiery subjected the greatest city in Europe to an indescribable sack. For three days they murdered, raped, looted and destroyed on a scale which even the ancient Vandals and Goths would have found unbelievable. Constantinople had become a veritable museum of ancient and Byzantine art, an emporium of such incredible wealth that the Latins were astounded at the riches they found. Though the Venetians had an appreciation for the art which they discovered (they were themselves semi-Byzantines) and saved much of it, the French and others destroyed indiscriminately, halting to refresh themselves with wine, violation of nuns, and murder of Orthodox clerics. The Crusaders vented their hatred for the Greeks most spectacularly in the desecration of the greatest Church in Christendom. They smashed the silver iconostasis, the icons and the holy books of Hagia Sophia, and seated upon the patriarchal throne a whore who sang coarse songs as they drank wine from the Church's holy vessels.

The estrangement of East and West, which had proceeded over the centuries, culminated in the horrible massacre that accompanied the conquest of Constantinople. The Greeks were convinced that even the Turks, had they taken the city, would not have been as cruel as the Latin Christians. The defeat of Byzantium, already in a state of decline, accelerated political degeneration so that the Byzantines eventually became an easy prey to the Turks. The Crusading movement thus resulted, ultimately, in the victory of Islam, a result which was of course the exact opposite of its original intention.

The disastrous future implications of this Latin assault upon Constantinople were indeed fully grasped by Pope Innocent III, whose long-term aspiration was actually to *restore* church unity between East and West—albeit under his own leadership. The pillage of Constantinople removed all possibility of such a rapprochement for—what he could not know—nearly a thousand years. As the pope himself wrote:

How is the Church of the Greeks, when afflicted with such trials and persecutions, to be brought back into the unity of the Church and devotion to the Apostolic See? It has seen in the Latins nothing but an example of perdition and the works of darkness, so that it now abhors them worse than dogs. For they who are supposed to serve Christ rather than their own interests, who should have used their swords against the pagans, are dripping with the blood of Christians. They have spared neither religion, nor age, nor sex and have committed adultery and fornication in public, exposing matrons and even nuns to the filthy brutality of their troops. For them it was not enough to exhaust the riches of the Empire and to despoil both great men and small; they had to lay their hands on the treasures of the Church...seizing silver valuables from the altar, breaking them into pieces to divide amongst themselves, violating the sanctuaries and carrying off crosses and relics.

The crusaders then imposed a Latin prelate over the city. The population meanwhile rejected the crusaders' candidate for emperor and popular anger against the "Latins" boiled over. But a Latin emperor nonetheless assumed the throne in Constantinople and ruled for fifty-seven years, until the city was recaptured by the Byzantines in 1261. None of these events have been forgiven or forgotten by the Orthodox Church. Subsequent efforts at reconciliation or establishment of theological union by the pope at various times following the sack of Constantinople were rebuffed by the Eastern Church; the strongest voice of rejection came from public opinion, which vilified any Orthodox priests who would even contemplate negotiations of potential terms of unity under Rome's conditions.

Some eight hundred years later, in 2001, Pope John Paul II expressed his sorrow to the Orthodox Church in his first visit to Orthodox territory, in Romania. In 2004, the apology was finally accepted by the Ecumenical Patriarch Bartholomew I. These actions constitute useful first steps in healing what is still a prickly relationship going back nearly two millennia. Rome's confrontation with Constantinople during the Crusades ranked at least as high in importance to the Eastern Empire as any confrontation with the Muslims, possibly more so since it came from ostensibly fellow Christians. In a sense, then, the Crusades wreaked incalculable damage upon the relationship between the Eastern and Western churches, which perhaps exceeded the anger sowed at the time between the Muslim and Western worlds. The world still lives with the legacy of both.

A Closer Look

We have concentrated on the nominally religious facet of clashes between the West, East, and the Muslim world. Now let's examine the case for alternate explanations of these same events that do not entail religion. The historical reality suggests there were indeed other powerful forces at work: a drive for expansion of Western power abroad and the force of economic, political, and social developments in Europe. If Islam had not existed—the ostensible rationale for the entire venture of the Crusades—could a form of Western Crusades against the East still have taken place?

Why are some of the nominal religious motives of Western crusader forces partially suspect? First, the timing of the Crusades is strange. After all, Jerusalem had fallen to Muslim forces as far back as 638 CE, yet here the Crusades were gearing up in response to that event some five hundred years after the fact. This was not even the first time that Christianity had lost Jerusalem to non-Christians: the Zoroastrian Sassanid Dynasty of Persia had seized the city in 614 CE, burned the Church of the Holy Sepulcher, and made off with the "true cross." Jerusalem was then recaptured several years later by the Byzantines in 629 CE, and then was lost again nine years later to Arab forces. Thus, Christians lost the Holy Lands twice—some five hundred years before the crusaders' response.

During that period of Muslim rule, Christian and Jewish worship had for the most part proceeded fairly peacefully in Jerusalem, and Christian pilgrimages had enjoyed regular access. This notable coexistence was broken briefly with the emergence of the Fatimid Shi'ite Dynasty in Egypt in the early eleventh century, whose zealous new ruler ordered the destruction of churches and synagogues in Jerusalem, including the Church of the Holy Sepulcher; this policy of persecution was later reversed as the Fatimids recognized the clear financial benefits in permitting reconstruction of the churches and restoring an unfettered flow of pilgrims to the Holy Places. This brief interlude of intolerance, however, probably set off a particular spark in the West on what had for centuries been a quiescent issue.

But in the West itself, powerful new forces provided an important *social* stimulant to launching the Crusades. Europe had experienced several centuries of constant, crippling internal raiding, skirmishes, and outright warfare among diverse barbarian tribes marauding across Europe. At the same time, onslaughts on Europe by the fierce Magyars and Vikings had generated a need for large numbers of warrior bands to defend European borders. Over time, with the lessening of the external threats, the need for these armed bands had greatly diminished, yet they continued to wander and fight among themselves, pillage villages, and devastate public order. The pope had struggled for years to end their attacks against local populations and their own destructive internecine warfare; an outlet was needed for their aggressive and expansionist energies. And at this point, traditions of "crusades" against Muslims had already become familiar through campaigns of Christian knights in northern Spain against the long-standing Muslim Empire in southern Spain. (Although it would not be until well after the Crusades, in 1492, that the final expulsion of Muslims and Jews from Spain, on pain of death, would take place.)

In his speech at Clermont, Pope Urban III notably referred to the need for "those who for a long time, have been robbers, now become knights." We also learn a good bit about the efficacy of inflamed religious rhetoric in galvanizing military expeditions against distant enemies. The religious symbolism of the "infidels" — never "Muslims" — and the affront to God of their actions provided the chief emotional and ideological basis for these foreign wars; the pope also appealed for Christian solidarity with their Christian brethren in the Middle East—who indeed often ended up being slaughtered by crusader bands, along with the Muslims.

What were the primary motives of the main players? They were diverse and complex. The Byzantines had lost control of the Holy Lands to Arab Muslim forces in the seventh century and continued to lose further territory to Islam as the Seljuk Turks in later centuries came out of Central Asia and moved deeper into Anatolia, further shrinking the empire. Constantinople desperately needed military assistance against both Turkish and Arab forces and had often turned to the West for aid in the defense of Christendom. But we have also seen how the Byzantines maintained fully justified suspicions about ultimate Western intentions. Many Western rulers, including the pope, nourished hopes of weakening Greek Byzantine rule and returning the Eastern Empire to "Latin," or Rome's control. If Rome could wrest the Holy Lands from Muslim rule, it would not only restore Christianity to the area, but would also serve as a redoubt for expansion of Rome's power against Constantinople itself. Who knew it could possibly lead to the reunification of the divided empire, this time fully under Rome's auspices? Thus, in seeking Western aid against the Muslims, was not Constantinople inviting the fox in to guard the chicken coop?

And then there were numerous economic factors. The great trading city-states of Venice and Genoa had a huge stake in the increase of military activity in the eastern Mediterranean. It was a win-win situation under any circumstances for them: boats and logistical supplies would be required in full measure, and these two cities were uniquely qualified to act as willing and experienced middlemen between the warring parties.

Additional geopolitical imperatives emerged with the First Crusade. Growing new social stability in Europe produced a new European warrior aristocracy, who formed the backbone of the "Princes' Crusade." After arriving in the Levant, some of these princes founded four separate kingdoms of their own on Muslim soil along the Mediterranean coast from Asia Minor to Egypt.

These so-called crusader states—Jerusalem, Antioch, Edessa, and Tripoli—represented perhaps the earliest form of actual European colonization in the heart of the Middle East. While their size and fortunes waxed and waned from battle to battle, three of these crusader states lasted for over 150 years; all of them were eventually to fall to Muslim armies. The establishment of Latin crusader power in these four new states also meant, incidentally, the expulsion of the Orthodox patriarchs from both Jerusalem and Antioch, a serious loss of key religious centers to the Orthodox Church.

It was therefore a convenient excuse that the lands conquered had been in Muslim hands. But can there be much doubt that restless European adventurers would not at some point have undertaken similar expansionist activities into the Near East if the whole area had been under Eastern Christian and not Muslim control? Other pretexts could have been found as various European princely forces were already picking off parts of Byzantine territory in the same period anyway. Indeed, the "Latin Massacre" in 1182 could have served as a perfect justification if the more obvious Muslim target had not been available. In short, European power was all armored up and ready to go someplace. It is hardly far-fetched to imagine a crusade in the name of the Latin Church against the despised Greek Church. Indeed, such an assault against the Eastern Church did take place in the Fourth Crusade, but the ostensible target was, of course, Islam.

Cultural interchange between the Muslim and Western sides tended to be somewhat limited, as most populations stuck to their own communities. Crusaders were impressed with the level of civilization of the Muslims, their fine arts, and their textiles, which all exerted influence upon European arts. And while Muslims were generally viewed only as infidels, a legend did develop in the West about Saladin, the Muslim commander who ultimately recaptured Jerusalem; he was seen to personify the character of honor and chivalry. Muslims, however, were less impressed by the crusaders, whom they regarded as rough, unkempt, smelly, not given to Muslim traditions of use of the public bath, and crude in their manners.

It's interesting to note that the First Crusade also marked the first vigorous use of a Muslim call for *jihad* against Western invaders. It came from 'Ali bin Tahir al-Sulami, a legal scholar and philologist in Damascus. Al-Sulami did not see the Crusades in isolation but as part of a broader threat against Muslim civilization, especially since they coincided with an ongoing struggle in Spain between Christian crusaders and Muslim states. The Crusades marked the first time when Muslim populations had frequent encounters with Westerners on Muslim soil; otherwise Muslim forces had up to that time mostly encountered Eastern peoples serving as Byzantine mercenaries. Byzantium was a well-known element, but the Muslim world was barely beginning to think in terms of a generalized challenge from the European West. And just as the pope blamed the failure of the Second Crusades on the sins of the crusaders, al-Sulami blamed Muslim defeats during the Crusades on Muslim abandonment of the true faith and urged Muslims to first turn to "inner *jihad*" — cultivating one's inner resources and control over one's baser instincts to be able to conduct a successful Muslim war (*jihad*) against the crusaders. Both sides portrayed their struggles in terms of holy wars, obscuring the geopolitical struggle. Al-Sulami's call for *jihad* was ignored by Muslim rulers, however; it was not until many years later in the Crusades that the linking of *jihad* with military expeditions was articulated by Saladin.

Northern Crusades

If there was any doubt about the nature of the crusading spirit and its restless expansionist nature, its highly political side is vividly revealed in several other Crusades of the period that were quite unrelated to Muslims. Simultaneously with the Second Crusade, some fifty years after the First, a new outlet for the crusading spirit was established within Europe itself. German tribes who did not wish to heed the pope's call to go to the Holy Lands were informed they could fulfill their religious obligations with an expedition of conquest and conversion against the few remaining pagan Slavic tribes in the Baltic.

The chief spokesman for the pope's crusade plans, Bernard of Clairvaux, proclaimed the need to battle the pagan Slavs until they were killed or converted. But typically, the crusade was not limited to conversion of pagans. The Catholic Teutonic Knights were eager to settle old ethnic and territorial scores with their *co-religionists* in Catholic Poland. The Christian kingdoms of Denmark and Sweden were also eager to extend their power south into the Baltic area. Even Orthodox Christian Russia was targeted by them. As a result of these various crusade campaigns,

> the east Baltic world was transformed by military conquest: first the Livs, Letts and Estonians, then the Prussian [Slavs] and the Finns underwent defeat, baptism, military occupation and sometimes extermination by groups of Germans, Danes and Swedes.

The Second Crusade thus provided a religious justification for Germanic forces to project their power and economic control east into the Baltic. Indeed, Pope Eugene III in 1147 issued a papal bull (*fatwa*) ascribing equal spiritual values and rewards to all those going on crusade, either to the Holy Land or against pagan Slavs.

In 1242, a body of Catholic Teutonic Knights marched against the Russian Orthodox Republic of Novgorod, near today's St. Petersburg, but were defeated, with a number of heavily armored

Germanic knights plunging through the ice in a battle on frozen Lake Ladoga. The event was perceived in popular Russian culture as one of many God-given victories of Orthodoxy defending itself against the evil forces of invading Catholicism—a deep theme in Russian national thought. Thus, even in Europe we see the branches and offshoots of this three-way geopolitical struggle among Islam, Western Christianity, and Eastern Orthodox Christianity.

Note throughout all of this that it was the *pope* who called for all of these wars and campaigns over a nearly two-hundred-year period. The pope in effect inspired, directed, and commanded the political and military actions of European princes. We are hard put to find any parallel of purely religious authorities in Islam directing the actions of Muslim armies. (Where the caliph commanded power, especially in the first few Islamic centuries, he first and foremost wielded secular power and was selected by quite secular means—power politics.) Muslim 'ulama may certainly have blessed Muslim military expeditions, but they did not inspire them or direct them. Once again, we find state and church intimately linked through the bulk of Christian history; far less so in Islam.

The Crusades in History

It must be noted that source materials, in any language, on the history of the Crusades are almost exclusively Western. The Crusades were entirely a Western project fought for Western reasons in a European political, social, and economic context. Europe was, in effect, ripe for a grand mission to the East that could absorb and safely redirect all the diverse drives of the swirling European political and social environment. Catholic Europe was ready to begin its restless eastward expansion—against pagan Slavs, Jews, Eastern

Orthodox Christians, or Muslims—regardless of what religion happened to be dominant in the Middle East at that point.

Most Muslims who did not live near the crossroads of the crusader movement or who were not engaged in military struggle were largely ignorant of the events. At the time they occurred, the Crusades were not perceived by Muslims as a "civilizational event" in the way that Europeans then perceived, or contemporary thinking has now come to perceive, it. Indeed, even for those Muslims affected by the ongoing battles for control of the Levant coast, the crusaders, or "Franks" as they were known, were often viewed by Muslims as just one more variant of the many Byzantine mercenaries or ethnic militias regularly pressed into service from around the Byzantine Empire.

This was the period as well when the word "Frank" was widely absorbed into the Muslim world to denote *all* Europeans. The word "firengi" or "faranji" is still a near-universal slang word all across Muslim Asia to refer to foreigners from the West of any sort.

Finally, the Crusades created sets of attitudes of each side toward the other, particularly in the West. As the Crusades scholar Carole Hillenbrand puts it:

> Contact with the Muslim world gave the Europeans a taste for all kinds of commodities, including ivory, inlaid metalwork and other luxury goods that came from the Arab world. Of these the most important were textiles: damask, fustian, muslin, organdie, atlas, satin and taffeta...
>
> Crusaders returning home from the Holy Land would speak of the exotic countries they had left behind. The phenomenon of Orientalism from the 18th century onward and its manifestations in Western art and literature, so powerfully described in recent times by Edward Said, fed on the heritage of the Crusades. The Muslim world was the place of deserts, walled cities, veiled women, harems,

eunuchs, bathhouses, intrigues, outlandish animals, clothing, languages, luxuries and an alien religion; in short, a land of romantic mystery and danger.

When asked his opinion of the French Revolution, Chinese Premier Zhou En-Lai in the 1950s famously remarked, "It's too early to tell." So, too, time never ceases to refract the past in shifting patterns that tell us as much about the contemporary observer as it does about specific past events. Over time, the Crusades have undergone various interpretations, both favorable and unfavorable. In the West today, there is a tendency among most secular-minded people to see the events as indeed a force of Western expansionism—a not-particularly-admirable moment in Western history. Conservative Christian commentators are more inclined toward arguments that justify Western intervention in the Holy Lands in response to serious challenges to Christendom from ongoing Muslim expansion. The roots of the present debate in the West about Islam are thus projected backward.

For Muslims, the historic shift of perspective has been more dramatic. Today, Muslims look back to perceive in the Crusades the earliest indicators of the imperialist urge in Western policies; Usama bin Ladin, among others, has described current Western actions in the Global War on Terror as "Zionist-crusader" aggression against Muslim lands. The concept was unfortunately reinforced by George W. Bush when he referred to "this crusade, this war on terrorism" in the first week after 9/11. Europeans, closer to the full historical implications of the crusader period, were dismayed by Bush's use of the term.

Our own views of current wars in the Middle East are, of course, also highly subjective; they hinge upon our sense of who is reacting to which earlier provocation, in an endless regression of blame backward into time—the eternal chicken-and-egg problem of historical politics. Islam today is a convenient shorthand to characterize the immense geopolitical complexities that made up the saga of the Crusades. The Crusades are now part of the pantheon of East-West tensions. Yet we noted some of the early foundations of this struggle well before the emergence of Islam in the regional rebellions inside the Byzantine Empire against Constantinople; these movements embraced various religious banners (heresies) as vehicles and symbols for what was basically a contest for territory and power. These tensions preexisted Islam, ran parallel to Islam, and still exist within the Middle East today. Could there have been Crusades without Islam? Perhaps not in quite the same form, but a restless and ambitious Europe would probably have found its way quickly enough to the East, in any case. It had already launched war against other border areas of Europe. If the distracting factor of Islam had never existed, the tensions between Rome and Constantinople would likely have been far more direct and confrontational than they were even at the time.

CHAPTER SIX

Shared Echoes: The Protestant Reformation and Islam

In a time of increasing domestic turmoil and foreign intervention, a group of fundamentalists seized power in a small city and established their own religious community, renaming the city in accordance with the sacred texts. A fanatic authoritarian religious leader backed by numerous followers placed himself at the head and undertook some eighteen months of harsh theocratic rule as the community imposed its vision of the requirements of the faith. They shared their possessions in common with those who were believers and readily accepted the use of force against those who were not believers. They practiced polygamy, and some had more than four wives. Even as their rebellion lay exposed to military siege from the outside by local rulers who feared that their own legitimacy was threatened, the insurgents promoted their millenarian and apocalyptic vision of God's political, social, and religious design in what they hoped was the beginning of a world crusade. The rebellion was ultimately snuffed out by the arrayed forces of external authorities, its leaders tortured and executed, and their bodies hung in cages. Orthodoxy in religion was restored.

This was not an Islamist fundamentalist movement. The place

was the German city of Münster, the date 1534, as the Protestant Reformation was heading into full swing. The movement and its leader were Anabaptists, the most radical of the three main trends of the Reformation, which included Lutherans and Calvinists. The Anabaptists had renamed their city the "New Jerusalem," but the radicalism of their message and methods was enough to unite Catholic and Protestant (Lutheran) forces, which surrounded the city and blotted out its dangerous doctrines.

This violent, revolutionary event marked an end to Anabaptist political activism. As in many Islamic movements after 9/11, after 1534 Anabaptist leaders were at pains to publicly dissociate themselves from the use of violence. Lutherans and Calvinists totally rejected the revolutionary program of the Anabaptists, and Europe was horrified at the zealotry behind the Münster saga. Consequently, the Reformist Protestants, once reviled as radicals by Catholics, began to appear more mainstream in comparison. And we find parallels today. Many Muslim fundamentalists were shocked by the events of 9/11 and their blowback; as the ultimate political and military implications of radical theology grew clearer, large numbers hastened to denounce the role of violence in their midst, even though they understood the grievances that had brought about the events.

So, in a book designed to look beyond the role of religion to find deeper causes in the history of events in the Middle East, why are we considering the Reformation and its progeny in Europe? In fact, the Protestant Reformation exemplifies, in a number of fascinating ways, many of the same concepts we raised earlier: the intensely *political* nature of events usually understood as being primarily religious in character. But again, religion is the vehicle of political confrontation and turmoil, not the cause. Political leaders attempt to maintain tight control over religion as a means to their own ends. Yet, the events of the Reformation also dramatically reveal to us the converse: what happens when the state or church *loses* control over the contents of religion or allows others, even the masses, to determine theology or to define its meaning and how to act on it. Christianity had vastly longer success in maintaining centralized, politicized control of religious doctrine than did Islam, until it slipped during the Reformation; the Roman Catholic Church still attempts to retain that control.

If there had been no Islam and the Eastern Orthodox Church had held onto its power in the Middle East, it would still have been only the Latin Church, *Rome,* that was challenged by the budding Protestant German princes and others in contestation for political power, wealth, and control of doctrine. Constantinople would likely have remained a bulwark of stern Orthodoxy, more convinced than ever of the misguided, dangerous, even disastrous course of Christianity in the West.

Islam did not, of course, undergo any Protestant Reformation, nor did most of the rest of the world. For the West, the Reformation was massively destabilizing to Europe as a whole; among other things, it led to the Thirty Years' War, one of the bloodiest wars in European history — ostensibly all about religion, in reality all about power struggles among states. The Reformation changed power relationships *within* states as well by unleashing many disruptive and sometimes even violent trends as in Münster. It was socially destabilizing in that it liberated people from centralized control over their religious ideas, empowered more individual thinking on political and religious questions, and ultimately unleashed some truly radical ideas.

Muslims, too, over the past century have developed much new thinking about the links between religion and politics; they, too, have generated a number of destabilizing forces, including sharp critiques of their own ruling regimes, creation of new organizations to achieve political and social goals, and even adopting the use of terror against selected domestic and foreign enemies and invaders. Al-Qa'ida is but one of these forces.

The Reformation was in many ways a period of democratization of religion: not that there were any functioning democratic political orders, but individuals were encouraged to examine the texts and think for themselves about the meaning of religion. This was really the beginning of the development of popular voices in political and social affairs. But this chapter also notes the radical consequences that can emerge when democratizing trends—everyone their own theologian—penetrate religious tradition. There are some striking echoes of Protestant radicalism in Islamic fundamentalism—and even in some contemporary radical Protestant interpretations of Christianity. The state, especially the authoritarian state, is threatened by these new trends toward freer and more activist thinking in matters involving religion. Indeed, there is close linkage between freedom in political thought and freedom in religious thought; each serves to liberate the other.

It's worth noting that nowhere did the Eastern Orthodox Church undergo a Reformation. This suggests that a Middle East without Islam—that is, one that remained Orthodox Christian—probably would not have become any more secularized and rationalized than the Middle East did under Islam. In fact, it is fairly evident that Islam in modern times has become in some senses *more* democratized, more involved in mass politics, than the Orthodox Church has. (Whether that is good or bad can be debated.)

Finally, this chapter looks at some of the extreme theological interpretations within modern Christianity that still exert significant impact upon contemporary Christian thinking, even if not mainstream. There are often striking parallels here with elements of radicalism in Islamist thinking. In this context, then, Islam again looks less and less like an exceptional, uniquely Middle Eastern phenomenon and more part of a global process of *religious* change with political implications; or, conversely, part of a process of *political* change with religious implications.

THE PROTESTANT REFORMATION of the sixteenth century blew apart the entire institution of the Western Church. It was arguably the most devastating schism in church history, even more important than the Great Schism between the Eastern Orthodox Church and the Latin Church several centuries earlier. It all happened within Europe. It resulted in deep, lasting divisions. A world of centrally controlled theological doctrine in the West was fragmented, creating new relations among church, state, and the individual. Neither the church nor the West would ever be the same again.

Yet the Reformation did not come as a complete surprise. In fact, its timing suggests a lot about its political character. When the monk Martin Luther nailed his ninety-five theses of accusations against the church onto the church door in Wittenberg in 1517, he crystallized in one sharp moment centuries-long dissatisfactions with the church. The newly emerging secular power of the German princely states and the north European states had long been raising objections to excessive church exercise of political and financial power. Europe had already witnessed many centuries of demeaning struggles among various states to capture the papacy for their own ends. The Reformation would never have happened if Luther had simply been one of a handful of dissident monks arguing theology; the success of his movement was due to the direct support of German princes who shared his desire to cut the power of the church down to size. The theological objections to the church, while quite real, provided intellectual and theological cover for a deeper political and economic assault against the church's power and corruption. Luther's theses, in other words, would clearly bring to a head a church-state crisis that the European political order had not yet been ready or willing to face in an earlier era; but by 1517, it was.

In its more moderate forms, the Reformation called for sharp reform of the church—doctrinal, organizational, hierarchical—and an end to Rome's centralized power. But as the process of change, decentralization, and independent-mindedness evolved, more radical formulations in thinking began to emerge; ultimately, some of these began to challenge the *entire validity* of the church, its body of theology, hierarchy, history, and operation as representing an apostasy from True Christianity from its earliest days.

Islam actually had no parallel to the intimate links between church and state in the West, where the church itself wielded great political and economic power. While Islamists today—those speaking for forms of political Islam—constantly emphasize the indissoluble unity of religion and state in Islam (*din wa dawla*), in fact, this perception is largely a modern ideological construct: state power in Islam was virtually always distinct from the clerics. Religious officials in Islamic states never appointed leadership or controlled the state. (Clerical domination of the state in today's Iran is a glaring exception, a modern Shi'ite innovation.) Even in Saudi Arabia the monarchy in most contexts is far more powerful than are clerical institutions.

To be sure, the legitimacy of Muslim rulers historically depended upon their implementation of Shari'a law, at least in theory, but a great deal of the time rulers did not seriously implement its spirit, and they rarely could be overthrown for such religious lapses. In fact, some medieval Muslim clerics inadvertently dispensed virtual carte blanche authority to misrule by secular powers by declaring that anarchy (*fitna*) was worse even than oppressive rule (*dhulm*). Indeed, no sultan or Muslim ruler in Islamic history ever kneeled to ask forgiveness before a grand mufti in the way that Henry IV was forced to do before the pope in 1077 in Canossa for challenging papal authority on some key secular matters. Henry VIII of England had to break with Rome entirely simply to secure the divorce he sought from his wife. Thus, intimate linkage between religious and state power marked most of Christian history in a way that has had no parallel in Islam.

———

EARLIER CHAPTERS HAVE EXAMINED the way in which expanding religions routinely absorb local religious traditions, shrines, holy figures, and practices of the earlier religion to smooth the transition to the new. Both Christianity and Islam experienced these pagan accretions as they grew; their reformers have sought to expunge such accretions and to get back to the pure, original faith. That was part of what the Protestant Reformation was about—a return to the pure message. Muslim "fundamentalists," too, attempt to get back to fundamentals, to basics, to purify the faith. Wahhabism in eighteenth-century Saudi Arabia was one of many such movements; they are often also referred to as "renewal" movements (*tajdid*). Renewal can actually cut two ways: it can refer to a movement back in time perceived as once purer, or it can look forward in time to interpret the traditional texts in the new light of contemporary understanding.

So how would the Middle East region differ today if it had remained Orthodox? Of the three religions—Islam, Western (Catholic) Christianity, and Eastern Orthodox Christianity—it is Orthodoxy that has perhaps changed the least. Some of the most divisive reforms over ritual were introduced in seventeenth-century Russia to bring Russian Orthodox practice into conformity with Greek Orthodox practice, essentially a politically driven agenda that caused much widespread popular opposition. Other Orthodox "reforms" strengthened Russian state control over the church. The Orthodox Church has maintained its remove from involvement in political affairs ever since the fall of Constantinople, and of the three faiths is probably the most "otherworldly" and the most subservient to the state. It has avoided becoming heavily involved in political and social agendas. A Middle East still under Orthodoxy today would perhaps have been more conservative on political and social issues than Latin Christianity or Islam.

Holy Texts as Source of All Law

The lessons of the Reformation left little doubt on one key issue: when the state, or powerful institutions like the church, loses control over religion, religion can quickly become an instrument for an attack on the state and its powers. In some of the radical Protestant movements—especially Calvinist and Anabaptist—the broader forces of democratization and individualism open the door to more personal and radical interpretations of scripture. This process has immediate implications for society and governance.

Islam, too, has undergone a process of liberation away from its state-controlled clerical thinking of the past and toward the emergence of diverse modern Islamist movements. And when state-controlled clerics lose credibility and legitimacy, others take over interpretation of Islam and can direct its message against the state. Some of these movements, however strict, harsh, radical, and violent, are a direct outgrowth of a process of *rethinking* Islam. No longer the purview of clergy working for the state, no longer limited to "safe" questions of ritual and purity, newer Islamic movements have emerged against the will of the state. They call for religion to play a role in combating corrupt, incompetent, oppressive, and unrepresentative regimes and in alleviating poor social and economic conditions, already under the strains and disruptions of the Global War on Terror.

The varieties of contemporary Islamism attempt to speak out boldly, to open up the political order, and even to aggressively change the status quo in line with the ideals of Islam. The process of opening the system has unleashed considerable pent-up radicalism and violence against the state. While some groups have moved toward more liberal interpretations of Islam in keeping with the contemporary world, many others have moved toward intolerance through insistence on taking the texts literally and attempting to apply them unchanged to contemporary conditions. As occurred in the Protestant Reformation, Pandora's box has been opened in Islam. A lot of intellectual shaking down will take place in Muslim societies as they ponder the relationship between religious values and societal improvement in today's polarized circumstances. The process is well under way: 9/11 and the Global War on Terror have accelerated radicalization and, simultaneously, the production of its ultimate antibodies.

With the collapse of the centralized theological authority of the Roman Church in the Reformation, the door was open: how could the contents of religious texts be applied to the creation of the good (and Godly) society? In reality no religious text offers a ready-made module of law for instant application to the workings of society: devout followers can seek only to glean values out of the texts and to craft legislation reflecting those values as best they can. Christianity and Islam have both struggled with application of the texts and values to society and governance — and continue to do so. Protestant Christianity in particular sought to found its theology and moral judgments for society on the texts themselves, not on the deliberations of unrepresentative church councils that played such a major role in the earlier Roman Catholic and Orthodox traditions.

Islam struggles with precisely these same questions: what is the role of the Qur'an in shaping the individual's understanding of Islam and in crafting Islamic legislation? Both Islamic reformism and Protestantism are interested in action and results, in *applied* religious values and their social implications, not in mere abstract theology.

CALVINISM, along with Lutheranism and Anabaptism, was one of the three main movements of the Reformation. John Calvin had undergone a powerful and mystical personal religious experience that pushed him strongly toward embrace of Protestant-style beliefs—"God subdued my soul to docility by a sudden conversion"—and he was convinced that he had a divine mission as God's instrument for the spiritual regeneration of the world. Viewed as a heretic in Catholic France, Calvin sought refuge in Geneva, which was struggling against powerful external forces for its independence. In 1536, the city took three astonishingly radical steps: the abolition of monasteries, abolition of Mass, and rejection of papal authority. Calvin strongly favored "magisterial rule" for the city, meaning rule by Protestant clergy—in effect a theocracy—seemingly prefiguring Ayatollah Khomeini's rule of the clerics in Iran. Calvin worked for fourteen years to win over the leaders of Geneva and to impose his authority over the form of his church's doctrine and organization, and the moral behavior of the congregation. We find here almost a blueprint for later Wahhabi thinking in Saudi Arabia. Calvin established a "City of God" in Geneva and proclaimed the Bible to be the source of all community legislation—parallel to trends in much Islamist thinking that supports the Qur'an as the sole source of all legislation; indeed, Saudi Arabia speaks of the Qur'an as its "constitution."

All elements of Calvin's religious services came entirely out of the Bible. As the Wahhabis would later do, Calvin opposed the use of musical instruments, church bells, and colorful vestments or artwork in religious services. Nearly all traditional church holy days and saints' feast days were abandoned. Fundamental to Calvin's thinking was a belief in the sinfulness and corruptibility of mankind. Strict moral principles were imposed, whose violations were punishable: excommunication and banishment for breaking religious laws, and the death penalty for blasphemy. Dress codes required simple garb. Taverns were closed, theaters and dancing were not permitted, and the general public was kept under close scrutiny by informers. "Morals police" (like Sa'udi *mutawwa'*, or "enforcers") visited neighborhoods to ensure that moral codes were upheld. All sensual pleasures were deeply suspect.

Calvin's goal was that Geneva should become the Kingdom of God on Earth and a community without sin or taint. And although Calvin and his movement were a vital part of the Protestant Reformation, his views directly contradicted the spirit of the Lutheran branch of the Reformation, which emphasized an individual's personal responsibility for interpreting and understanding the Bible and God's message. Calvinism employed authoritarian means to impose Calvin's moral vision. He himself led a strict, rigorous, and seemingly joyless life, replete with constant health problems.

Whatever dissatisfactions may have existed among part of the population of Geneva, John Knox, the leader of Scottish Protestantism, described the city as "the most perfect school of Christ." Geneva also became a center for training; missionaries schooled in Calvinist principles fanned out across Europe, in effect to "export the revolution." The movement soon took on an international status through the use of underground messengers and clandestine communications, enabling its spread to points in northern Europe and later to America.

The Antihierarchical Christianity of John Calvin

Again, parallels with fundamentalist Islam abound in the strict interpretation of religious text as the basis for legislation and social organization. Wahhabism, in its insistence upon a return to the basic *texts* of the faith, bears considerable resemblance to both Lutheranism and Calvinism. The movement in later forms advocated the priesthood of all believers. Wahhabism also denounces blind adherence to earlier clerical interpretations of texts and practices, and even reflexive perpetuation of family and traditional religious practice. Instead, it insists that each Muslim has a responsibility to seek a personal understanding of the texts.

It would surely seem to be a feature of enlightened modernism to stress the individual's responsibility in seeking a personal, reflective understanding of his own faith and moral values, as opposed to uncritical acceptance of inherited tradition. But the experience of the Reformation—and fundamentalist Islam—demonstrates that when individuals believe themselves empowered and able to interpret sacred texts, then alternative, unauthorized, and even bizarre views may emerge and possibly run rampant. Senior theologians, Catholic or Islamic, then lose control over what the "correct" meaning of the texts is. Indeed, in Lutheranism the clerics are very much supposed to lose control and relinquish authority to the individual believer. We return here to the permanent dilemma of revealed texts in the Abrahamic faiths: To whom is understanding vouchsafed? Who can determine genuine orthodoxy? No single source can ever be viewed as authoritative, and a theological free-for-all can easily ensue, with irresponsible and even dangerous consequences. That is exactly what has happened in both the Reformation and some fundamentalist Islamic movements. Fundamentalist Islam does not reveal here some strange or unusual characteristics but is instead moving along predictable lines in the evolution of revealed religions.

The issue is as vital now as it was during the Reformation or the emergence of Wahhabi thought. Today, many clerics outside Arabia seek to denigrate trends toward independent thinking as "Wahhabi," suggesting they represent a "foreign import" contrary to local tradition and understanding. As in Christianity, there is genuine tension between centralized "authoritative" understanding of religion, and local, traditional, or "unauthorized" personal views. Individual interpretation may lead to a deeper understanding of scripture, but it may also grant license to ignorant radicalism.

In the Reformation, fears of possible "religious ideas run wild" were quickly justified: early Protestantism witnessed a sudden proliferation of sects, with often wildly diverse understandings of biblical texts. Ideas have consequences. Many new interpretations created radical new political and social groupings that turned to violence and were often exploited by local powers as weapons against other powers.

The (Protestant) *Dictionary of Christianity* estimates that 20,800 different Protestant denominations are in existence today; the *World Christian Encyclopedia* places the total at a staggering 33,820. While the precise figure can be debated, these numbers undeniably represent the fruits of the seeds sown by the Reformation. They fully validate Catholic fears about the consequences of loosened centralized control over church doctrine and hierarchy.

And in Islam, the Sunni branch in particular is characterized by a lack of centralized theological control or even of a single authoritative voice like a pope. So, in one sense, it shares the same dilemma as Protestantism. There is no one figure in Sunni Islam who can speak with absolute or binding authority on questions of interpretation of Islam. The rector of the religious faculty at al-Azhar University in Cairo enjoys some respect, but even his voice owes more to tradition and Egyptian state power than to any real authority. A leading Muslim Brotherhood resident scholar in Qatar, Yusif al-Qaradawi, enjoys perhaps more respect than any other figure due to his weekly TV program on al-Jazeera, in which he tries to clarify orthodox Islamic perspectives on religious issues under contemporary conditions.

The Reformation spawned numerous radical groups several centuries ago. But apart from some historical fringe groups in

Islam, not until the twentieth century did more-sweeping radical interpretations emerge in political and social thinking. These ideas planted seeds that were later carried to far greater extremes in such radical groups as al-Qa'ida. The radical group *Takfir wa'l Hijra* in Egypt—literally "to denounce others as Unbelievers and to seek refuge for oneself from an impure world"—parallels Calvinist thinking, although Calvinism did not practice terrorism. This sect preaches that there is little true Islam in this world and that the only option open to the individual is to denounce contemporary Muslim society as "ignorant" or nonbelieving and to take refuge, either in a special righteous community (like Calvin's City of God) or, more commonly, within oneself, to find purity of belief and action against the corrupting influences of society.

And who is the target of all this preaching? Strikingly, in both the Christian and Muslim cases the goal is not to create converts from other religions. For the majority of Islamists, *da'wa,* or missionary work, is aimed at changing other *Muslims* whose understanding of Islam is seen as flawed or incorrect; they seek to call them back to the true faith. In the eyes of many of these fundamentalists, contemporary Muslim society is deeply corrupted, has lost its moral path, and is even referred to as *jahili,* or "ignorant"—a term originally applied to pre-Islamic Arabian society, a state of ignorance before Islam. The term was reinterpreted by Egyptian Islamist thinker Sayyid Qutb in the mid-twentieth century to refer to the *overall state* of contemporary Muslim society as he saw it—that is, wallowing in ignorance of the true faith.

Perhaps the most radical of the three main Protestant trends during the Reformation were the Anabaptists, who share with many Islamists a strong commitment to missionary work. Anabaptism literally means "baptism anew," the idea that baptism is meaningless unless it represents a conscious adult decision to establish a new and personal relationship with God. Anabaptists called for "rebaptism" of adults, who this time would be fully conscious of the nature of their decision to embrace their personal God. Central to Anabaptists, too, was *empowerment* of the individual and the rejection of routine, often empty acceptance of inherited faith via family tradition. And similarly, for many Islamic fundamentalists, inheritance of faith through the social environment does not suffice; only Muslims who personally understand their newly found commitment as a Muslim, through personal study of the texts, can be considered a true Muslim. And like Islamic fundamentalists, Anabaptists were known for their formidable knowledge of scripture. The Anabaptists reached the pinnacle of radicalism in the eighteen-month Münster Rebellion described at the outset of this chapter.

Similar social conditions help spawn similar religious reaction in diverse societies. For all of the period's intense focus on theology, it was its political and social forces that drove the Reformation. This was a time of great change: the crumbling of a feudal order associated with social and economic injustice, the emergence of cities and a new urban life free of the norms of feudalism, an environment which fostered the emergence of new bourgeois values and conscious assertion of rights for the individual. These changes were resisted by feudal forces, sometimes by princes but sometimes not, depending on their interests. The newly emerging states sought to seize control of church finances and take them over. Above all, the Reformation carried huge and deliberate political implications for the German princes and other northern European rulers. Where you stood on Reformation theology depended on where your economic and political interests lay.

We have seen this in the turmoil of a changing Mecca, the shift from tribal to more mercantile values, and the loss of more traditional tribal safety nets and the emergence of Muhammad; Jesus, too, was emerging in a new social environment in which, among other things, Galilee was hostile to the economic and religious power of Jerusalem.

The common theme through all of this is the relationship of the state and state power: what happens when the state loses control over doctrine. We see it almost invariably releases popular participation in political and social events, often unleashing radical activism, especially when conditions are bad.

The Great Apostasy

Perhaps the most extreme and sweeping assault ever against the foundations of the Christian Church is the concept of "The Great Apostasy," a body of ideas that has captured the thinking of a small but articulate and vocal minority and that receives considerable time on the airwaves of Christian broadcasting and publishing. This approach condemns the very *institution* of the church, nearly from its beginnings, and levels a series of bold and diverse charges:

- The church's original teachings and practices began to be distorted, changed, and even corrupted extremely early on, even perhaps during the lifetime of some of the Apostles; the church went on to compound these errors by persecuting and expelling advocates of the original principles of Christian faith.
- The church began to move inexorably down the road of worldly corruption with the official adoption of Christianity by the Roman Empire; this event wed the church to state power, and the state manipulated the church and its doctrines for its own end. The church has not only committed grievous errors but it also is fundamentally incapable of change or reform in this respect.
- The church compounded its errors when it then propounded the doctrine of church infallibility on doctrinal issues; and yet again when the church extended this

infallibility on doctrinal issues to the pope himself. The
reality is that the church, both Catholic and Protestant, will,
in fact, *never be able to speak infallibly* until the end of time.

- "Human weakness is naturally drawn to a form of
false religion that is worldly, pompous, ritualistic,
anthropomorphic, polytheistic, infected with magical
thinking, and that values human accomplishment more
highly or more practically than the work of God (divine
grace) is valued." Humans are also inclined to accept *tradition*
as being on par with the written testimony of the Bible.

These concepts represent a revolutionary, even subversive critique
of the church in various strands of radical Protestant thinking
that has included at various times Anabaptists, the Church of
Jesus Christ of Latter-day Saints, Adventists, and Jehovah's Witnesses. It has also shaken up the thinking of liberal denominations
of the church in its direct charge of corruption of religion through
power. Interestingly, classical Shi'ism is right on message here: a
belief in the inevitable corruption of the true faith through clerical
association with the state and power (even though violated by the
ideology of contemporary Iran). Today, radical Sunni Islam calls
for Muslims to think for themselves, even to resist the state when
the state clearly is not Islamically legitimate. But this is all relatively new to Sunni Islam — and is almost Jeffersonian in its belief
in the obligation to overthrow unjust and illegitimate government.

Reconstructionism

The Reconstructionists, another branch of radical Christian
thought, get right down to the heart of it: how much coercion is
appropriate in establishing morality within the social order? The
very existence of the state, by definition, acknowledges the necessity

of coercion to maintain society and order and to prevent anarchy; the only unknowns are the *degree* of coercion required, the methods to be used, and who is to sanction it. We have here a sociopolitical question as well as religious one, because all states legislate on certain elements of morality in society, such as murder, crime, vandalism, theft, and sex with minors.

The state is an attractive target for any reformer of society, religious or secular, for its capture provides the means—persuasive or coercive—to impose and implement religious values within society. Indeed, the values need not be solely religious: Leninists saw the capture of the state as the indispensable prerequisite for implementing a system of political, economic, and social communism. Some Islamists, too, particularly in earlier eras, were enthusiastic about the prospect of using the powers of an Islamic state to impose a truly Islamic society. Over time this idea has come to lose favor with many Islamists, some of whom, through experience, are now more inclined to let God, and not the state, punish the sinful. "The state is not responsible for keeping the gates of hell closed; they should be free and open to all," as one Turkish Islamist put it to me.

Some elements of Christianity, even in the West, present clear parallels. Over the past hundred years, a "reconstructionist" movement has emerged that again theorizes about the actual creation of a state based on Christian values. Just as the Qur'an is seen by many Muslims as the source of legislation, so, too, the Bible—not the US Constitution—for Christian reconstructionists is the document that should guide the future of the United States. Moral principles are to be derived from the Bible to serve as the basis of law for the family, community, and civil government—shades of Calvin in Geneva. Some reconstructionists argue that Christian clerics should be in charge of government, similar to Iran's theocracy, or rule by clerics. Government itself would be subject to the moral principles of the Old and New Testaments. Some reconstructionists support the recriminalization of abortion and homosexuality, and, while not necessarily advocating the death penalty for it today, note that there were some twenty offenses in the Old Testament punishable by death, including incest, prostitution, adultery, blasphemy, Sabbath breaking, and worshiping gods other than the One God. Progress cannot be made through compromise with those who deny the Christian faith, they argue, because we share no common ground. Pluralistic political organizations are not acceptable because they imply cooperation with those whose ethical and moral principles are not based on the Bible.

Just as many Muslims believe that one day—simply due to its innate doctrinal superiority—Islam may ultimately become the religion of all mankind, so do reconstructionists believe that one day Christianity will be acknowledged by all and will thus come to dominate the world. Imposition by force is undesirable, unnecessary, and counterproductive to the longer goal; it will simply come.

For reconstructionists, *tolerance* is not a neutral concept that acknowledges equal validity of all religious belief before the law; instead, they speak of a "Christian tolerance" that permits equal treatment but not equal *acceptance* of all doctrine. Reconstructionists would not seek to regulate personal *beliefs*, but would regulate *public actions* and behavior. This view is remarkably similar to some Islamists who advocate Shari'a law under nearly identical terms. In this view, tolerance within an Islamic state means just that— the state will *tolerate* other beliefs, but that does not imply acceptance of equal doctrinal validity.

The number of self-acknowledged reconstructionists represents a small segment of Christians, but their overall influence on the political views of the Christian Right has been major, creating a much broader trend known as "Dominionism."

According to the sociologist Sara Diamond, the defining

concept of Dominionism is "that Christians alone are Biblically mandated to occupy all secular institutions until Christ returns." This version of Christianity transcends the realm of religion and enters into the secular realms of politics and even nationalism. Researcher Frederick Clarkson has characterized Dominionism as promoting a celebration of "Christian nationalism," urging that the United States return to its status as a "Christian nation" in which the Ten Commandments play a central role in the legal system and governance. Books abound on "Christian patriotism."

Debate swirls around these Christian movements in the United States, and many of their critics accuse them of seeking to impose a Christian totalitarianism, a charge the Dominionists stoutly deny. The debate is reminiscent of some elements within the Islamist movement that argue about the place of compulsion in reforming, or "Islamizing," *Muslim*—not Christian—countries.

The Qur'an, of course, is quite explicit and unambiguous in its statement that "there is no compulsion in religion" (*La ikrah fi'l-din*—Qur'an, Sura 2:256). At the same time, critics of Islam rightly point out that what the Qur'an says is one thing, and the social practice or state institutions from place to place another. There are many competing texts in the Qur'an, each of which reflects revelation from different periods and under varying conditions, addressed to varying issues. All who seek to impose rigid or intolerant interpretations of scripture upon others can always find ample theological grounds to do so. Or, as Luther famously said, "The Devil can quote scripture to his own ends."

Even during the Reformation, the question of religious orthodoxy and Christian relations with Islam came up in one dramatic case involving Michael Servetus, the prominent physician, theologian, and scientist. He took sharp issue with Calvin over the nature of the Trinity: Servetus argued that Jesus and the Holy Spirit were just manifestations of God with no independent existence—old stuff. But Servetus went on to proclaim that the concept of the Trinity in Christian theology had been a consistent barrier to Christian relations with Muslims and Jews. A Catholic prosecutor charged him with favoring "Jews and Turks," and he was accused of reading the Qur'an. In 1553, Calvin had Servetus burned at the stake in Geneva. Today, Servetus is viewed as the first Unitarian martyr.

Christian Shades of Modern Political Islam

These political and ideological conflicts of the Reformation, then, highlight themes that first emerged in the early days of Christianity. Heretical issues from that early period nearly all resurfaced in more potent form in the sixteenth century, this time driven by the new social and economic imperatives of emerging European urban centers, thriving mercantile activity, new nationalisms, and the political ambitions of nascent nation-states and rulers. Islam grapples with quite similar issues, indicating to us the abiding nature of these concerns across religions. And these struggles are taking place at a time of intense pressure and stress in the Muslim world. Any religion institutionally linked to the state order faces similar dilemmas: the relationship between religion and political power, the role of compulsion in morality, and the problem of implementing moral values in society and governance through political action. Yet, when religion is liberated from state or official control, it will quickly be used as a political tool to challenge the state and demand reform—in the name of religious values.

———

WE HAVE SEEN in earlier chapters how struggle for control of religious doctrine was an essential element in the struggle for power. The Reformation represents the high point of that struggle in the West. In the past, Islam's religious figures could never really determine the leadership and policies of state power in the way

Christianity did for fifteen hundred years in the West. It is today, with the "reformation" of Islam, that the story is changing. With the emergence of modern fundamentalists, Islam is no longer the exclusive purview of the state; "lay" clerics exercise ever greater voice and influence, for better or for worse. These self-trained theologians challenge the state over the proprietorship of Islam. "It is not your Islam, it is *my* Islam," as one street placard put it. It is the fundamentalists, trained or untrained, who seek to apply Islam and lend it relevance — to use it as an instrument for political and social reform, to change or overthrow the state that they see as serving neither Islam nor the people.

So in looking at fundamentalist Islam today, we're not dealing with some strange religious product of the Middle East. Islam and Christianity show remarkable parallels of development here as similar forces come into play — typical of the evolution of most religions in attempting to coexist with power. In a modern democratic era, it should be no surprise that "the people" are attempting to take control of their religions out of the hands of the elite, or the state, that dominated it for most of history. That same thing would have happened in an Eastern Orthodox Middle East, without Islam. These are features of an "Islamic Reformation." For better or for worse.

PART TWO

MEETING AT THE
CIVILIZATIONAL BORDERS
OF ISLAM

Samuel Huntington, in his book *The Clash of Civilizations*, employed the infelicitous phrase "Islam's bloody borders." In a world that is fairly bloody overall, it's worth remembering that it generally takes two to make a border bloody. We're now going to take Islam further afield than its Middle Eastern birthplace and look at how it interacted with four major cultures as it came into contact with them and established varying forms of coexistence: Russia, Europe, India, and China.

First, I'd like to step back a bit from the usual use of the term "Islam" to recognize that as the religion spread, we're really talking about *Muslims*—what they thought, said, and did and how they related to non-Muslim cultures. It matters more how Muslims see their own culture and religion and act upon it than what other people think Islam is. *Islam, in the end, is what Muslims say it is, and how they act upon it.* That can be many different things.

Through examination of Muslim interaction with some key non-Muslim societies, we will better understand how Islam functions under diverse circumstances, its flexibility, and variety of forms. And as we look at these interactions, we again note that religious doctrine is almost never the issue at stake, whereas ethnicity and community are. Did Muslims maintain some kind of implacable hostility and posture of religious war toward these non-Muslim cultures? Or maybe a cold truce—or possibly coexistence? Or did they share some common interests with the non-Muslim cultures?

Most of the cases of "borders of Islam" that follow are not really about borders but about Muslim relationships *inside* non-Muslim cultures, essentially as minorities. In every instance, Muslims have developed creative relationships in living with non-Muslim power. They have not, however, swerved from one overriding principle: the preservation and protection of Islam and Muslim society within these states. That means an unwillingness to relinquish their Muslim identity or to become so culturally absorbed and assimilated as to vanish as a culture. That does not mean they will not become fully integrated as active and involved citizens in their societies. Jews have undergone very similar experiences throughout their history in struggling to pro-tect their community and maintain the uniqueness of their own remarkable and gifted culture, while consciously resisting assimilation, absorption, and disappearance. We find that Muslims have managed to coexist and even share in cultural cross-fertilization in societies that have often not been very multicultural in spirit. As we examine these four cases, we perceive different Muslim strategies: adaptation, fusion, sometimes resistance when threatened, but a realistic acknowledgment of the reality of their Muslim minority status in non-Muslim states.

But Huntington's phrase about borders was not entirely off the mark either. He reminds us — although not the first to do so — that throughout history "civilizations" can in fact represent significant fault lines. Fault lines are really *boundaries* of any sort that can flare up into conflict: they can exist within a clan, a village, a region, a country, or between continents or civilizations. "Civilization" is simply a kind of community writ very large.

How strongly does a civilization or a community cohere? It depends on the circumstances, since under certain kinds of stress almost any community can break apart into narrower components. But just what is it that creates the boundaries between communities — and how firm are they? It's highly situational. An old saying captures the sense of it: "Me against my brother, me and my brother against my cousin, me, my brother, and my cousin against the other clan."

All of this matters because Islam is not necessarily the delimiting border to which Muslims respond every time. The *actual* communities that may end up facing each other across battle lines can vary. In one situation, it could be Christians against Muslims, or Muslims against Hindus; but it could also be Sunni Muslims against Shi'ite Muslims. Or Turkish Muslims against Kurdish Muslims. Or struggles among various Iraqi Shi'ite militia. The unit of solidarity is constantly shifting, as it would with Catholic or Protestant communities. We could even imagine a badly divided globe suddenly uniting in solidarity to repel an invasion of Martians.

Not surprisingly, it is *local* conflict that is everywhere more common than wide-scale conflict. That's where the rubber hits the road—conflict emerging from proximity, just people rubbing up against others. Conflicts among Muslims themselves, or among Christians themselves, are vastly more commonplace than any "civilizational conflict." These grand "civilizational conflicts" that Huntington talks about are often highly theoretical, or imagined. It's hard to engage an entire civilization into a conflict against another civilization—but it has, in fact, become easier in modern times, where communications greatly facilitate a sense of group solidarity on an ever-bigger scale. You can show the distant enemy on the TV screen in the living room and work up emotions long distance. "It's the Muslims," or "it's the Christians," or "it's the West." The Crusades were probably the closest thing to a "civilizational conflict" the world had ever seen up to that time— luridly articulated in the stirring speeches of Pope Urban II about the threat from "the infidels." But most Muslims hardly knew it was going on at the time.

All this matters as we consider the question of Muslim minorities living in other societies. How will they interact? As a tight Muslim bloc? Perhaps not, unless they are under serious pressures or heavy discrimination precisely *because* they are Muslim. Just as likely, it might be all the citizens of a southern region against those of a northern region. Or mixed Muslim-Christian or Muslim-Hindu communities of one linguistic group joining against those ethnics of a different linguistic group—such as Shi'ite and Sunni Kurds against Shi'ite and Sunni Turks. You can't predict. It is all situational and changing as people and communities constantly reassess their self-interests. Thus, it becomes fairly foolish to posit automatic Muslim hostility to non-Muslim neighbors, unless some very bad things are going on between them—which can periodically happen. Thus religion — especially Islam versus other religions — is an elusive basis for conflict. To posit permanent Muslim conflict with non-Muslims is absurd. And so even "a world without Islam" leaves us plenty of other fault lines along which communities can clash, have clashed, and will clash. Over long human history, ethnicity might be at the top of such a list, however we define "ethnicity" — itself a consciously constructed identity.

A Monopoly on Anti-Westernism?

Examination of Muslims in other societies also matters because it touches on another mantra of those predisposed against Islam: that Islam is fundamentally anti-Western. The truth is that *most of the world* has found reasons over time both to admire, and to hate, the West. Anger at the West is hardly a Muslim monopoly — although the specific conditions of the Global War on Terror in the first decade of the twenty-first century happen to have induced a particularly strong period of anti-Americanism among Muslims. It will eventually pass. But anti-Americanism or anti-Westernism can flare up again, as it has in the past in other cultures, such as Chinese or Latin American.

Thousands of books have been written on the subject of anti-Western thinking — essentially asking "Why do they hate us?" — and simplistic answers are routinely offered. The crux of the debate is really, do "they" hate us for things that the West has done? Or do they hate us for reasons that reflect their own confusion, jealousy, and lack of understanding? Whom do we blame, ourselves or them, for not liking us?

The question is unanswerable. More accurately, it deserves multiple answers. These questions lie at the heart of this very book. On the one hand, "they" — Muslims and others — do indeed hate us because of what we have done to them: invasions, colonies, empire-building, wars, coups, political, economic, and cultural domination, seizure and exploitation of resources, arrogance, lack of concern, failure to respect and understand non-Western cultures. We have heard these arguments before and there is a great deal of truth to them.

For those Americans who are uncomfortable in acknowledging *any legacy* of ongoing destructive and damaging US actions against the rest of the world, the temptation is to reply, "That's right, blame America." So we then search out self-serving and comforting answers: they "hate us for our freedoms," they envy our wealth and our way of life, they prefer to blame the West rather than taking a hard look at themselves and their own shortcomings, And all of these arguments contain grain of validity as well. But they basically don't tell most of the story.

Whatever the roots of anti-Westernism may be, the phenomenon still remains a problem for the West and the United States. How does all this fit into Islam's view of the world?

A combination of admiration, respect, fear, and anger characterizes the views of most developing nations toward the modern West and especially the US. The West is admired for its surge of economic and political development beginning in the sixteenth century. But it was specifically the West's technological and military advancements that were responsible for thrusting the West out into the habitat of other civilizations.

So how broadly shared are the components of anti-Western feeling, then? Could a broad front of anti-Westernism ever coalesce to any meaningful degree against the United

States? Are we moving into a world now better defined as "the West and the Rest"? These, too, are all abstractions. There are many "West"s out there, often at war among themselves for most of history. Similarly there are many "East"s, many "Islam"s, and of course many "Rests of the world." Such terms really aren't useful until they coalesce into some kind of specific, meaningful political force capable of changing things that matter to us here and now.

These days some kind of ad hoc coalition of "the Rest" against "the West," or against the United States, is already partly in evidence. The Muslim world today—galvanized, radicalized, unsettled, unnerved, and overwrought from the Bush administration's Global War on Terror—presents a greater degree of self-conscious "solidarity" than it probably ever has before in history. Perhaps that kind of emotional solidarity cannot be directly exploited by any single state, but it can produce turmoil, periodic terrorist actions, and strong foot-dragging against US goals at the international level. The imperial visions of the Bush administration, explicitly propounded by neoconservative strategists, and softer forms under Clinton, generated further anti-US feeling throughout most of the rest of the world— in the Muslim world, Russia, China, and Latin America. And even if these forces could never coalesce into a coherent military threat against the United States, they can easily focus on thwarting American global strategy; indeed, they already have. Their passive-aggressive attitudes alone sharply limited the Bush administration's influence and blocked its ability to get things done.

Thus, the more we think about "Islam's bloody borders," the more we find we are really talking about a complex set of phenomena and events: preservation of cultural communities from external onslaught, shared resentments against aspects of aggressive Western actions, and the effort of states to homogenize their populations. To single out Islam as somehow the operative factor in community conflict is to turn a highly selective microscope on some specific cases of world conflict at this particular moment in history. To believe that such anti-Western impetus would not be present if there were no Islam is naive. Three of the four other civilizations we will look at here—Russia, China, and India—all have deep roots of anti-Westernism in their own right. Muslims fit into those patterns to one degree or another.

First, we will turn to Russia in some detail, a pivotal state in our story. It matters perhaps more than any other of these three states: Russia directly inherited the jaundiced Byzantine worldview of the West and intensified it, it came to include a very large number of Muslims inside its own borders, and it has thrashed around over the centuries about the best way to deal with them under imperial, then Communist, and then post-communist governments. Finally, Russia is still intimately involved with the Middle East, which in some ways represents a shared distrust of Western actions.

CHAPTER SEVEN

The "Third Rome" and Russia: Russia Inherits the Orthodox Legacy

As the fifteenth century approached, the handwriting was on the wall: Byzantium was dying, its few lasting remnants of empire soon to be snuffed out by the Ottoman conquest of 1453. But the concept of the Orthodox Church, the great mother church, had been powerfully implanted across the region; it would not die. In this chapter, we will see how the Byzantine torch was, fatefully, passed on to Russia, where a flame of resentment and suspicion toward the West would be nourished and take on new character over the next five hundred years down to today. Anti-Westernism in the Orthodox Church was maintained even as Islam took over the imperial mantle in Constantinople.

Islam had now largely completed the assertion of its dominant role across the entire former Byzantine Empire — the Ottoman Empire would resemble the Byzantine in many respects, only now in Muslim garb. The Ottomans inherited and perpetuated numbers of Byzantine ruling institutions in its management of the multireligious and multiethnic empire. While the psychological blow to Eastern Christianity of defeat and loss of power was huge, it is important to note that Islam did not become the eternal deadly enemy of Christianity in these Eastern reaches of the world; they all lived too close together for that. Whatever the now-subject Christians felt about it, there was little choice but intimate coexistence on both sides. Certainly, there were numerous discontents here and there, local uprisings and revolts periodically, especially as the Ottoman Empire itself gradually weakened and separatist nationalist movements, encouraged by Europe, grew. Some rebellions were put down with great harshness. But local Christians had periodically revolted against Byzantine rule earlier on. And there were also local revolts by Muslim populations against Ottoman rule as well over this long period.

Large empires are never free of periodic violent discontent in one locale or another. Given a thousand years of Orthodox distrust of Rome and the West on the one hand, and the new imperative of Orthodox coexistence with Islam on the other, Islam's final attainment of power across the region seems to have brought remarkably little dislocation. Indeed, large communities of Christians in the Arab regions had already been living under Islamic rule for some six hundred years even before Constantinople fell. The year 1453 may be perceived as a symbolic watershed, but it disguises the power of continuity in the region. Whoever sat in possession of Anatolian, Levantine, and Balkan territories inherited some built-in geopolitical legacies of tension with the West. And in Russia we will see strong elements of this legacy passed on to the eastern Slavic world, creating new complex relationships between Muslim and Christian.

———

ACCORDING TO ANCIENT RUSSIAN historical accounts, both Catholic and Orthodox missionaries had made their way over a thousand years ago to Kiev, the birthplace of the early pagan Russian state. In a victory for Constantinople over Rome, the Bulgarians and several other Slavic peoples had already opted for Orthodoxy over Latin Christianity in an earlier century. Prince Vladimir the Great of Kiev is said to have dispatched envoys to the centers of each of the great religions in order to assess the suitability of each for official adoption by Russia. Rich anecdotal accounts narrate the envoys' reactions as they reported back:

> Of the Muslim Bulgarians of the Volga the envoys reported there is no gladness among them; only sorrow and a great stench, and that their religion was undesirable due to its taboo against alcoholic beverages and pork; supposedly, Vladimir observed on that occasion: "Drinking is the joy of the Rus."

Vladimir sent envoys to the Jews as well, "questioning them about their religion but ultimately rejecting it, saying that their loss of Jerusalem was evidence of their having been abandoned by God." Finally the choice lay between Catholicism and Orthodoxy. "In the gloomy churches of the Germans his emissaries saw no beauty; but at Hagia Sophia [in Constantinople], where the full festival ritual of the Byzantine Church was set in motion to impress them, they found their ideal: 'We no longer knew whether we were in heaven or on earth,' they reported, 'nor such beauty, and we know not how to tell of it.'" Thus was the fateful choice made with huge civilizational implications for the future, although we may be sure that there were major political as well as theological gains to be had for Vladimir through an alliance with Constantinople.

The conversion of Russia was a huge geopolitical prize for Orthodoxy: to this day, Russia remains the single largest Orthodox communion in the world. Russia is also the only religious link the Orthodox Church possesses to a major world power. At the same time, an expanding Russian Empire would take in larger and larger Muslim populations under its control, transforming Russia into an important Muslim state as well.

The Ottomans had been in no doubt about the historic and cultural character of the prize they had acquired from the Byzantines; they had long been familiar with the Byzantine ruling and administrative system as they gradually incorporated outlying parts of the empire into their own. Sultan Mehmet quickly sought to reestablish Constantinople as an international and multicultural capital. He invited all those Christians who had fled to return and restore the city to its former character. The patriarch of Constantinople was granted authority to oversee all Orthodox communities within the empire. In fact, the new power of the patriarch and his administrators under the Ottoman Turks came to be resented by some outlying Orthodox communities as an infringement upon their former autonomous authority. But the Orthodox Church was now settling in for a long four-hundred-year coexistence within the Ottoman Empire that would change them both.

At the same time, the church paid a high cultural price. Even though it was able to operate with considerable religious authority within the Ottoman Empire, its *political* power, shorn of the backing of an Orthodox state, had been greatly reduced. The church grew isolated within the empire, and its contacts with intellectual and theological trends in the West diminished. The church grew more introverted and continued an earlier drift away from intellectual and "rational" pursuits to emphasize what had always been a hallmark of Orthodoxy—the importance of faith and religious mystery in personal spiritual life. The church developed a deeper feeling of dichotomy between Eastern and Western Christianity: in Orthodox eyes, Latin Catholicism and the West were imbued with materialism, rationalism (the mind over faith and spirit), individualism, and corruption through close papal and church association with power, leading to a spiritual emptiness. The Orthodox Church saw its own spirit as emanating directly from the earliest teachings of Jesus himself, unsullied by the politics of the Latin Church and papacy. Orthodox spirituality and otherworldliness were perceived to reflect what the West lacked in its alleged spiritual impoverishment. These themes ran deep in the Orthodox psyche and persist in its rhetoric to this day.

Russia and Third Rome

The Eastern Roman Empire had come to an end, but the *imperial* tradition of Orthodox faith could not be allowed to perish with Constantinople. It was quickly taken up by Tsar Ivan III of Russia, who moved to declare Moscow the "Third Rome"—successor to the Roman and Byzantine Christian seats of power. To strengthen his claim, he forged a vital dynastic link to Constantinople through his marriage to Sophia Paleolog, the niece of the last emperor of Byzantium. Ivan III also adopted for his own use the Byzantine coat of arms—the double-headed eagle—which still remains on the Russian coat of arms today.

The assumption of the title of "Third Rome" denoted far more for Moscow than mere imperial pretension: it represented a *messianic vision* of a new civilizational and spiritual role, an obligation that had now fallen upon Russia to preserve the true faith of Christianity against the heresies and evils of both Roman Catholicism and Islam. The messianic flavor of this new Russian mission is perfectly captured in a letter from the monk Philotheus of Pskov to Tsar Basil III:

> The Church of Old Rome fell for its heresy; the gates of the Second Rome were hewn down by the axes of the infidel Turks; but the Church of Moscow, the Church of the New Rome shines brighter than the sun in the whole universe. Thou, Basil, art the one universal sovereign of all the Christian folk; thou should hold the reins in awe of God; fear Him who hath committed them to thee. Two Romes

have fallen but the Third stands fast; a Fourth there cannot be. Thy Kingdom shall not be given to another.

Continuities, with or without Islam, do not stop there. The concept of "Third Rome" was not lost on the Ottomans either. In a fascinating fusion of Muslim and Christian historical visions in the Eastern Mediterranean, Sultan Mehmet II, after the conquest, began to refer to himself as the successor to Byzantine imperial tradition and adopted the title *Kayser-i-Rum* (Emperor of the Roman Empire). He drew on selected Byzantine court and administrative customs for his own empire, including maintenance of its multinational, multireligious character. In a fascinating extension of the same theme, the Turkish historian İlber Ortaylı suggests that Mehmet now saw Ottoman Constantinople itself as the "Third Rome"—successor to pagan Rome in Italy and to Eastern Orthodox "Rome" in Constantinople—now an "Islamic Rome" in Istanbul. In this view, Islam did not represent a rejection of Eastern Christianity; rather, in powerful continuity, it picked up and smoothly adopted much of the Eastern imperial tradition from Christianity and integrated it into what would be the world's biggest and longest-lasting Muslim empire. *Empire* looms larger than faith in this great transition.

A recent reviewer of a book on the Ottomans and the West comments:

> ...the skirmishes and the pitched battles that raged between the Hapsburgs and the Ottomans [around the gates of Vienna], and their numerous vassals on both sides, represented not so much a "clash of civilizations" as a collision of empires. For all the pious sloganeering that accompanied it, the struggle was only incidentally one between Islam and Christianity. Territory was the aim, along with something less tangible but equally compelling: the right to

claim the legacy of the Roman Empire....Had not... Mehmed the Conqueror toppled the Byzantines and seized Constantinople two centuries before? Far from wishing to obliterate the Byzantine past, the Ottomans meant to assume it as their own...

Russian Orthodox Suspicions of the West

Ever since the early pagan Russians cast their lot with the Eastern Orthodox faith over Catholicism, the Orthodox Church went on to stamp Russia powerfully with its cultural outlook; this included a new Russian mission for the salvation of all mankind through propagation of the True Faith. These themes pervade Russian culture: the deep reservoirs of Russian mysticism, traditions of ecstatic belief, wandering holy men, belief in the Christlike simplicity of the Russian peasant and the purity of the Russian soul, the place of the holy fool in Russian society (indelibly portrayed in a powerful scene in the opera *Boris Godunov*), and Russia's *mission civilisatrice*. All of this bolstered the deep conviction of Orthodox believers in the spiritual superiority of their faith and church over that of an aggressive, expansionist, materialist, coldly analytic, individualistic, and corrupted West, which thirsted for power and vainglory. These themes in Russian folk belief are later elevated in the nineteenth century in Russian philosophical systems of thought extolling the world vision of Orthodoxy and pan-Slavism.

Russia to this day remains schizophrenic toward the West— part of its struggle for identity. Pro-Western views have long clashed with pro-nativist—later framed as a struggle of Russian "Westernizers" versus "Slavophiles." In one sense, the Slavophiles came to represent a Romantic vision of Russian culture and its unique spiritual tradition standing up to a rationalistic and aggressive West. The fear was not ungrounded: after the Mongol-Tatar threat to Russia receded in the fourteenth century, the most dangerous foreign threats to Moscow consistently loomed from the West, either from Roman Catholic Poland, the Teutonic Knights, Napoleon's France, Protestant German states and Sweden, or Hitler.

Russians similarly developed a sense of inferiority toward the West, its technological accomplishments, its powerful nation-states, and its economic and military power. In their insightful book *Occidentalism*, Ian Buruma and Avishai Margalit point out that the roots of much Slavophile anti-Western philosophy is borrowed from German Romantic philosophy, which itself partly represented a reaction against dominant French economic and military power in the eighteenth and nineteenth centuries. With the French Revolution, France had come to symbolize Enlightenment-derived exaltation of reason and science over religion and intuition. And it was this same rational France under Napoleon, seemingly the embodiment of the West, that then launched an all-out invasion of Russia and torched Moscow before suffering an ignominious defeat by ragtag Russian forces and by "General Winter" — the primeval force of Nature working in tandem to save Holy Mother Russia.

It was not surprising that Russian thinkers should view the driving ideology of this expansionist and crusading Western state of France as a threat to Russia and its values. German Romanticism, with its appreciation of the role of emotion, intuition, folk art, and Nature against the brutalisms of industrialization, was more in tune with Slavophile Russian thinking. The eternal character of nativist Russian values were extolled in the novels of such literary giants as Leo Tolstoi and Fyodor Dostoyevsky. And Russia in the nineteenth century produced a large body of philosophic thinking that critiqued the materialist, even nihilistic basis of Western philosophy. (It also produced an impressive body of counterarguments from Russian philosophers linked from among the Westernizers.)

One of the more fascinating examples of this brand of Russian thought is found in the writings of the nineteenth-century conservative philosopher, the monarchist-aristocrat Konstantin Leontiev, who propagated the concept of "Byzantinism"—the idea that Russia's true roots lie in Byzantium, the monarchy, and the Orthodox Church, and that Russia must oppose "the catastrophic egalitarian, utilitarian and revolutionary influences from the West" and instead direct Russia's "cultural and territorial expansion eastward to India, Tibet, and China." Leontiev's writings also happened to contain several remarkably prescient insights made before the beginning of the twentieth century into the future evolution of the West, including the belief that Germany would soon cause "one or two wars" in Europe, that there would be a "bloody revolution in Russia led by an 'anti-Christ' that would be socialist and tyrannical in nature, and whose rulers would wield more power than their tsarist predecessors." He also made the fascinating prophesy that "socialism is the feudalism of the future."

Many in the West readily dismiss anti-Westernism as mere pathology rather than reasoned evidence-based argument—after all, "How could one be anti-Western on a rational basis?" But if there are elements of pathology to anti-Westernism, so, too, the character and actions of Western power itself, in its will to conquest and domination and its racial discrimination, contain their own pathology. The West may not be unique in demonstrating these qualities, but it has exercised such qualities in its global policies more sweepingly than any other powers of the world for most of the modern era. Thus, it is the West as supreme practitioner of these negative values in the world that stirs up hostility. While some may describe this process as a "clash of civilizations," it is very clear that the clash has little to do with civilizational values and everything to do with certain realities of powerful and aggressive Western confrontation with the East over the past five hundred years.

As unwelcome as it may be to American ears, the Byzantine scholar Vasilios Makrides at the University of Erfurt argues that "anti-Westernism reached its peak in the violent anti-American attacks of the 11th September 2001 in the United States. These forms of anti-Westernism are mostly the direct corollary of the Western political, economic and cultural expansion across the world in modern times in the wake of imperialism and colonialism."

Furthermore, notes Makrides:

> It is particularly interesting to observe certain anti-Western coalitions [across] otherwise incommensurable lines which took place at that time, namely between Orthodox and Muslims in the Eastern Mediterranean area.... Orthodox and Ottoman anti-Westernism were far from being identical, but their eventual "cooperation" was not out of the ordinary.... An analogous attitude towards Muslims and Western Christians can be observed in thirteenth-century Orthodox Russia. Tsar Aleksandr Nevsky gave preference to a coalition with the Tatars and Mongols over an anti-Muslim alliance and a union with Rome, which had been proposed to him in 1248 by Pope Innocent IV.

THE ORTHODOX WORLD — Russia, Eastern Europe, the Balkans, and pieces of the Middle East — has unquestionably lagged behind Western Europe in modern industrial and economic development, creating a sense of inferiority vis-à-vis the West. The West has reinforced this through its arrogant display of imperial power against most of the rest of the world during the Age of Imperialism, including China. Much of this anti-Western anger emerged *outside* the Muslim world, such as in nineteenth-century China, but is shared by Muslims as well, helping to foster a kind of solidarity among anti-Western thinkers.

The West in turn has itself maintained a generally distant, condescending, and sometimes hostile view of the Orthodox world. After the Great Schism of 1054, the Eastern Church had in effect become a clear rival, if not quite an outright enemy to Rome. The borderlands between Roman Catholicism and Orthodoxy in Eastern Europe and the Balkans have remained contested to this day—witness tensions and divisions between Orthodoxy and Catholicism in Ukraine, and the perpetual cultural divisions and hatreds between Orthodox Russia and Catholic Poland that have taken on a geopolitical character.

Over past centuries, Europeans have practically defined "Europe" to mean *Western* Europe. They viewed even Eastern Europe as a different world, a backwater, rarely integrated with the rest of Europe. Only the Catholic/Protestant cultures of the Czechs, Poles, and Hungarians were viewed as just acceptably within the borders of cultural Europe. When Eastern Europe, both Catholic and Orthodox, fell under control of the Soviet Empire, the cultural gap between the two worlds was further reinforced. The European Union has encountered far greater problems in trying to integrate the Orthodox states of Eastern Europe than those of Catholic or Protestant faith. Thus Poland, the Czech Republic, Slovakia, and Hungary are easier for Europe to digest; Orthodox Romania, Serbia, Bulgaria, and, of course, Ukraine and Russia are far more uncertain quantities.

Cultural differences were even expressed in terms of church ritual and art. The West allowed musical instruments in the rites of Western churches, supplanting the strict Gregorian plainsong chants of the Eastern rite. In architecture, the West abandoned the traditional domed Orthodox church design—later absorbed into the design of many Muslim mosques—and adopted what was seen in Orthodox eyes to be the seemingly "harsher and sharper" lines of Gothic architecture. Religious art in the East maintained the highly idealized and stylized forms of painting of the Byzantine world, in sharp distinction to the later realism and literalism of Western religious painting, including their frequent bold (blasphemous?) portrayals of even God himself.

The New Russia

Since the collapse of the Soviet Union in 1991, the new Russian state that emerged from its ashes is in the process of restoring its traditional identity and the place of the Russian Orthodox Church. And while the church suffered immensely during the Soviet period and was heavily politicized in its obligatory service to the state, it nonetheless shared with the Russian Communist Party a traditional fear and antipathy toward the West—the church feared Catholicism, while the Communist Party, based on Marxism-Leninism, saw the West as the bastion of capitalism. Both were vividly aware of the history of attacks from the West on Russia, designed to overthrow the Russian state.

Cultural attitudes endure. Not surprisingly, we see again within the new Russian Federation a resuscitation of those same fears, suspicions, and antipathies toward the West, shared anew with a reinvigorated Orthodox Church. The post-Soviet Russian state quickly embraced the Orthodox Church again as a symbol and integral part of Russian nationalism. The church still possesses a magnetic liturgical power to stimulate nationalist feelings—the old blend of religion, salvation, ethnicity, and nationalism.

Contemporary Orthodox fears of the West have not been without foundation. Emotions were intensified when Western Roman Catholic and Protestant missionaries rushed into Russia after the fall of the Soviet Union to fill the post-Soviet spiritual vacuum by seeking to convert Orthodox believers to Catholicism or Protestantism. Considerable Western funds were devoted to facilitate the conversion of Orthodox believers at a time when economic hardships in the former Soviet Union were severe. The

Russian patriarch accused Rome of attempting in effect to buy conversions and maintain their centuries-old goal of penetrating the Orthodox world to establish the dominance of Catholicism. One Western observer in Russia commented:

> Here in the capital, as well as in St. Petersburg and other large Russian cities, it is difficult to miss the parade of preachers, proselytizers, para-churchmen and visiting gurus streaming in from the United States, Western Europe, Korea and India. Their messages wallpaper subway stations, line mailboxes, pepper the airwaves and draw the curious to campus crusades.... It is hardly surprising that many Russians feel exposed and unprepared for the foreign "god-bearers." Some would like to curb the religious flood, if not to dam it up totally. Recently the Russian parliament unveiled two amendments to the religious freedom act that echo these sentiments.

At a World Council of Russian Peoples in 2001, several speakers noted the spread of alien religious beliefs and cults in Russia. The Russian Parliament passed bills restricting the freedom of foreign proselytizing in Russia—aimed at Western Christianity, not Islam. Most Russians strongly supported this defense of the native faith against outside influences, whose goals and intentions were suspect. The Orthodox Church therefore makes it difficult for Catholic, Protestant, and especially Evangelical churches to proselytize in Russia, open churches, or organize. Once again *traditional national religion* becomes a key vehicle for cultural pride and nationalism; this phenomenon entirely parallels the role such pride plays in the Muslim world when the Muslim community confronts a rich and powerful West, similarly perceived to be operating to weaken Islam. This is not about religion, but about identity, tradition:

> Proudly, [the Orthodox Church] points to a 1,005-year-old tradition of faith, liturgy, music, saints and iconology. While that does not necessarily make it a state church, many within Orthodoxy see themselves as the state religion. They argue that Russia can only be Orthodox and that historically it has been a state church.

The Russian state is thus revivifying its nationalism, national traditions, and glories in particular through the magnificent cultural vehicle of the Russian Orthodox Church.

Christian themes are now restored to the once-atheist Soviet political scene; few politicians in the post-Soviet period fail to invoke the importance of religious values. Grigory Yavlinski, the head of the political movement Yabloko, commented that "lack of faith is the prologue to corruption and bureaucracy, which produce terrorism.... Economic reforms in a nation that does not believe in God are totally impossible."

The writer Valery Ganichev, chairman of the Russian Union of Writers, proclaimed his fears that "Russia is cloning the cells of immorality that it grasped from Western culture" and called for popular demand that the government "help save the nation from depravity." These tensions were further reinforced by the bitter so-called Uniate controversy, still ongoing, between Catholicism and Orthodoxy over who should control the Nestorian and Monophysite churches in Ukraine and Belorussia—an issue now inevitably entangled in the geopolitical struggles between Russia and the West.

Orthodoxy Fights Back

Conversion can be a two-way street, and the Orthodox Church worldwide notes with satisfaction a growing interest in Orthodoxy and conversions from other Christian sects to its own "purer" religious message. It proclaims that religion is about spirituality, the mystery of God that provides inspiration to fill one's life with godliness, even to strive to *become* God in one's personal life (*theosis*). Salvation can come in this life and need not be delayed to the afterlife if the Holy Spirit can liberate the individual from sin and fill the soul with spirituality. The liturgy, therefore, is designed to stir the heart with the mystery of God, thrill and inspire the senses through incense, music, magnificent iconography, richness of liturgical garments, cultivation of ecstatic joy, the emulation of God in one's personal life, the enrichment of contemplating mysteries within the depths of the faith, a sense of knowing and participating in God's divine energy on this earth rather than waiting for the afterlife — in all, a religious experience designed to move the soul. Orthodox believers believe these spiritual qualities of the church are diminished in the highly secular environment within which the Catholic and Protestant churches operate in the West, with their sometimes trendy "social" concerns and political activism. The American scholar Nikolai Petro suggests that "if twenty-first-century Europe ever develops a religious complexion, it will be predominantly Eastern Orthodox." He is referring to its primarily spiritual focus.

In a very real sense, then, the chasm between the Orthodox and Latin Christian world is older and in some ways deeper than that between Islam and Christianity. Both have been profoundly influenced by geopolitical considerations of power and have used theology as the symbol, or vehicle, of the rivalry. Theological differences indeed do exist, but they have taken on new substance through linkage with contesting nation-states and the forces of nationalism.

A further striking echo of these emotions can be found on the crowded religious spectrum of Lebanese religious communities today — Sunni, Shi'ite, Maronite Catholic, Roman Catholic, Protestant, Eastern Orthodox, Druze, and others; it is especially the Eastern Orthodox Christians among them who instinctively possess the best intuitive feel for the psychology and politics of Muslims. It is no accident that the position of foreign minister of Lebanon is always reserved for the Orthodox community. Eastern Orthodox Lebanese instinctively understand the balance between Christianity and Islam and their subtle interplay in international politics. They enjoy the confidence of Muslims more than any other Christian sect does. This Orthodox sensitivity stems in part from a slight wariness toward Western policies and an awareness that Muslims and Orthodox, even when relations have not always been fully cordial, indeed share a certain intimate past and a shared worldview. Eastern attitudes transcend mere Islam.

But how has Russia handled its relations with its own large indigenous Russian Muslim population and the evolution of ethnic and ideological tensions?

CHAPTER EIGHT

Russia and Islam: Byzantium Lives!

Russia and Islam

Russia itself has lived intimately with Islam for nearly a thousand years; it contains the largest population of Muslims of any Western country—some twenty million, between 12 to 15 percent of the overall population. Furthermore, these Muslims are not immigrants as they are in Western Europe, but part of the indigenous population who became part of the Russian Empire through Russian conquest. Muslims represent the largest religious minority in the new Russian Federation, and Islam remains the second-biggest religion in Russia after Orthodoxy. The city of Moscow now has the biggest Muslim population of any city in the entire West. By dint of its large Muslim population, Russia now seeks to be an observer within the Mecca-based pan-Islamic Islamic Conference Organization.

Perhaps the most significant reality is that in Russia virtually all Muslims are ethnically *non-Russian*, that is, they belong to other ethnic—primarily Turkic—groups. Some of these same Turko-Tatar-Mongol peoples had invaded Russia in the thirteenth century and are remembered for their harsh rule when they controlled Muscovy for several hundred years. Thus, in Russia a religious difference nearly invariably signifies an *ethnic* difference as well—a powerful factor in reinforcing distinctiveness. That they are largely Turkic may ultimately be more important than the fact that they are Muslim.

Since it was Muslim Turks and Arabs who brought down the Byzantine Empire, it would be reasonable to assume that Russians would be strongly hostile to Islam and Muslims. But it is hard to blame the fall of Constantinople on Islam. Can we really believe that if the Ottoman Turks had not been Muslim, they would have opted not to invade and conquer Greek Byzantium, a rich and weakened state, regardless of whatever religion Byzantium practiced?

The harsh atheist policies of the Soviet period were designed to destroy all religion on Soviet soil, but while the Soviets severely weakened the practice of Islam, they could not destroy it. And predictably, Islam reemerged as a major issue for Moscow immediately after the collapse of the Soviet Union. Six Muslim republics gained their independence and ceased to be part of Russia—the Central Asian "Stans" and Azerbaijan. Russia has alternately viewed its own Muslim populations first as enemies, then as pillars of the Tsarist state, or as loyal members of the Russian Empire, or as potential leaders of communist anti-imperialism in the East, or as ideological partners against Western imperialism, or as unreliable nationalists, dangerous secessionists or terrorists, or, once again, as potential allies against US imperial power. The Russian case also shows how Muslims, in differing ways, have adapted to life within a Christian country under violently shifting Russian realities. They may still be discovering some new geopolitical commonalities today.

With the end of official atheist campaigns and greater freedoms and cultural autonomy after the fall of communism, the profile of Islam rose substantially in the Russian Federation. Muslim activists from outside the former USSR entered Russia to propagate Islamist ideas, with clear political intent—mostly non-violent, but some highly violent. Russian Muslim populations actually needed such religious missions, since most of them, under Soviet repression for over three generations, had lost much knowledge of religious rituals and their meaning—even knowledge as basic as how to pray properly. A huge spiritual vacuum all across Russia was revealed, with all populations hungry for new spiritual content and meaning in their lives.

Contact with Islamists from outside the country intensified Russian Muslim consciousness of their religion as well as their historical ties with the outside Muslim world. Muslims began once again to make the pilgrimage to Mecca (*hajj*) and, more important, to reacquaint themselves with contemporary Islamic thinking across the spectrum and to reintegrate themselves into the Muslim world, which was now much more politicized than Muslims of Russia had ever previously experienced. While some of these new Islamic trends were radical, most were nonviolent. But the North Caucasus remains a major exception, where various ethnic microgroups, especially the Chechens, resumed their long-term armed struggle of 150 years for political independence and once again invoked Islam in the cause. Their brutal fate at the hands of Russian troops in the 1990s became a lesson for all other peoples in Russia who might entertain secession—the destruction of their capital city, Grozny, and other towns, with tens of thousands dead. The city has been subsequently rebuilt, and Moscow this time wisely granted a considerable degree of autonomy to Chechnya within Russia; nonetheless, great quantities of Chechen blood have been spilled, while Chechen frustration and fury have led a number of its warriors to embrace more radical versions of Islam, including al-Qa'ida.

While it seems that the Chechens' long quest for independence is likely never to end, this struggle may not be fully representative of all other Muslims in Russia. But this time there was an important difference in the character of the armed struggle. In the past, it was Sufi brotherhoods who spearheaded the efforts for independence—mystical movements that could, when necessary, resort to armed resistance when their culture was threatened from outside. This time, many international Muslim *jihadis*, often veterans of other armed struggles such as in Bosnia, Kashmir, or Afghanistan, went to Chechnya to lend support and to propagate more radical *jihadi* doctrines.

Sometimes struggles broke out between the more traditional Sufi warriors and the new Islamist militants, who were often indiscriminately referred to as "Wahhabis." Some terrorist operations were carried to the heart of Russia itself in retaliation for Russian brutality in Chechnya. Chechen terrorism against Russians has been perhaps the biggest source of current Islamophobia in Russia.

Following 9/11 and Washington's declared Global War on Terror, Moscow and Beijing were quick to join ranks to proclaim their own local separatists and Islamists as terrorists; the "war on terror" provided legitimacy for implementing much harsher policies that under different circumstances would have been perceived as human-rights violations. In Uzbekistan in May 2005, the Uzbek government indiscriminately fired on unruly crowds of Islamist protestors, killing hundreds—all of whom were described as "Wahhabis"; the Uzbek state press linked them all to international terrorists, even as the evidence suggested that they were largely homegrown Islamist dissidents, protesting the harshly authoritarian character of the Uzbek regime.

As of today, the Muslims of the former USSR and today's Russia have now become intellectually integrated into the flow of global Muslim thinking. Islamic identity is on the rise, yet is evolving almost completely within the confines of the Russian federation and its multicultural character.

Under conditions of oppression, Islam provides an important

element of common identity that helps to unite diverse Russian Muslims, but it would be a mistake to assume that Islam can bridge all ethnic and language lines among Muslims. Even the ethnically Turkic peoples have rivalries among themselves and have not yet shown strong Turkic political solidarity, much less notable Islamic solidarity. Thus, Islam is only periodically a uniting factor—as strong as Russian policies make it. But it is abundantly clear that even if the Turkic peoples of Russia had never been Muslim, they would have retained a powerful independent identity and would likely still foster secessionist impulses in an age of nationalism and Russian misrule.

How did Islam become subject to Russian rule? Islam reached parts of Russia even before Christianity did. Russia's initial relationship with Islam developed on the battlefield, as the Russian Empire inexorably expanded south and east in the gradual conquest and absorption of Muslim Turkic states. One of the more dramatic events was Ivan the Terrible's conquest of Kazan, the capital of the Tatar Khanate in 1552. (The siege is vividly narrated in a stirring aria by the drunken monk Varlaam in Mussorgsky's opera *Boris Godunov*.)

It was actually the Orthodox Church militant that first stimulated these Russian campaigns of conquest to the East, advocating the spread of Christianity into the well-established Muslim Kazan Khanate. Immediately after the conquest the church established a strong institutional presence in the Tatar regions and planned for the forced conversion of its Muslim population to Orthodox Christianity. Russia's conquest of Kazan was a momentous "civilizational event"—marking a first major step in creating a Russian Empire and the transformation of the Ruler of Moscow into a Tsar (or Caesar) over new regions and new populations. The Tsar's legitimacy and power were seen to emanate from his role as propagator of the Orthodox faith. The metropolitan of the church, Makarii, led the campaign:

> Under Makarii's influence, the war against the Khanate was fought as a religious struggle of the Church Militant. Once military maneuvers began, he exhorted more virtuous behavior from Ivan's army stationed in Sviiazhsk, the Muscovite fort near Kazan'. Makarii promised the army God's blessing for their holy work, because the Tatars of Kazan' had "shamed the word of God" and "desecrated" the faith. For the Muslims' impiety, Makarii predicted the "furious wrath of God," which would bring victory for the army, fulfilling their new role as holy defenders of Orthodoxy.

Note how the early Russians, just like the Crusaders, did not think of Muslims as being adherents of another religion but rather as heretics from Christianity.

Despite its establishment of churches, monasteries, and religious institutions in the newly conquered regions, the church was to be frustrated in its goal of imposing Christianity on Muslim turf. While the church saw the conquest and conversion of Muslim Tatars as a holy mission, the Muscovite state did not. The campaigns were strictly part of the expansion of state power. If these Tatar areas had not been Muslim, Moscow would just have readily marched against them. Thus, for Moscow religious conversion was little more than pious pretext for imperial expansion.

But Moscow's Tsars soon grasped the complexity of attempting conversion of such a large and established population, especially given Islam's ability to resist conversion. Geopolitical considerations also entered the picture: the Ottoman sultan expressed his concerns for the welfare of Muslims in the Khanate, over whom he exercised a religious responsibility. The Tsar assured him he would permit their continued practice of Islam. Practical realities took precedence over Orthodox religious fervor.

Even though the new relationship was between Christian conqueror over Muslim conquered, a kind of coexistence emerged. By the end of the eighteenth century, Empress Catherine the Great actually rebuffed the church's wish to drive out Islam and convert all Muslims—a goal that would surely have led to unending hostility and rebellion within the empire. Instead, in a momentous new experiment in Russian imperial multiculturalism, Muscovy instead chose to enlist religion into its structure of empire by directly engaging Islam in forging a pact for national cohesion and social stability. Catherine adopted a broadminded and tolerant policy that sought to incorporate existing Islamic religious and secular structures into the broader imperial polity. Religion would be the foundation of imperial political and social organization based upon a commonly shared acceptance of One God and Enlightenment concepts of religious toleration. Moscow sought to "transform religious authority in each community into an instrument of imperial rule."

The Russian imperial plan thus promoted the creation of religious communities, instead of ethnic groups, as the basic sociopolitical unit of the empire. (The Ottoman state had earlier pioneered this principle in organizing its own empire along the lines of religious communities.) Social and political order in the Russian Empire was best preserved through maintaining *religious conformity* within each community, overseen by its state-anointed leaders. Any form of religious or doctrinal dissent in any religion thus became tantamount to political dissent—a familiar concept from Byzantine history. The cohesion of each community depended upon preserving a common body of unchallenged religious beliefs central to the community's identity. Muslim communal leaders in turn would call upon the police powers of the Russian state to enforce their own decisions, maintain religious orthodoxy, and thus social order.

But how legitimate in Islamic terms was it for Moscow to appoint the leadership of a Muslim community? The ultimate legitimacy of 'ulama who work for a Christian state is eroded by their very appointment and support to the state. They lose their independence and can readily be accused of being "puppets." Indeed, one of the political demands of Muslims at the time of the Russian Revolution was the right to appoint their own grand muftis.

During the three hundred years of the Romanov Dynasty then, the Russian state persisted in claiming its ruling authority as "grounded in religion." The Romanov state project came to be based on a "shared moral universe." These policies largely succeeded. Just as secular rulers in Islam must uphold the principles of Islamic society and law to claim legitimacy, the non-Muslim Romanovs could in principle be accepted as rulers over Muslims, as long as they permitted Muslims to maintain their Islamic way of life and upheld Islamic principles within Russian Muslim communities. Muslim subjects were even encouraged to bring their grievances and disputes to the Tsar for adjudication, thereby both legitimizing the Tsar and preserving the unity, well-being, and satisfaction of the Muslim population. The expectation was that over time, the Muslim population would come to view the Russian monarch as "legitimate" even if not Muslim, and would come to owe him loyalty. The Russian state had come to play the role of "defender of the faith," not just of Orthodoxy, but also of Islam, Judaism, Buddhism, and later Protestantism and Catholicism.

The Tsars' decision to acknowledge religious differences and overlook ethnic differences ended up strengthening religious bonds of solidarity among Russia's Muslims over that of ethnic ties. But Muslim loyalty would be tested as Moscow's military expansion brought it into direct conflict with external Muslim states. This amounted to upward of fifty battles fought over three centuries between Russia and the Ottomans, and four major wars with

Muslim Persia (in which the British and the French periodically supported the Persians as part of their anti-Moscow policy). Since Russian Muslims were both predominantly Turkic and heavily Sunni, they had far more sympathy with the Ottoman Turks than with the Persians. But their loyalty to the Tsar largely held until the turmoil of World War I and the Russian Revolution.

This coexistence of Islam and Orthodox Christianity within the Russian Empire is a significant experience in the history of Islamic peoples. The Muslims of the empire could extend their loyalty to the Russian state precisely because they were *not* being forced to assimilate, or to give up their personal and communal identity for a Russian Christian one. And, of course, the Muslim communities of the Russian Empire were not in any case homogeneous; each evolved through its own distinct historical and cultural experience, as did the significant Protestant, Roman Catholic, Jewish, and Buddhist communities in Russia, who similarly were not pushed into assimilation.

Religion versus Ethnicity in the State

However functional at the time, the idea of administering the state through religiously based communities strikes the contemporary observer as outmoded, the product of a different, more religious age. Yet, what then should the basis of *identity* be within the state? Ethnicity (language) or religion? One or the other of these two concepts has constituted the main organizing principle in most complex multicultural societies for millennia. In the contempory West, the reigning concept of identity within the state tends to be membership via "citizenship"—a kind of "don't ask, don't tell" identity—where one professes loyalty to the state but need not disclose anything about one's personal characteristics.

Despite its many wars with neighboring Muslim states, the Russian Empire nonetheless actively engaged in diplomacy with the Ottoman state, with Iran, and served at the same time as official protector of Orthodoxy in the Holy Lands of Palestine under Ottoman control. Moscow cared greatly about the opinion of foreign Muslims toward Russia; at the same time Moscow sought to enlist Russian Muslims to advance Russian foreign policy goals in the Middle East, so that Moscow could speak as a "Muslim power" as well as a Christian power. Thus, rather than hindering the expansionist vision of the Russian state, Islam actually facilitated it.

The Russian Orthodox Church itself, however, was far less happy with the situation; it did not approve of the ecumenism of the Russian state that hindered the church from pursuing Christian goals across the empire. Russian nationalists such as the writer Dostoyevsky saw the Orthodox Church as representing the "soul" of Russia and were opposed to Russian state accommodations with Muslims. Dostoyevsky criticized the state for "extolling Muslims for monotheism," which he called "the hobby-horse of a great many lovers of the Turks." He believed that Russia was destined to dominate the Orient.

The degree of Muslim acceptance of Russian rule often depended on the Russian policies of the moment. The breaking point seemed to come in 1917, when Moscow finally lurched into the Bolshevik Revolution and the long, unhappy Soviet experiment. But during all those previous centuries, no serious bloc of internal Muslim resistance ever emerged, even during Russian campaigns against Muslim neighbors. In many cases, Muslim fighters, or *"jihadists,"* fought their own traditional local rulers— shades of the Middle East today. And a number of Russian Muslims who could not religiously support Russian foreign wars against Muslims on the borderlands decided to emigrate from Russia to Turkey, sometimes even to fight on the opposing side.

And yet nearly all imperial powers around the world at some point have attempted to recruit local Muslim elites into supporting the colonial regime and fending off local rebellion. Thus the Hapsburg Empire before World War I sought out pliable Muslim rulers in the Balkans. The German Kaiser during World War I sought unsuccessfully to foment revolt across the entire Muslim world against British and French imperial rule. The French, equally unsuccessfully, sought Islamic legitimacy for their conquest and annexation of Algeria; as did the Germans in their invasion of the Caucasus during World War II. The Japanese before and during World War II attempted to ally themselves with the Muslim populations of South and Southeast Asia to fight against Western armies there. In World War II, the Germans won over the mufti of Jerusalem in an effort to gain Arab support against Allied forces in the Middle East. The United States today supports numerous unpopular and nonelected rulers in the Arab world to help promote unpopular US policies.

But the Russian engagement with Islam is older, deeper, more extensive, and more complex than Europe's. One key reason is that the Russian Empire encountered Muslims as a result of *contiguous* overland expansion east and south, unlike the European imperialists who encountered Muslims only through distant voyages of conquest overseas. Russian forms of coexistence with Islam persist and always will, simply because they inhabit common space. Russia remains the sole state in the West that embraces a significant *indigenous* Muslim community among its citizenry.

The Jadidists

Muslims in Russia always pursued the goal of maximum cultural autonomy, but they also lived inside a Russia that was itself undergoing intense intellectual and political ferment. Muslims could not remain immune to the fierce debates on issues of importance to them. It was toward the middle of the nineteenth century that the first serious reform movement emerged among the Muslims of

Russia—the *Jadidist* movement (from the Arabic *jadid*, or new) that sought renewal of Muslim society. The Jadidists were, in fact, one of the most important early Muslim reform movements anywhere in the Muslim world, reflecting perhaps crosscultural stimulus with Russian society.

The Jadidists emphasized the importance of education and the inclusion of practical subjects such as mathematics and the sciences into the curriculum. Schools spread, newspapers sprang up, books began to be translated into the local languages. But Russian imperial authorities greeted this movement with ambivalence, fearing the emergence of possible subversive, separatist, or pan-Islamic ideals, even as they were linked with liberal elements of Russian society. Opposition to Jadidists came also from old Muslim elites, often feudal in outlook, who feared any movement that might educate, inform, and empower a new elite and change the ossified social order. And that was exactly the Jadidist goal, but without recourse to revolution or violence. The Jadidists did not even promote a separatist agenda, but sought to strengthen their position within the broader Russian political framework.

One of the leading Jadidists, the Crimean Tatar Ismail Gaspirali, clearly envisaged Muslim activism *within* a reforming Russian political order and, in turn, urged Russia to work with the Muslim world:

> ...If Russia could have good relations with Turkey and Persia, she would become kindred to the entire Muslim east, and would certainly *stand at the head of Muslim nations* and their civilizations, which England is attempting so persistently to do.

In short, Gaspirali saw Russia as potentially a great *Muslim* nation as well as a Christian one. At the same time, this was one of the first and greatest integrationist experiments between Muslim and

Christian cultures. Religion, in this case, seemed to facilitate rather than hinder a grand vision of Russia's place in the world. But even without religious differences, without Islam, Russia would still have faced the serious problem of integrating large Turkic populations.

The Muslim movement for education, reform, and political participation in Russia accelerated dramatically as the nineteenth century drew to a close. Elites engaged in fierce debate over identity in a new political age that emphasized ethnicity. Even Russians themselves were unsure whether they belonged to "the West," or to a distinct Orthodox world, or even to Asia in some sense. Muslims asked similar questions: Were they primarily Muslims, or Russian citizens, or Turks, or Tatars, and in which order? Did they "belong" in Russia?

After the 1905 revolution in Russia, Tsar Nikolai II was forced to make major political concessions toward liberalization, which included the opening of a parliament, or Duma. Russian Muslims organized their own political movement, on the basis of religion rather than ideology, in convening the First Congress of the Union of Russian Muslims in 1905 to discuss strategy. Their two key goals were greater religious and cultural autonomy and equality of status with the Russian population. We should remember that a key reason the Russian Muslims—primarily Turkic—chose Islam as the unifying element was because religion, and not ethnicity, had been the organizing principle of the Russian Empire.

This movement's policies were moderate and centrist. It sought the unification of all Russian Muslims for common goals that included fair distribution of land; an end to state expropriation of Muslim land; freedom of the press, congregation, and religion; and a constitutional monarchy. The party's leadership sought a place on the Russian political scene and promised the Minister of Interior that the party was not anti-Russian or separatist, and was loyal to the Tsar. The union succeeded in winning between thirty to forty seats in the Duma over several elections. In the religious sphere, the union interestingly called for radical reform of the Muslim hierarchy of 'ulama and for the direct *election* of a grand mufti by the population—a dramatic first in any Muslim country. These measures helped break the hold of traditional and conservative ranks in the 'ulama. Within a few years, however, the Muslim Union began to fracture, partly along ethnic and regional lines, and partly ideological in the face of some delegates who adopted a more leftist stance in keeping with the Russian Socialists. In short, Islam was no longer adequately functioning as the social glue, and Russia's Muslims were behaving along more expected lines of ethnic, regional, class, and ideological differences. The Islamic identity no longer predominated under conditions where Muslims could operate freely across a broad political spectrum. More than a million Russian Muslims joined the Russian Army in World War I, many of whom fought against Ottoman forces in the south—and this despite Ottoman *fatwas* calling on all Muslims to support the Ottoman Empire against Christian aggressors in its hour of need.

The key features, then, of this Tsarist imperial period were the relatively successful integration of Muslims into a Christian empire, Muslim ambivalence between an ethnic or religious basis for political organization, and a relative sense of loyalty to the Russian political order. Their politics were relatively mainstream, later described as "bourgeois nationalist," with few leftist or strong religious parties. Above all, there was no "bloody border" at work. Here is a leading case where Muslims, given a chance to participate as a minority within a reasonably acceptable political order, will do so. They will even support broader political parties that are political/ideological and not simply Muslim blocs. But they will also not generally yield up their religious identity as a key feature of their communal identity. The Soviet period would put all this to the ultimate test—to the breaking point.

The Russian Revolution and Bolshevism

The Soviet period reveals a new and violent chapter in the complex evolution of the Russian Muslim community. The new communist (Bolshevik) rulers could not initially decide whether to recruit Islam to their side, crush it, or try to subvert it through creation of ethnic rather than religiously based political structures. They ultimately opted for an ethnic approach—with some success. Meanwhile, a Muslim Turkic revolt of serious and long-term proportions had broken out in Central Asia in 1916, a year before the Russian Revolution; the uprising was in sharp reaction to new Tsarist policies that tried to force Muslims into military service, and to other grievances linked to the war economy. This so-called Basmachi Revolt would continue to smolder and periodically flare up for another ten to fifteen years, primarily inside the Uzbek and Tajik areas of the Soviet Union, driven by new nationalist and religious aspirations for independence among many Muslim Central Asians, who had become fiercely hostile to Soviet dictatorship and its militant atheism. While the revolt was eventually crushed by the Red Army, it exposed deep grievances among Russian Muslims. It was also abetted by support from renegade ex-military officers from Turkey, and by British intelligence—tarring the Muslims with the issue of questionable loyalty vis-à-vis foreign powers. The Basmachi movement offered a clear indication that Moscow would have to handle its Muslim population with great caution—in both its ethnic as well as religious aspects.

Indeed, in the early days of Soviet rule, the Communist Party engaged in some fascinating efforts to *exploit* Islam to its own ends and to enlist its own Muslim citizens to promote the agenda of worldwide communist revolution and the overthrow of Western imperial rule across Asia, Africa, and Latin America. One of the key Soviet targets was British-ruled India, on the Russian doorstep, a colony that had already witnessed earlier Muslim-sparked anti-British rebellions.

Thus, in an epic and colorful gathering in 1921, the Baku Congress of Peoples of the East, the Soviets brought together nearly two thousand delegates from colonial and semicolonial countries around the world to plan revolutionary action against Western colonial powers. While carefully scripted by the Bolshevik leadership in Moscow, the conclave nevertheless gave powerful voice to the anticolonial struggle. Moscow perceived Muslim countries to be potentially at the forefront of these revolutionary contests and sought to capitalize on them to further Soviet foreign policy interests against the West.

Islam did not directly figure in the proceedings of the Baku conference; Moscow was more intent upon aligning the distinct *nationalisms* of the Muslim peoples with communism as an anticolonial instrument. But as we have noted, Islam is invariably allied in spirit to nationalist impulses when engaged against *non-Muslim* forces. So Soviet strategists, particularly Lenin and Zinoviev, sought ways in which to skirt the conservative elements of Islamic society and to stimulate revolutionary forces within them. Even the term *jihad* was appropriated for use, this time in a more secular sense, as speakers referred to "holy war against imperialism," and referred (blasphemously, in fact) to a new kind of "pilgrimage" to the new center of world revolution in Moscow, which would bring liberation to all the oppressed peoples of the East. Nonetheless, Moscow was also well aware that Islam and nationalism represented perpetual double-edged swords that could be turned equally against Soviet rule in the Muslim areas of the empire, and had already been linked with the Basmachi Rebellion.

Mirza Sultan-Galiev: The Communist-Muslim-Nationalist

The encounter of Marxist-Leninist ideology with Muslim societies is perhaps personified most vividly in the figure of Mirza Sultan-Galiev, a Muslim Tatar from the Volga region who had joined the Communist Party at the time of the Bolshevik Revolution in 1917. He went on to become a major figure in the Bolshevik anti-imperialist movement. Sultan-Galiev urged formation of an "all-Muslim communist party"—a near oxymoron—arguing that ethnic differences among various Muslim peoples within the Russian Empire would be overcome by their shared Islamic culture. He believed that Marxism could reach the Muslim masses if given an Islamic face. He therefore envisioned a powerful Muslim communist party which could promote communist revolution against European imperialism across the Muslim world. Religion and ethnicity were now becoming closely enmeshed.

Sultan-Galiev was himself an atheist, but he had studied the Qur'an and Shari'a and warned Soviet authorities about the power and depth of Islamic culture in Muslim life. He rapidly rose in the Soviet system to ultimately become president of the People's Commissariat for Nationalities and had a major voice in nationalities policy under the direction of Josef Stalin.

Sultan-Galiev's early belief in the Communist Party was based almost entirely on his own impassioned anti-imperial hopes, in which he saw the Bolsheviks, initially, as the only savior:

> I now move to my cooperation with the Bolsheviks....I go there because with my whole spirit I believe in the rightness of the Bolsheviks' cause. I know this; it is my conviction. Thus, nothing will remove it from my soul. I realize that only some of the Bolsheviks were able to implement what was promised at the beginning of the revolution.

[But] they were the ones who stopped [World War I.] Only they are striving to return the nationalities' fates into their own hands. Only they revealed the cause of the world war. They also declared war on English imperialism, which oppresses India, Egypt, Afghanistan, Persia and Arabia. They are also the ones who raised arms against French imperialism, which enslaves Morocco, Algiers, and other Arab states of Africa. How could I not go to them? You see, they proclaimed words that have never been voiced since creation of the world, in the history of the Russian state. Appealing to all Muslims of Russia and the East, they announced that Istanbul must be in Muslims' hands. They did this while English troops, seizing Jerusalem, appealed to Jews with the words: "Gather together quickly in Palestine, we will create for you a European state."

But Stalin and the Soviet leadership ultimately rejected the idea of an all-Muslim communist party as an unacceptable and dangerous compromise with bourgeois nationalist forces in the Muslim community. Moscow insisted that only a party based on the unity of "the proletariat" could lead such a movement—even though a proletarian class scarcely existed among the agricultural and mercantile Tatars. At this point, Sultan-Galiev saw the handwriting on the wall and realized that the Soviet Communist Party would never share his vision. He became convinced that Muslims had exchanged Tsarist oppression only for a new kind of oppression under a so-called Russian proletariat; he now came to believe that Tatar interests were not compatible with Russian imperial interests and that Communism offered no freedom from imperialism, merely a new form of it. Sultan-Galiev was eventually arrested by Stalin; he was executed in 1940, along with many thousands of other Muslim-Turkic nationalists.

Sultan-Galiev was an outstanding example of a prominent

communist activist, theoretician, and important spokesman for the Muslim left. The events that led to his denunciation, jail, exile, marginalization, and later execution provided dramatic evidence of the "nationalist" character of Islamic culture when confronted by European—even Soviet—imperialism. Indeed, the phenomenon of Sultan-Galiev's break with Stalin and his subsequent embrace of Muslim *nationalist* interests was given its own nomenclature within the Communist Party, "Sultan-Galievism," that would forever invoke communist fear of the latent elements of nationalism that existed within the Muslim communities of Russia. "This, you see, is what happens when nationalism is allowed to displace Marxist-Leninist ideology" was the refrain. And the Soviets themselves had inadvertently pressed so hard as to turn Islam into an "ethnicity." US policies have done much the same in the Global War on Terror.

Thus, for all the revolutionary potential of the Russian Muslim community in carrying a communist anti-imperialist message to the oppressed peoples of the East, the experiment was a terrible failure: Muslims remained deeply hostile to subsequent Soviet policies and Soviet oppression of Muslim Turkic culture. By 1926, Moscow had come to see Islam as a basically anti-Bolshevik force and organized a Union of Militant Atheists to foster atheist propaganda among Muslim populations and to remove all believers from positions of power. Soviet official promulgation of atheist ideology and suppression of all religions constituted the greatest sin the Soviet regime could commit in the eyes of Muslims. Muslims sought to protect and practice their religious rituals and customs in an underground fashion; Sufi networks were instrumental in keeping some knowledge of Islam alive during the dark years of Soviet rule.

Where Tsarist Russia had promoted religion as the basis of political and social organization of the empire, the Bolshevik communists now dramatically changed direction and sought to

encourage narrowly defined ethnic groups as the basis for organization of the Soviet Empire in a divide-and-conquer process.
Hence, instead of working with a broad Turkic ethnicity, for
example, the Soviets developed separate political republics for
each separate Turkic language—Uzbek, Tatar, Kazak, Kyrgyz,
Turkmen, Azeri, and so on. Ethnicity had now become the tool by
which to destroy the Islamic identity and possible pan-Turkic
nationalist ideas.

The Soviet struggle with Islam took on vivid new foreign-
policy dimensions with Moscow's invasion of Afghanistan in 1979
to shore up a new communist regime there. Very quickly, armed
rebellion spread across Afghanistan, fighting a holy war in the
name of Islam against the Soviet occupation. The West, and especially the United States, lent major support to the anti-Soviet *jihad*
that succeeded in driving out the Soviets eight years later. Many
Soviet troops there, however, were themselves Soviet Muslim and
felt some ambivalence toward Soviet policies designed to crush an
Islamic resistance movement. And later, with the Soviet withdrawal in failure from Afghanistan, Afghan and foreign *jihadists*
were to proclaim that "Islam had defeated a superpower." The
message did not go unnoted among unhappy Russian Muslims.

The collapse of the USSR in 1991 was a turning point for
Muslims of the Soviet Empire. Quite quickly, five Muslim republics—all but one Turkic—achieved full independence as new
"nations," now on a nominal ethnic basis—most of them were
varieties of Turks, after all. The remaining Muslim peoples, who
still lived within the borders of the new and much-diminished
Russian state, were granted greater autonomy—again along strict
ethnic lines. Unrest in several of these areas, particularly in
Chechnya, demonstrated that the nearly 150-year-old struggle for
independence of the Chechens—who regularly fought in the
name of Islam—had hardly been extinguished. While most Muslims remaining in Russia realize that separation from Russia is

not practical—they represent large, ethnically distinct Muslim islands in the middle of a Russian sea—they are restoring Islam to a prominent place in their national identity, while celebrating their separate ethnic distinctiveness as well. These various Muslim ethnic groups are not, in fact, united on an Islamic basis, even though some Islamists wish it to be so.

And the perennial question about tiers of identity remains: Are these peoples first of all Muslims, or are they ethnic/national groups of Tatars, Uzbeks, Kakaks, Tajiks, and so forth? Or are they part of a larger pan-Turkic group? Or citizens of Russia? The reality is that they can be any and all of these things depending on circumstances. They are not mutually exclusive. Which identity will dominate at any given time depends upon circumstances.

Muslims around the world have been generally aware that the Soviet Union itself severely persecuted Islam. At the same time, they valued the vital role of the USSR in providing a geostrategic balance against the colonial and imperial forces of the West. The mere existence of the USSR and a bipolar world provided maneuvering room for small states, preventing formerly Western imperial states from extending total domination over them. The subsequent collapse of the USSR dismayed the Muslim world and most neutral nations—not because they favored communism, but because it spelled the end of a bipolar world and rendered small states more vulnerable to the remaining single global superpower's will.

Eurasianism

We conclude this chapter with a look at the ideology of Eurasianism: strange new bedfellows—Russia, China, and Muslims—potentially emerge in the shifting post-Bush strategic environment, sharing a common anti-Western, anti-American focus. Clearly this anti-Americanism has everything to do with geopolitics and little to do with religion. There are hints of a latent new convergence between some radical elements among Russia's Muslims and among some Russian ethnic nationalists, based on a shared suspicion of the West as a neo-imperial force. This is not a mainstream movement, but could take possibly interesting new directions in the future.

The phenomenon of Eurasianism demonstrates some key arguments of this book: the existence of deeply engrained anti-imperial anti-Western trends that are not just limited to the historic geopolitics of the Middle East but spread across Asia more generally. The diverse cultural strands of Russian, Chinese, and Muslim cultures indeed differ as much as they coalesce, but common anti-American, anti-hegemonic themes often serve to bring them together.

Eurasianist thought goes back to earlier Russian thinking that takes its Asian face seriously, a fusion of ideas that includes distrust of Western intentions and alienation from the West. It emphasizes an alternative world of Russian ambitions and culture, a mystical sense that Russia represents a more profound and spiritual project than the West. Above all, it preaches that Russia shares a place in the deeper traditions of Asia, which bestow upon it a special role and mission in world history—a Russian Manifest Destiny, if you will. It suggests that Russia is truest to its identity and traditions in an alliance *against* Western domination, to restore a balance of power in the world, and create an alternative vision of life. The Byzantines might be proud.

Russian fear of Western encirclement took on greater urgency as the administration of George W. Bush moved to establish US military bases in Uzbekistan, Kyrgyzstan, Georgia, Azerbaijan, and Tajikistan as part of the Global War on Terror, and in the attempt to incorporate into NATO as many of the former Soviet Republics as possible. From a Russian perspective, all of this was highly provocative, even aggressive, in seeking to bring American power right onto the Russian doorstep; such events suggested the need for Russia to look to new sources of geopolitical support to resist American strategic encroachment. That new area of support would come from the Muslim world and the East.

This vision of Eurasianism combines traditions of Russian Slavophilism with Russian Orthodoxy; in its broader formulations, it reaches out to a loose concert of interests that includes Muslim states and China, possibly even India and Japan. It may seem a bit extraordinary to contemplate convergence or cooperation with four civilizations that have, over much of the past, been antagonists, rivals, or even opponents of the Russian Empire. Yet it is a measure of the distrust of the Western—now American— drive for hegemony and global dominance that Eurasianism seeks common new interests to replace past antipathies with key Asian states.

Eurasianism originated in the 1920s, drawing on earlier Slavophile roots. The scholar Dmitry Shlapentokh interprets Eurasianism as an argument that "Russia is a unique blend of Slavic/ Orthodox and Muslim, mostly Turkic people. Russian *Muslims*, not Slavs outside Russia, are Russia's natural allies." Eurasianists see Russia not as a part of Europe, but of a Eurasian continent whose two main ethnic elements are Russian and Turkic. The old working coexistence between Russian Orthodoxy and Islam that we saw in the political structure of the Russian Empire survives in this new vision. Undoubtedly, there still remains a considerable legacy of suspicion among these parties, and none is willing to cede dominance to the other. At the popular level, there are deep anti-Muslim strains—even racism—in Russian society. Nonetheless, striking new political and geopolitical rapprochement between Turkey and Russia over the past decade lends much substance to this interesting ideological school of thought. Ancient geopolitical suspicions of the West in the Middle East have thus repeatedly emerged in all three cultures: Byzantine Orthodox,

Russian Orthodox, and Islamic—all with common roots. These are persuasive indicators of how a world without Islam might react toward the West even today.

Russia will never wish to lose its own unique historical character that is rooted in Orthodoxy. Russia has never been truly accepted as part of the West by the West. Nor can Russia's strategic orientation ever lie solely with the West; it will continue to seek partners from Eastern cultures to bolster it—emphasizing Russia's abiding Eurasian and Orthodox character. Russia's serious engagement in the Sino-Russian-dominated Shanghai Cooperation Organization further demonstrates this geopolitical orientation, which includes many Central Asian states and a strong expression of interest from Afghanistan, Iran, Pakistan, and Turkey. Geopolitics transcends religion—Islam, in this sense, is mere frosting on the broader geopolitical cake that is driven by suspicion or fear of Western power and intentions, deeply rooted in history.

With or without an explicitly Eurasian doctrine, Russia remains deeply engaged in the Middle East, both to portray itself as a friend of the Muslim world to recruit support against American hegemonic expansion in Asia, and to utilize its own Muslims to this end, as well as placate them within the Russian Federation. Russia's close ties and support to Iran are important indicators of this engagement, as are deepening Russian ties with Turkey over the past decade. The politics of the situation would be readily recognizable to Persians and Semitic peoples going way back in defending the Middle East region against the encroachments of Alexander the Great of Greece, or the Roman Empire's deep thrusts into Eurasia. Islam has simply joined the game. And whatever this complex relationship between Russia and Islam is, it can hardly be summed up as one of "Islam's bloody borders."

CHAPTER NINE

Muslims in the West:
Loyal Citizens or Fifth Column?

The dramatic force of the events of 9/11 focused attention on Muslim communities in the West like nothing before. That the 9/11 plotters drew up many of their attack plans in Germany and had spent a lot of time in the West raised the already troubled profile of Muslims in Europe to unprecedented levels. Were Muslims in the West now enemies inside the tent, fifth columnists lying in wait for the signal to strike? Open expression by Europeans and Americans of latent and visceral anti-Muslim sentiments now became more acceptable in the smoldering fears of the new security-driven environment.

Then violence did indeed come to Europe itself. In March 2004, a series of bombs ripped through several commuter trains in Madrid, killing 191 people and wounding over 1800. The conspirators were ultimately traced to Muslims from North Africa with inspiration from, but no clear links to, al-Qa'ida. In November 2004, Holland was shocked by the brutal knife murder in broad daylight of the Dutch writer and film producer Theo van Gogh; his murderer was a Moroccan-born Dutch citizen who had become radicalized through the Iraq war. Van Gogh, an equal opportunity bigot who had previously mocked Jews, was also out-spokenly anti-Islam and had made a short film in which passages from the Qur'an were projected onto the body of a writhing naked woman as a protest against "Islam's discrimination against women." The murder understandably sent a chill through even liberal European circles about the presence of a community of foreigners for some of whom religion mattered enough to commit murder.

In July 2005, several British Muslims carried out suicide bomb-ings in the London Underground, killing 52 and wounding some 700 people. The bombers were allegedly influenced by British involvement in the war in Iraq. Then in June 2007, two Muslims, one a British-born doctor of Iraqi origin, drove a truck with pro-pane canisters into the entrance at the Glasgow airport. No one was killed, but several were injured. The motivation again seemed linked to Iraq events.

In November 2007, riots broke out for days around Paris by African and Arab immigrants angry at their problems in trying to assimilate into French culture and economy; a lot of property was destroyed, although no terrorist tactics were employed.

All of these events brought to front and center the presence of Muslims in Europe, raising questions about their loyalties and their willingness and ability to assimilate. Questions naturally arose: is there something "different" about Islam that puts Mus-lim immigrants into a special category from other immigrants? Or we might turn the question around: if they were not Muslim, would the problems and issues be fundamentally different? The answer seems to be a qualified *no*.

Tariq Ramadan, a leading European Muslim, warns against what he calls the "easy pitfall of 'Islamizing' problems," that is, identifying problems of the Muslim community as somehow linked to Islam. "We have social problems, we have economic problems, and we have urban problems. They have nothing to do with religion. They have to do with social policies.... But when we have politicians who do not have social answers, they tend to essentialize the problem claiming that these social ills stem from the fact that these people are Muslims or Arabs." In short, Europe would face, indeed does face, considerable problems with immigrants from the developing world in this era of globalization, even if there were no Islam.

Europe presents a very different "frontier" for Muslims compared to Russia, India, or China. Muslims in Europe are not indigenous; they are modern immigrants who individually and voluntarily left their homelands to migrate to non-Muslim countries to work and raise families. While some saw employment in Europe as a temporary move for financial reasons, increasingly their decision has become permanent: they seek citizenship and accept their status as minorities.

Life in contemporary multicultural Europe of course differs sharply from life in most other parts of the world and raises new and complex identity issues. In most cases Europe represents the first contact of Muslims with an essentially post-ethnic and post-religious European society in which ethnicity and religion had seemingly ceased to be important aspects of life, until massive immigration began. And the European experience was quite new for Muslim immigrants, as well—and to most of the rest of the developing world.

Unlike North America, Europe is not by nature an immigrant society; it had consisted of old and well-established Western European nationalities and cultures often set in conservative patterns of life. Europe was, of course, long familiar with the Muslim "Other" as the historical enemy—but usually a distant enemy. Europe had repelled Arab forces from Muslim Spain at Poitiers in 732 CE—considered to have ended forever the prospect of a Muslim invasion and any potential Islamization of Europe. Europeans met Muslims on the battlefields of the Crusades. King Ferdinand and Queen Isabella in 1492 put a harsh end to nearly seven centuries of a largely pluralistic, Muslim-Jewish-Christian multicultural society in Spain by unleashing modern Europe's first program of ethnic cleansing of Muslims and Jews. Polish forces stopped the advance of Ottoman armies at the 1683 siege of Vienna, the high-water mark of the Ottoman move into Eastern Europe. Then Europe itself had gone on to invade and dominate virtually every Muslim country in the world. Still later, Europe struggled to put down anticolonial resistance of Muslim populations; Europe dominated oil exploration and production in Muslim lands before nationalist movements eventually took them over. The French effort to retain control of Algeria was an intensely bloody affair and Algerians became objects of hate in France. So European historical memory of its interactions with Islam were not positive. But now, by the second half of the twentieth century, an entirely new and unexpected relationship with Muslims began to emerge with the arrival of large numbers of Muslims as immigrants.

Who Are the Muslims of Europe?

Muslims make up about 5 percent of the total EU population. France has the largest number of Muslims, about 4.5 million, followed by 3 million in Germany, 1.6 million in the UK, and more than half a million each in Italy and the Netherlands. Under half a million each live in Austria, Sweden, and Belgium. Of all this Muslim population, approximately half are foreign-born.

The first serious immigration of Muslims into Europe occurred in the 1960s, sparked by Europe's need for menial laborers to perform the kinds of work that Europeans did not want to do. Thus began the era of the "guest workers." What was initially seen as a temporary arrangement by both sides soon became semipermanent. Numbers increased when European states began to permit the guest workers to bring family members to join them. A key problem for Europe lay in the socioeconomic background of the immigrants: a high proportion of them were unskilled and poorly educated workers who were less able to adapt and integrate into the European social order; they have subsequently often drifted into ethnic ghettoes. The predominantly working-class origins of European Muslims contrast significantly with the more professional backgrounds of Muslim immigrants to North America.

These populations come from different parts of the Muslim world: in France, the majority is from North Africa; in the UK, the majority is from South Asia; in Germany, most are from Turkey, and later from Bosnia and Kosovo. By ethnic breakdown, Arabs make up 45 percent of total European Muslims, followed by Turks and South Asians. Other Muslim groups are represented in much smaller numbers. Clearly, the Muslim population is diverse both regionally and linguistically and cannot be considered monolithic.

As the Sorbonne political scientist Jocelyne Cesari points out, "the socio-economic condition of European Muslims is one of great fragility," particularly as reflected in unemployment rates. Unemployment among Muslims is considerably higher than among non-Muslims. In the Netherlands, 31 percent of Moroccans and 24 percent of Turks are unemployed. More disturbingly, in 1995 unemployment rates for Muslim youth were twice that of nonimmigrants at the same level of education. In the UK, Bangladeshi and Pakistani immigrants had triple the unemployment rate of nonimmigrants, and in the inner cities, nearly half of the Bangladeshis are unemployed. Worse, "this marginality is passed on to the generations born and educated in Great Britain."

The problem is self-reinforcing because working class and poorly educated Muslims are not easily able to assimilate or even engage in European culture; as a result, they feel marginalized, are viewed as outsiders, often feel alienated, and retreat into their own cultural shell, thereby reinforcing stereotypes of Muslim resistance to assimilation. Resentments grow and the symbolism of different clothing, food, and language become more emotive on both sides. The Netherlands may represent one of the most serious examples of this problem. A Dutch parliamentary report in 2004 determined that "multiethnic society had been a dismal failure, huge ethnic ghettos and subcultures were tearing the country apart and the risk of polarization could only be countered by Muslims effectively becoming Dutch." This is a depressing conclusion since the proposed solution—"Muslims...becoming Dutch"—is ill-defined. What does it mean to become "Dutch"? To be indistinguishable from traditional Dutch citizens, except for visible physical characteristics? Or entirely stripped clean of former linguistic and cultural characteristics of their original homelands? Or are there certain minimal "Dutch" characteristics that should be required, while others not? Judging by patterns in any number of countries, assimilation is a process that requires several generations even for serious acculturation to occur, let alone actual assimilation.

Yet Islam is not directly relevant to the problem either, since *any* uneducated group of workers of color from the developing world pose similar problems of assimilation. Nonetheless, we cannot dismiss the Islamic factor entirely out of hand either, due to a striking social factor that has now appeared among them: the emergence of a *new identity as European Muslims.* Algerian, Turkish, or Pakistani immigrants with direct ties to their countries of origin have now given way in the first generation in Europe to an entirely new "Muslim identity"—quite distinct from an ethnicity based on original national origin. This Muslim identity comes as a direct response to their loosening ties with their countries of origin—the now distant and irrelevant culture of their parents. A Muslim identity provides a common link across ethnic lines, with shared social experiences including discrimination as new minorities in Europe. This young generation is European-born, speaks European languages natively, is schooled in Europe. And yet they are alienated and marginalized for socioeconomic reasons and now turn to "Islam" as a new interethnic identity in the absence of any other one that works for them. Their turn to an Islamic identity, however, creates suspicions in a post-religious Europe.

The crisis is a two-way street. As a result of its immigration dilemma, Europe is now in the middle of an identity crisis of its own, painfully reassessing the whole process of facing globalization and de facto multiculturalism. The violence of the broader Middle East does not involve the Muslim population in Europe in most cases, but all it takes is a handful of violent incidents involving Euro-Muslims in Europe to whip up yet deeper European fears of Islam—that in turn reinforces the immigrants' Muslim identity. It is potentially a vicious cycle. Is the adoption of a new *nonethnic* "Muslim" identity a step forward toward broader assimilation? Or a step toward reinforcement of a new social solidarity that will be harder to eventually assimilate?

European worries about assimilation processes are not without foundation. Muslims may, in fact, now be one of the more difficult cultural groups to fully absorb, precisely because of the inherent long-standing strength of that culture, its pride and historical self-consciousness, and its strong resolve to protect Islamic culture and the community. Beyond that, Islam would seem to add a certain new social strength to these first-generation migrants that enables them to better weather the hardships of the assimilation process.

Today, the question is more about retaining a "Muslim" identity than it is an ethnic or even linguistic one. One may happily learn Dutch and work within Dutch society but not want to give up being Muslim. Complete assimilation is no longer a viable concept for most non-Western minorities if it means becoming culturally indistinguishable from Dutch, that is, with a total loss of original culture. The issue is how to be both Dutch *and* Muslim, surely not an impossible feat. If it means accepting Dutch civic values, being upright citizens, willing participants in Dutch society, and contributing to the life of Holland, then it is very possible to become Dutch. And over many generations, the issue may lose its poignancy.

The dilemma finds striking parallels in earlier Jewish concerns about aspects of assimilation into American society. As the American scholar Eric Goldstein points out:

> The last decades of the nineteenth century brought Jewish immigrants from Central Europe unprecedented opportunities for social integration. While these opportunities made Jews ebullient, they also raised anxieties about what borders were to remain between them and the rest of society. Much of this anxiety stemmed from the tension between Jews' impulse for integration and their desire to maintain a distinct Jewish identity. Jews' history of persecution and social exclusion had imbued them with a strong minority social consciousness that was not easily surrendered and that led them to place a high value on group survival. Since social ties were seen as the protective force that had guaranteed Jewish continuity in the past, most Jews were reluctant to break these bonds.

These are legitimate concerns of the Jewish community—an accomplished historical and cultural minority that is generally unwilling to become so assimilated that it disappears. Jews were very poorly assimilated into American and European culture for long periods and were the object of much discrimination, even within people's living memory. Additionally, for many decades Jews were associated with radical movements and anarchist terrorism that had a grip on the Western imagination in the early twentieth century, with echoes of Muslim terrorism today.

Today the position of Muslims differs considerably from Jews in numerous respects, of course. Muslims are now the object of intensified overt and covert suspicions, sometimes even discrimination on a de jure basis, on anything that smacks of security issues. Muslims in the West have yet to receive the benefit of public political correctness; their characteristics and culture remain open season for spoof, lampoon, derision, and hatred in ways no longer tolerated by Western society in respect to African-Americans, Jews, or Native Americans.

The key argument, then, revolves around problems of large-scale migration of people of color, at a particular time of intense geopolitical tension in the Muslim world itself. Beyond that, there is little doubt that Islam does create a stronger social glue and broader international links than is the case of most other immigrant groups. But the United States has seen previously "indigestible" or "unassimilable" minorities before—Hungarians, Italians, Irish, Chinese; indeed, Jews were once routinely referred to as "clannish." Clannishness, to a considerable degree, reflects the absence of a social alternative.

An Unholy Alliance of Left and Islam?

New fears have emerged in recent years among neoconservative and pro-Zionist groups that a dangerous and unholy alliance of the Left and Islam is emerging: a European-based alliance in which "the deal is that the Leftist parties get a number of new clients, I mean voters, in return for giving Muslims privileges and subsidies, as well as keeping the borders more or less open for new Muslims to enter."

The second convergence is perceived to be a "hatred of America" that the Left allegedly shares with Islamists. Thus, the Islamists are said to buy into the Leftist critique of America and the West, while the Islamists fortify the same anti-American instincts on the Left. The American commentator William S. Lind writes: "What made possible the recent bombings in London [July 2005], and the many more that almost assuredly will follow in Europe and the United States, is the Marx-Mohammed Pact. Once again, two sworn enemies, Marxism—specifically, the cultural Marxism commonly known as Political Correctness—and Islam, have made a Devil's bargain whereby each assists the other against a common enemy, the remnants of the Christian West."

Intriguing in these arguments is that the neoconservatives have, in fact, captured one small element of reality that is accurate: a potential collaboration among diverse political groups in the world that oppose Western traditions of dominance and US hegemony and indeed do seek to cooperate to block their effect. The neoconservatives, however, like to describe the US bid for permanent preservation of unipolar American hegemony as "maintaining the Judeo-Christian tradition." While the Judeo-Christian tradition indeed represents a part of Western culture, American global hegemony is about a great deal more than that, and raises concerns on the part of other powers that involve much more than "hatred of Israel and the Judeo-Christian tradition." One right-wing anti-Muslim website observes:

> Iranian-in-exile Amir Taheri, too, has noticed this "red-black" cooperation. According to him, Europe's hard Left "sees Muslims as the new under-class" in the continent: "The European Marxist-Islamist coalition does not offer a coherent political platform. Its ideology is built around three themes: hatred of the United States, the dream of wiping Israel off the map, and the hoped-for collapse of the global economic system."

Thus, the battle lines are drawn, complicating Muslim integration into European society and inserting global ideological struggle into the perception of European Muslims.

Muslim Engagement in the Non-Muslim Community

Numerous British commentators portray UK Muslims as standing outside the British political order. For an early generation of immigrants, this was in fact usually the case when, in their own experience, political involvement was a dangerous process in their home country and may even have led to the necessity of their fleeing their homeland for security in a foreign culture.

But Amin Nasser argues that first-generation Muslims in the UK are indeed politically aware and are organizing community support for legislation and civil liberties that affect them. This is especially true in the area of antiterrorism legislation that brought hardships to the Muslim community through restriction of free speech under the Blair government.

And in a surprising example of adaptation, perhaps 10 percent of the entire Muslim student population in France now attends private Catholic schools. One reason is the relative paucity of Muslim schools. But more important is that Muslim parents believe that Catholic schools offer a more sympathetic view of the role of religion in life and show greater understanding of Islam than state secular schools. Muslim parents also like the stress on moral behavior. They seem *not* especially concerned about the particular Catholic theological aspects of instruction, and the Catholic schools have no ban on girls wearing headscarves to class, unlike French state schools. Thus, on the religious level, there is healthy coexistence in these schools that may provide a good basis for the next generation to experience multireligious understanding.

While the administration of George W. Bush pursued ruinous policies in the Muslim world that exacerbated and deepened the crisis, American society itself has actually been much more successful in integrating Muslims into society than the Europeans. First, as we have already noted, Muslim immigrants to North

America are largely professionals, better educated and more capable of making the cultural transition than their working-class counterparts in Europe. Additionally, North American societies are immigrant societies and therefore by definition far more multicultural than Europe. With the exception of a minority of American chauvinists who believe that the United States must remain essentially a white, northern-European Protestant society, most Americans do not really feel that the arrival of new immigrants is going to fundamentally change the culture. European societies such as Scandinavia, Holland, or Belgium, however, possess considerably smaller populations; there the arrival of significant numbers of immigrants can actually begin to change the carefully preserved nature of their traditional culture. These countries had never expected to be multicultural in any significant way, and the process has been something of a shock.

One of the leading scholars in Europe on Islam, Tariq Ramadan, stresses that integration is a two-way street. He believes Muslims must first address their *responsibilities*, and only then their rights in their new societies. In his view, Muslims who emigrate freely to Europe are under obligation not only to accept but also to understand European culture, its languages, and its psychology deriving from the European historical experience. Muslims cannot live outside that experience or hold the culture at arm's length — although that does not have to mean full Muslim acceptance of all aspects of European lifestyles. Ramadan notes among European Muslims the existence of "literalists and traditionalists who do not want to be involved in the society. And of course we still have people saying, 'Anything European is against the Islamic tradition.' But the [Muslim] mainstream, made up of those who feel at home in Europe, is a big part of the European reality." And this reality is in a constant state of evolution and integration as new generations of Muslims are born and grow up in European societies.

Ramadan notes that Europe represents a culture of great personal freedom for the individual to do as he or she wishes; no one compels Muslims to pursue the lifestyles of others. If they believe that changes should come about in European lifestyles, they must turn to the ballot box if they wish to introduce change. But Europeans, too, must understand that integration does not compel Muslims to live just like traditional Danes or Dutch. Europeans need to understand how the nature of "integration" is also changing: Europe is not a static and frozen culture, in which Muslim immigrants suddenly represent a jarring force. European culture has been formed over two millennia by a great variety of cultures, invaders, barbarians, wars, and external influences. Islam contributed heavily to the development of medieval European culture and the transmission of Greek philosophy. Thus, Europeans, too, must expect to change and find their traditional culture evolve as it encounters globalizing forces.

Ramadan also deals with questions of identity, referring to the well-known reality that we all have multiple identities. Therefore, it is not reasonable to ask Muslims "Which identity comes first, Muslim or German?" Ramadan identifies himself as "a Swiss, an academic, a male, a Muslim, of Palestinian origin, European by culture," and so on. Different identities emerge in accordance with the situation.

These problems are familiar in America as well, where social challenges often shade off into racism when they are simply attributed to "the Mexicans, or the blacks" or, in earlier eras, to Italians, Hungarians, Irish, Roman Catholics, Jews, and Chinese, who in previous years were considered "unassimilable." There are indeed social issues involved in integrating Muslims into American and European societies, and the problems are often of a different character in each place and with each group. But these problems essentially resolve themselves over time through the process of integration and acceptance. The election of Barack Obama in America represents just one such American watershed of assimilation, as was the election of the first American Roman Catholic president, John F. Kennedy.

Western Anti-Islamism

The situation is not improved by the presence of others in the West who see Islam and Christianity as locked into an implacable struggle — the mirror image of the worldview of the al-Qa'ida zealots. Take Pastor Rod Parsley of the huge World Harvest Church of Columbus, Ohio, a spiritual adviser to the Republican presidential candidate John McCain in 2008. Parsley writes:

> I cannot tell you how important it is that we understand the true nature of Islam, that we see it for what it really is.... I do not believe our country can truly fulfill its divine purpose until we understand our historical conflict with Islam. I know that this statement sounds extreme, but I do not shrink from its implications. *The fact is that America was founded, in part, with the intention of seeing this false religion destroyed,* and I believe September 11, 2001, was a generational call to arms that we can no longer ignore.
>
> It was to defeat Islam, among other dreams, that Christopher Columbus sailed to the New World in 1492. Columbus dreamed of defeating the armies of Islam with the armies of Europe made mighty by the wealth of the New World. It was this dream that, in part, began America.

Famous evangelist Franklin Graham told NBC news following the September 11, 2001 attacks: "We're not attacking Islam but Islam has attacked us. The God of Islam is not the same God. He's not the son of God of the Christian or Judeo-Christian faith. It's a different God, and I believe it is a very evil and wicked religion."

Bernard Lewis, the well-known neoconservative scholar of Islam, has raised the specter that the present demographic trends in Europe may well end up producing a Muslim Europe. Yet the real figures don't add up. Other right-wing commentators brandish the specter of a future "Eurabia." Alarmists about Islam bolster their case by pointing to what are genuinely incendiary remarks by a small group of radical clerics, such as the sensationalist Syrian Sheikh Omar Bakri Muhammad, once the darling of London shock television:

> Why should I condemn Osama bin Laden? I condemn Tony Blair, I condemn George Bush. I would never condemn Osama bin Laden or any Muslims....We don't make a distinction between civilians and non-civilians, innocents and non-innocents. Only between Muslims and unbelievers. And the life of an unbeliever has no value. It has no sanctity.

Or the remark of Dyab Abu Jahjah, a Lebanese settled in Antwerp, who denounced the Western ideal of assimilation as "cultural rape," and aims to bring all the Muslims of Europe into a single independent community.

Many of the remarks of radical preachers who have taken up positions in some mosques in the West, especially the UK, are indeed outrageous and provocative. They make good press, as do extremists in all democratic societies. Unfortunately, in the middle of a Global War on Terror, such remarks have been doubly incendiary and can actually have impact on a handful of youthful would-be violent extremists. Nonetheless, any limits on free speech must carefully and thoughtfully delineate legal thresholds. But the speech of a small group of unrepresentative extremists must not be taken to represent the true nature of Islam in Europe or anywhere else. What is a minor problem must not be exacerbated into a major problem.

Unfortunately, some Muslims living in psychological despair and ghetto isolation can be ready recipients for bloated conspiracy theories and exaggerated interpretations of past Western colonial villainies—events that possess many elements of truth but lack historical perspective and proportion. At the other end of the spectrum, we in the West are generally socialized into believing that the Western colonial experience was essentially positive, benign, and well-intentioned for colonials; thus, even accurate charges of Western brutality during the colonial period are often rejected by Westerners out of hand as intemperate, or marginal. For Muslims to present their historical case regarding the past, therefore, is not an easy sell in the West; even *Western* critics of Western policies are often rebuffed or ignored in the US mainstream press.

What is most disturbing is that we now face quite extraordinary remarks from an entire class of right-wing ideologists who actually challenge the fundamental *humanity* of Muslims—as products of a culture that is *fundamentally incapable of joining global civilization*—as if Islam had had no major part in creating it. Has this kind of charge ever been leveled against any other civilization in the past? Such language was indeed invoked against Jews during the terrible nineteenth- and twentieth-century pogroms in Eastern Europe that led to mass slaughter. And in those cases, of course, it was not mere ethnic discrimination; entire racist theories were spun about Jews as a culture. Such events are still within living memory.

We now hear seemingly serious discussions about whether Muslims are capable of modernization, whether they have excluded themselves from modernity, whether basically there is a place for them at all in the West. Fears are openly expressed that Muslims plan to take over the West demographically; that they plan to impose Islam; and that a militant Islam will sweep away the enfeebled Christianity practiced by ineffectual Europeans, who in their heady liberalism lack any will to resist. Battle lines have been drawn by some and the banners raised high. Worryingly, there could indeed be a reprise of the Jewish experience, and Muslims have very much become the new Jews in European society, in many senses. It is noteworthy that quite a number of Jews themselves recognize in the current campaigns of Islamophobia hints of the same mentality and mood of pre-Nazi Germany and the European pogroms; greatly to their credit, they find it frightening and speak out.

Euro-Muslims and Secularism

What of the frequently debated issue of Muslim problems with secularism? The very existence of a "Muslim" identity, especially in France, challenges the French notion of secularism, or *laïcité*. *Laïcité* does not imply strict legal separation of church and state as in the United States, but rather state *control* of religion. This strict secularism has caused France to clash with its Muslim population in several areas, especially education, where the state does not tolerate personal religious expression in public school; hence girls by law are not allowed to wear headscarves—a major issue of concern, and cultural symbolism, for the Muslim community. The presence of a large new minority to whom religion matters a great deal—as a symbol of identity—has forced the French, and Europeans in general, to rethink the meaning of *laïcité* when the imperatives of multiculturalism now clash with French secularism. Europeans, who have a generally low rate of religiosity, are now forced to reexamine the role of religion in society and the life of the community. The issue is sometimes a painful one, with the resurrection of an issue that Europeans believed they had put to bed after the bloody "religious wars" of the past.

Ironically, the Catholic Church has noted this phenomenon, and not without some approval. Cardinal Jean-Louis Tauran, head of the Catholic Church's department for interfaith contacts, said religion is talked and written about more than ever before in today's Europe. "It's thanks to the Muslims.... Muslims, having become a significant minority in Europe, were the ones who demanded space for God in society.... We live in multicultural and multi-religious societies, that's obvious. There is no civilization that is religiously pure.... Religions are condemned to dialog."

Strong proponents of secularism—often explicitly nonreligious in their private lives—tried to bring the issue to a head in the notorious Danish cartoon incident, when a few liberal secular Danes resolved to damn political correctness and demonstrate their freedom of speech and antireligious attitudes by publishing cartoons demeaning the Prophet Muhammad. The reaction in the Muslim world, to what was perceived as a calculated and deliberate act of disrespect and blasphemy, was angry, hurt, harsh, and predictable.

What should we make of this incident that pits freedom of speech against religious sensitivities? The Danes were utterly within their rights to exercise freedom of speech, on any topic. But the real question perhaps should be, How wise and how sensitive was it to mock the Prophet, simply to show it could be done? And this at a time when the whole Muslim world felt itself under the siege of war in the Global War on Terror. The cartoon incident did not pit believing Danes against nonbelieving Danes, but rather nonbelieving Danes against the supreme cultural symbol of a small, disadvantaged, and frightened minority that lacks voice or status in Europe—in their eyes, a direct assault against their very being and a mockery of their presence. Such events might be akin to mocking Jews as the Chosen People of God, and making comedies and satires about the Holocaust. (It is against the law in Germany to deny the Holocaust. And in France, the National

Assembly in 2006 passed a bill outlawing denial of the Ottoman genocide against Armenians in World War I.)

At a minimum, this Danish exercise showed lack of judgment, sensitivity, and social perception, even though entirely legal. Not all that is legal is wise. In fact, the West is faced here with the irreconcilability of two sacred and quite unchallengeable values: in the West, discussion of even the possibility of the curtailment of freedom of speech is unthinkable—the right is sacred. Among Muslims, even nonreligious ones, discussion of even the possibility of mocking and blaspheming Islam and the Prophet is unthinkable—this is sacred turf. (One positive note: Muslims are developing their own stand-up comedians in Europe and North America who are able to start gently satirizing their own Muslim societies in a way that does not directly stir Muslim fears of anti-Muslim hatred and discrimination.)

The distinguished International Crisis Group perfectly encapsulated the dilemma in its analysis of the 2006 rioting in Paris as follows:

> Youthful radicalism and rioting, at least in France (and probably in the UK too) reflects not the *presence* of political Islam, but its *absence, its failure.* . . . Political Islam has signally failed to solve the problems that the contemporary situation poses. As a result, youth have turned to Salafism, a narrow, scripturally focused movement that stresses individual adherence to Islam in a narrow interpretive base that encourages withdrawal from non-Muslim society and an inward turn that rejects French society and culture. The struggle thus gravitates towards a culture war rather than a political one. This in turn creates a de-politicization of social and economic problems, a dangerous political vacuum, an *unwillingness* to engage the system through

political channels to express dissent and seek redress. This leaves a dangerously disillusioned, angry and inchoate, unorganized mass of youth whose grievances are "increasingly expressed through jihadi Salafism and rioting, fueled by precarious living conditions, rampant unemployment, social discrimination and, more recently, the perceived vilification of Islam."

A UK Muslim convert writes:

We [Muslims] need a new agenda. And it is essential that this not be defined as an Islamic liberalism. Liberalism in religion has a habit of leading to the attenuation of faith. Instead, we need to turn again to our tradition, and quarry it for resources that will enable us to regain the Companions' [of the Prophet] capacity for courteous conviviality.

It is no less evident that *da'wa* [missionary work on behalf of Islam] is impossible if we abandon tradition in order to insist on rigorist and narrow readings of the Shari'a. Our neighbours will not heed our invitation unless we can show that there is some common ground, that we have something worth having, and, even more significantly, that we are worth joining. Radical and literalist Islamic agendas frequently seem to be advocated by unsmiling zealots, whose tension, arrogance and misery are all too legible on their faces.

There are other heartening signs. Open up a Muslim website, such as the very popular Islam Online, based in Qatar, and look at its question-and-answer section. This website is associated with one of the most authoritative clerics of all, the Shaykh Yusif al-Qaradawi.

One recent exchange went as follows:

Question: Dear scholars, as a Muslim living in the United States, I need to know my duties towards my people here, I mean towards my country. How do I support it in the face of the surrounding crises, side by side with upholding my religious duties? What does Islam say on this?

Response: by Dr. Muzammil H. Siddiqi, President of the Fiqh [Jurisprudence] Council of North America:

We have to understand that after September 11, America is not the same America. A lot of things have changed, are changing and will change. Now we Muslims have to assess ourselves and change some of our own ways of thinking and behavior. We must come out of our isolation. We must put aside our petty differences and work together. We have to introduce ourselves, our Islamic values and principles and we have to participate fully in this society for the sake of peace, harmony, good will and good community, not only for ourselves but for all Americans.

...It is important to build good families and keep good family ties, but we must go beyond our own family and treat all people as one family....

Religion is not just some rituals but it is building good conduct and good morals. It is to care for the poor and needy. It is to love our neighbors and be good to them....

We must work for justice and harmony among all people. Our vision must be universal and not parochial....

Justice requires that the wrong should be corrected with right means. Injustice cannot be removed by another injustice. Two wrongs do not make one right and ends do not justify the means.

Dr. Taha Jabir al-Alwani, president of the Graduate School of Islamic and Social Sciences and president of the Fiqh Council of North America, comments:

> Renowned Muslim scholars have made it clear that every Muslim living in the West, in general, and the US, in particular, has a role to play in the process of establishing a better life for all the people living together as members of the society, regardless of whether they are Muslims or non-Muslims. Islam urges Muslims to be active and proactive in any society they reside in.... But being proactive in the society does not mean that a Muslim has to jeopardize his religious teachings when some policies of his government run counter to them; he must champion right and justice wherever he finds himself and in any post he occupies.

Finally, as in all religions, many Muslims wish to know the views and judgments of their own religious authorities, but in the end, they make their own judgments about how to maintain Islamic principles in Western society and where compromise is necessary without being harmful. (The pope forbids birth control, yet Catholic believers in Italy have one of the lowest birthrates in Europe.) Muslims, in the end, will balance their own common sense against traditional clerical interpretations. Even more likely, many will simply lead their own lives and not worry about possible contradictions. Most Muslims do not accept all clerical judgments as irrefutable dogma; clerical judgments furthermore differ. In voting with their feet in coming to the West at all, many millions clearly believe it is fine to live in non-Muslim countries and will get on with their Muslim lives there as best they can, learning as they go, integrating ever more closely with each generation.

This is not about Islam at all, but about the complex and shifting dynamics of integration and multiculturalism. And Europeans must accept Muslim culture as part of the new Europe — much as Jewish, Hindu, or Chinese culture is now also being accepted as part of Western multicultural richness. We must be wary of Islamizing the problems of multiculturalism and immigrant integration.

One final note on multicultural progress: the UK journalist and writer William Dalrymple writes, "It seems almost unbelievable in the world of 9/11, bin Laden, and the *Clash of Civilizations*, that the bestselling poet in the US in the 1990s is a classically trained Muslim cleric who taught Shari'a law in a madrasa." He was referring, of course, to the Persian/Turkish medieval poet Jalaladdin Rumi, one of the most beloved Sufi poets, whose poetry is a spiritual balm to the world. Indeed, Islamic spiritualism is one of its glorious contributions to human civilization. It would be great if there would be more room for those spiritual themes in the troubled political and cultural lives of both Muslims and Westerners, as the debates swirl over religion, identity, citizenship, tolerance, and belonging.

CHAPTER TEN

Islam and India

The world has seen three wars between predominantly Hindu India and Muslim Pakistan over the past fifty years; the next such war could even unleash a nuclear exchange. The Kashmir conflict has long been the major seed of contention, an ongoing proxy war between India and Pakistan as Kashmiri Muslim liberation groups fight a guerrilla war against perceived oppressive Indian rule. Additionally, violent Islamist groups, usually with links to Pakistan, have conducted several bloody terrorist operations inside India. Neither Indian nor Pakistani populations have forgotten the bitter partition of India, engineered by the British in 1947, in which millions of Hindus, Sikhs, and Muslims died in savage three-way attacks during the vast transfers of populations—Muslims from India to the new state of Pakistan; Hindus and Sikhs from the new state of Pakistan to India. If this is not the locus of a "clash of civilizations," then what is?

Of all the "borders" between Islam and other cultures, India—the third such case in our discussion of Islam's contacts with other major civilizations—is one of the most critical. Islam not only borders on India (in Pakistan and Bangladesh), but large numbers of Muslims have lived *within* India for over a millennium, with their own rich and complex relationships with Hindus. Over time, Muslims have played highly diverse roles on the Indian stage: peaceful traders propagating Islam in the south; conquering warriors out of Central Asia in the north; founders and cocreators of one of the great "fusion civilizations" of history between Islam and Hinduism that produced the brilliant Mughal Empire; and finally a defeated Muslim minority divided in 1947 into a new Pakistani state or minority status within India. In India the community has been the object of de facto discrimination and suffers second-class citizenship. India also represents the first *non-Christian* border with Islam that we will look at.

In our alternative scenarios of a world without Islam, the lines in India are less clear. In one sense, things would be quite different without Islam: the world would have been deprived of the brilliance of the Hindu-Muslim fusion civilization of the Mughals. At the same time, it might have been spared some of the ugly religious struggles between Hindus, Muslims, and Sikhs that have characterized recent history. So, in this context, the more interesting question might be, Was the religious strife between Hindus and Muslims inevitable? Did this have to be a bloody border? Why are we where we are today? And how much is really about religion? Or can the roots of the problem also be traced to the self-serving policies of British colonial rule in India?

ISLAM'S INITIAL ENCOUNTER with India represented a major new intellectual frontier for Muslims: Hinduism was not only an ancient, vast, complex, and multifaceted religion, but was also the first religion Islam encountered that was quite unconnected with Middle Eastern religions and "People of the Book." Hinduism represented a sharply different experience for Muslims, with its explicit polytheism, its profusion of unconventional religious images, and the startling combination of animal, human, and mythological characteristics, elements of nudity or near-nudity in the religious art of numerous Hindu sects—all of this combining to make Hinduism perhaps the most "shocking," in Islamic terms, of any religion the 'ulama would ever encounter. Yet the demands of reality soon created compromises and an uneasy coexistence between Hinduism and Muslim society was established.

Not surprisingly, we find differing schools of interpretation about the entire record of Islam in India. All nationalisms read history retroactively; that is, their historians go back and mine the past for evidence to buttress their nationalist and territorial claims of today and tomorrow. For Hindu nationalists, the Hindu religion is as deeply rooted in Indian soil as anything can be; any other religion intruding on that soil is either absorbed into its embrace or seen as an unwelcome foreign intruder. Thus, both Islam and Christianity are seen in this latter light—more on political and cultural grounds than on theological grounds. Both Islam and Christianity sought to roll back Hinduism in their own favor. The fact that the most widespread international symbol of India today should be the quintessentially Muslim architecture of the Taj Mahal rankles Hindu nationalists deeply. Yet an India without its Mughal fusion civilization would have been a culturally far less rich place.

More liberal-minded accounts of that same history take pride in the rich fruits of Hindu-Islamic civilization. Each culture markedly influenced the other in profound ways, suggesting the creative absorptive power and malleability of both. Yet today, Indian Muslims have become disadvantaged minorities within the great Indian society they once ruled and helped shape. They've come in from outside, been at the top, fallen to the bottom, and are now mulling over their place as a minority in the new conditions of the modern Indian state. Maybe it is this diverse historical trajectory that has given Indian Muslims the most subtle and complex vision of Islam in multicultural society to be found anywhere.

———

India touched Muslims in particular ways. First, it is one of the many areas of South and Southeast Asia where Islam did not initially come by the sword. Trading connections between Arab seafaring merchants and the southwest coast of India were well-established long before Islam. According to Hindu records, the first actual Muslim settlement on the Indian subcontinent took place in the early seventh century in just one such Arab trader settlement. Reportedly, the first mosque was established in Kodungallur in today's Kerala province in 612 CE, during the Prophet's lifetime.

Historians draw major distinctions between the nature of Islam in the north and in the south of India. In the south, Islam came on the scene early via trade and missionary work; in the north, Islam entered many hundreds of years later as one of the many invaders of north India from Central Asia. As a result, tensions between Muslims and Hindus are more pronounced in the north than in the south, where the Muslim population gradually integrated into the local culture, as opposed to the Muslims who invaded the north with their armies of mixed Persian, Arab, Turkic, and Mongol blood.

Muslim Arab armies first entered northern India under the Umayyad Dynasty from Damascus and conquered Sind, the westernmost province of the subcontinent. Further Muslim military invasions came out of Afghanistan in the tenth century; finally, the great Turko-Mongol commander Babur, from Central Asia, founded the Mughal Empire with the fall of Delhi in 1526. The Mughals would control nearly all of India at its height. The Mughals themselves represented a fusion of Turko-Mongol and Persian culture and both languages were brought to India, where they exerted a huge impact on Indian culture and language.

As the Brookings Institution scholar Stephen P. Cohen has written:

> Although each of these conquerors [Greeks, Huns, Scythians, and Muslims] viewed the Subcontinent as an extension of their exogenous power base, they later came to view the world through Indo-centric eyes. The absorptive power of Indian society has always been impressive.... [Islam] also brought new military technologies, theologies and political ideas but it did not destroy Indian civilization as it had destroyed pre-Islamic Persian culture. Eventually, under the Mughals, India was again unified, within an imperial system. With this new order even Islam was powerfully influenced by this Hindu culture, just as Islam shocked and transformed Hinduism.

Sufi Islam, with its mixed syncretic character, appealed to many Hindus and helped soften the initial impact of Islam. But the Muslim clerical class never reached consensus on how to deal with Hindus and Hinduism. The outstanding Muslim scientist and polymath al-Biruni spent time in India in the mid-eleventh century observing the society; he remarkably concluded that in the end, Hinduism, with all its multiple deities, was basically a monotheistic faith:

> The Hindus believe with regard to God that he is one, eternal, without beginning and end, acting by free-will, almighty, all-wise, living, giving life, ruling, preserving; one who in his sovereignty is unique, beyond all likeness and unlikeness, and that he does not resemble anything nor does anything resemble him.

But what of the multiple "idols" worshipped in Hinduism? Al-Biruni believed that their worship essentially reflected the theological ignorance of the lower classes that clung to them, but that Hinduism as a higher philosophical concept shares an essential monotheism with Islam. Whether one agrees with this interpretation or not—and most 'ulama certainly did not—this conclusion is indeed striking coming from a Muslim scholar himself.

For most of the 'ulama in India, inclusion of Hindus among the "People of the Book" seemed an impossible theological reach, but if they were not, then forced conversion to Islam was appropriate. Some 'ulama were zealous and did compel conversion and even argued that death was appropriate in the case of noncompliance. There are accounts of the destruction of Hindu temples in various parts of India, while many others were transformed into mosques. Indeed, more commonplace than the use of violence were reports of Mughal emperors raising the level of the poll tax to squeeze poorer Hindus into conversion to Islam, to gain relief from the tax. Even more typically, however, many lower-caste Hindus converted to Islam to escape the rigid caste system of Hinduism itself, or simply to become part of the ruling cultural order. But in the end, the Mughals could not convert most of the country—and knew they could not—so the situation settled down into a kind of cool coexistence, at least from the point of view of the 'ulama. In some functional sense, then, Hindus did become a kind of *nominal* "People of the Book," even if it was in principle theologically unacceptable and incompatible.

On the other hand, while few Muslims would visit a Hindu temple, most Hindus were comfortable visiting Muslim shrines as part of an expression of Hindu syncretism or pantheism. Islam simply joined the pantheon. Nor did Hindus have any interest in seeking converts to Hinduism—their religion is a closed system that basically admits no converts; one must be born into the system. If one seeks to convert to Hinduism, functionally it must be to a specific caste and community; but lacking community or blood ties, into which caste would the outsider be legitimately accepted? Without specific caste association from birth, one is left floating in a theoretical Hindu social limbo. And other unanticipated fusions took place. At the formal level, Islam certainly does not welcome integration of other religious traditions into it. Yet India saw at least one fascinating experiment in the fusion of Islam with Hinduism, the brainchild of the innovative mind of Mughal emperor Akbar the Great (1542–1605), Babur's grandson. Akbar emerges as the most remarkable of all the Mughal rulers over a four-hundred-year period.

Akbar was well aware of the welter of competing faiths within India, including Islam (Sunni, Shi'ite, and Isma'ili), countless sects of Hindu faiths, Jainism, Zoroastrianism, Christianity, and Judaism. He was tolerant, fascinated with religion, and thrived on religious discussion, bringing together adherents of various religions for debate of theological and moral issues. From these exchanges, he reportedly concluded that no religion had a monopoly on the entire truth; he therefore took the revolutionary step to create on his own a new religion, Din-i-Ilahi, or Divine Faith, which represented a fusion of Islamic, Hindu, and other Vedic beliefs, as well as beliefs from Christianity and Judaism. Through propagation of the Divine Faith, he hoped to forge a unity within the country that would no longer be beset with religious differences—a kind of religious Esperanto.

Muslims, of course, were already familiar with the Jewish and Christian antecedents to Islamic theology. Din-i-Ilahi also contained elements of mysticism, philosophy, ethics, and nature worship, with emphasis on tolerance of religious diversity. It recognized no gods, prophets, scriptures, or priestly hierarchy. The admixture of these "pagan" ideas, however, was quite offensive to most of the 'ulama, who saw the entire project as utterly blasphemous, though they had to be circumspect about what the emperor propounded.

In the end, the new religion did not make it outside the palace walls; it was simply too bizarre and lacked social or cultural foundation. Nonetheless, it represented a remarkable vision of ecumenical thinking before its time, and Akbar is well remembered by Hindus, even though his admirers among the 'ulama are few.

If religious fusion seems abstruse, not so the Mughals' brilliant architecture, which combined Hindu and Islamic style with a strong Persian flavor, perhaps the most famous and enduring contribution of the empire. The great Mughal public buildings to this day remain glorious works of art, of which the Taj Mahal has achieved the greatest perfection, but is rivaled by dozens of palaces, forts, mosques, and madrasas, frequently worked in red sandstone. The Mughal style has gone on to influence Muslim architecture around the world and even graces large numbers of public and private buildings across Britain—a symbol of the mighty British Raj period in India.

The Mughal Dynasty also created great poetry and established the foundations of Indian classical music. The most familiar Indian cooking in the world today is that of northern India, a superb fusion of earlier Indian cuisine with Persian cooking, known still as *Moghlai* cooking. The two sister languages Hindi and Urdu both represent the same fusions of Persian, Arab, and Turkish vocabulary grafted onto a north Indian grammatical base; they remain the dominant languages of northern India and Pakistan today. In short, modern Indian civilization is inconceivable—almost unrecognizable—without the Mughal element. Yet this fact does not sit well with some Hindu nationalists.

In terms of counterinfluence, one major cultural impact of Hinduism upon Islam was less felicitous: that of the Hindu caste system on Indian Muslims. Within the Hindu caste system, one is born into a specific place in the caste hierarchy for life; these caste positions are fundamentally unchangeable in ritual and social terms. A Brahmin (upper caste) may not have any physical contact with an untouchable (Dalit), and if so, is required to perform ritual purification. One's place in the caste hierarchy determines the range of permitted occupational and social parameters. Indian Muslims, exposed over long periods to this caste system, eventually absorbed some elements of it, in which Muslim society came to be informally divided into Ashraf (noble) and Ajlaf (lower) castes. While the Muslims in India were originally a very small percentage of the population at the time of the first Muslim invasions from the north, over time there were Hindu converts to Islam in much larger numbers, often bringing social vestiges of their lower caste status with them. By the time of partition, the number of Muslims in India had reached some 14 percent.

In Islam, by any theological measure, a caste system among Muslims is unacceptable; the Qur'an makes clear that the only individual superior to another in the eyes of God is the more pious. But in India we observe the de facto cross-cultural impact of religions living side by side.

Several striking perspectives, then, emerge from all of this. First, when Islam entered India via traders and missionaries, as in the south, there was no friction. Muslims in South India are generally ethnically identical to their Hindu neighbors. But in the north, the seat of Indian political power, ethnic differences did exist: essentially Turko-Persian Muslims from Central Asia represented identifiable foreign conquerors, often viewed with resentment by those displaced from power. A second phenomenon is how "incompatible" theologies under situations of daily human intercourse managed to coexist over time and even influence each other, although cases of interreligious violence certainly occurred. Third, a fusion culture emerged of great brilliance — one to match an equally brilliant fusion of Islam with Persian culture in Iran, and of Turko-Islam with Byzantine culture in the Ottoman Empire.

"Bloody borders," then, hardly captures this extraordinary dynamic, one that involved rich ethnic cross-pollination as well as cultural and religious influences. Would Zoroastrian Persia have abstained from conquest in India? In what ways would its conquest of India have been different? Would *non-Muslim* Turks from Central Asia shrink from joining other groups to invade India from the North? Islam does not appear to have been a central factor.

Partition: Where Are the Muslims Now?

With the gradual collapse of the Mughal Empire in the face of encroaching British imperialism, the Mughal system began to lose its power, and with it came a gradual decline of Muslim status. The British, too, perceived a greater degree of resistance to their rule from Muslims than from Hindus and hence began to give preference within the system to the Hindus, whom they felt were more "reliable" or "pliable."

Muslims were indeed quite active in the many acts of resistance against the British Raj, including a central role in the Great Indian Mutiny of 1857, when Muslim sepoys rioted over the rumor that pig fat was used in making the bullet cartridges for their muskets. But the Hindus, in the end, demonstrated the same powers of resistance. Political and social discontent in British India were ripe enough for a small spark like this incident to set off a national rebellion. Muslims and Hindus were generally united in opposition to British power and rule, although their tactical approaches to the problem often differed.

As princely Mughal power gradually broke down or was conquered by the British, Muslims soon found themselves a minority without power within the Indian system and partially suspect in British eyes. Some British speculated about whether Muslims were simply "naturally rebellious to foreign rule." As the date of Indian liberation from British rule approached after World War II, Muslims became primarily concerned about protection of their minority rights within the coming independent India; they were fearful that in a straightforward democratic order, they would become a permanently outvoted minority. As a result, Muslims favored some kind of confederal system in which they would not always be in permanent minority status (a classic dilemma of all democratic systems in which minorities can rarely change the system through the ballot box). Muslims within India were furthermore not homogeneous but themselves divided by class, regional, and even linguistic differences.

In the end, the actual partition of India into Indian and Pakistani states had not been the preferred Muslim goal. But under the force of events, and Hindu concerns over what limitations Muslims might place on the centralized power of the future independent Indian state, partition suddenly loomed as the likely option for all.

Interestingly, many of the Muslim 'ulama in India did not favor the partition of the country or even the formation of a new independent Muslim Pakistani state. They correctly perceived that not all Muslims would depart for Pakistan and that those Muslims left behind would become an even smaller minority in the hands of a then overwhelming Hindu majority. Approximately fourteen and a half million people crossed the newly created borders either into or out of India in this great British-run process of ethnic cleansing in 1947 called Partition. Massive and horrifying violence took place during the transfers of populations, with many terrible massacres on the part of all three religious groups — Sikhs, Muslims, and Hindus — upon each other. The result was that the new immigrants — Muslims moving into Pakistan, Sikhs and Hindus coming into India — were often traumatized and embittered through the process and proceeded to number among the most religiously intolerant in each new society. Politics created religious time bombs in both countries. Indeed, for the Muslims who did not transfer to Pakistan but remained in India, the situation did, in fact, become worse: they had not only lost numbers and thus political clout, they also now had their ultimate loyalty to the new Hindu-dominant state cast into doubt. In the three wars between Pakistan and India in the years to come, Indian Muslims were often perceived in Hindu eyes as untrustworthy, a potential fifth column.

The situation in Kashmir was equally volatile. Kashmir was a Muslim-majority province (some 77 percent Muslim in 1947) with its own distinct historic and ethnic character. It had been promised by the British in 1947 the right to a referendum about whether to stay with India or join Pakistan; in the end, India reneged on a genuine referendum, which it would surely have lost. The majority Muslim Kashmiris remain angry and still continue to agitate for their right of choice; Indian authorities have ruled with an iron hand and have administered Kashmir unwisely and insensitively. Given three wars between Pakistan and India, partly over Kashmir and all of which Pakistan lost, the area offered fertile ground for Pakistani pressure upon India through covert support to violent Kashmiri separatist movements. This long-running battle poisons Pakistani-Indian relations to this day and is a key source of regional terrorism.

Muslims in India today are back up to some 13 percent of the overall Indian population. The Muslim community is now regrettably divided: on the one hand, the more religious elements press for establishing a separate self-contained Muslim community that could live apart from the Hindus — a fantasy given how scattered Muslims are across India. This policy of promoting communal identity at all costs has increased the isolation of the Muslims. On the other side, a smaller group of Muslims seeks to move beyond communalism and become integrated into the secular Indian state. To find refuge in communalism is an act of insecurity and fear; to work for secular integration is an act of confidence and optimism. Both sides can find valid arguments in support of their position.

But the choice is not solely up to the Muslims: a formidable *Hindu* ethnic/religious nationalist movement has emerged and targeted non-Hindus, especially Muslims, whom they perceive as blocking the way to the formation of a Hindu religious state. The intolerant Bharatiya Janata Party (BJP) has controlled Indian national politics in the past, may do so again, and controls many state governments. The violence of the Hindu nationalists is a serious threat to the Muslim community, which drives them together into an intense and isolated communitarian posture.

Hindu nationalism—*Hindutva*—can only be based on religion since there is no "Hindu" ethnicity per se; Hindus come from hugely diverse ethnic backgrounds and languages, as do Muslims. Hindu nationalists, unlike the more secular Hindu leadership, had strongly favored partition in 1947 specifically to expel Muslims, thereby leaving no barrier to establishing a Hindu state. Part of their resentment against Muslims, Sikhs, and Christians as well is that by their very presence they require maintenance of a secular and multicultural Indian state that the Hindu religious nationalists seek to abolish. And ironically, it is the Muslim population that today overwhelmingly supports a *secular* state, more keenly than in any Muslim country; as a minority, they clearly grasp the benefits of a secular state for preservation of their own culture, society, and religion against an official Hindu state. Indian Muslims generally feel their culture within India is richer than that of Pakistan, which had long been largely a feudal backwater with little cultural heritage; all the cultural glories of Mughal India remained with India after partition, except for the city of Lahore.

In this atmosphere, communal outrages have not been lacking. The city of Ayodhya in northeastern India has become a site freighted with emotion for both sides. It is one of the six holiest Hindu sites in India, known for its beauty and impressive temples. Nine hundred years ago, it was attacked by Muslim forces from Afghanistan and looted. Later Babur, the founder of the Mughal

Empire, was said to have built a mosque there. Hindus claimed much later that it was built on the site of a temple to Rama, although the evidence for that is uncertain. This was the location chosen by the Bharatiya Janata Party in 1992 when it resolved to create a key Hindu challenge to the concept of Mughal and Muslim India. After a long build-up campaign, it organized a mob of some 150,000 Hindus, armed them with picks, and attacked the Babri Mosque, pointedly demolishing it into small pieces. The symbolism was intense for both sides, and unleashed cycles of retaliation around India. In Ayodhya, it found its response in 2005, when five armed Muslim gunmen attempted to bomb the makeshift new Rama temple on the site, killing only themselves in the process.

The emergence of the Hindu nationalist party, Shiv Sena, which is based in Mumbai (Bombay), has further polarized religious and ethnic emotions in the state of Maharashtra. Strongly hostile to south Indian migrants to Mumbai, the movement has particularly targeted Muslims, who make up some 15 percent of the Mumbai population. The movement has adopted ultranationalist values and rhetoric and specializes in recruiting street thugs for intimidation purposes against Muslim neighborhoods, while at the same time managing to run the city government somewhat capably. Serious anti-Muslim riots in Mumbai occurred in 1992, in which 900 people, mostly Muslim, died, many burned alive; an official investigative commission identified Shiv Sena as behind the riots. Then, in response to these riots, in March 1993 thirteen powerful bombs went off in Mumbai, in which 250 people were killed; the bombings were traced to a Muslim mafia organization. Tit for tat violence has sporadically occurred in other locales as well.

Then in December 2001, a brazen attack took place when five Muslim gunmen attacked the Indian Parliament building in New Delhi in broad daylight; fortunately, the death toll was limited to security guards and all the gunmen. But the national shock from the assault on such a major public symbol was immense. The gunmen were identified by Indian authorities as belonging to the Lashkar-e-Tayiba and the Jaish-e-Mohamed, groups based in Pakistan that have received Pakistani support in past years for operations in Kashmir.

The year 2002 then saw ferocious anti-Muslim riots in Gujarat that were particularly horrific—up to two thousand Muslims died in them. According to the UK *Guardian:*

> Two hundred and thirty unique Islamic monuments, including an exquisite 400-year-old mosque, were destroyed or vandalised during the recent anti-Muslim riots in the Indian state of Gujarat, according to a local survey. Experts say the damage is so extensive that it rivals the better publicised destruction of the Bamiyan Buddhas in Afghanistan or the wrecking of Tibet's monasteries by the Red Guards. In other disturbances, Hindu gangs have smashed delicate mosque screens, thrown bricks at Persian inscriptions, and set fire to old Korans.... "This has been a systematic attempt to wipe out an entire culture," said Teesta Setalvad of Sapara, a body opposed to communal strife, who compiled the list.

Thus, the terrible terrorist attack of Muslim *jihadists* in Mumbai in December 2008 needs to be seen as part of a series: this one outrage indiscriminately butchered some two thousand people at random, in multiple attacks on public places and big hotels—the kind of incident that has played back against the Muslims of India, even though few if any seem to have had a hand in it. All these incidents intensify Muslim communal insecurity and serve to impel the core Muslim identity into a hunkered-down and defensive mode that now typifies Muslim communities across much of the Muslim world.

A 1995 study of communal tensions in India prepared by the

US Library of Congress attributes most of this communal violence in India not so much to "ancient hatreds" or to religious
fundamentalism but to the interaction between socioeconomic
problems and the irresponsible strategies and tactics of India's
politicians since 1980. This study identifies the destabilizing character of rapid urbanization, and increased competition among
diverse groups for livelihoods. The Library of Congress study also
singles out changes in the nature of India's political process that
lead politicians to dangerously exploit religious sentiments and
appeal to chauvinistic caste biases among the Hindu majority, all
for short-term gain at the polls. Violence by Muslim guerrilla
groups in Kashmir and by Sikhs in Punjab have also contributed
to the sentiment among the Hindu majority that "religious minorities employ aggressive tactics to win special concessions from the
government." The study concludes, "The manipulation of India's
religious tensions by militants, criminals, and politicians high-
lighted the extent to which religious sentiments in India had
become an object of exploitation."

Special coverage in *Time* magazine in 2003 on rioting in India
reported a disturbing divide between the Hindu and Muslim populations in India. In terms of violence alone:

> India's Muslims are far more likely than Hindus to be
> victims of violent attacks. In all the communal riots since
> independence, official police records reveal that three-
> quarters of the lives lost and properties destroyed were
> Muslim, a figure that climbed to 85 percent during [the
> 2002] riots in Gujarat.

Yet in the nearly six thousand deaths resulting from Hindu
rioting (as of 2003), there had been hardly any prosecutions of
those guilty of rape, arson, or murder. The tacit support of Indian

local or national government under the BJP to Hindu-sponsored violence is scarcely concealed.

Time also noted that in the cities, 40 percent of Muslims exist at the lowest end of the income scale, compared to 22 percent of Hindus. Although Muslims make up 13 percent of the population, they occupy only 3 percent of government jobs, and even fewer are employed by Hindus in the private sector. In the cities, Muslims also have an illiteracy rate of 30 percent, as opposed to 19 percent among Hindus. An Indian leader of a moderate Hindu party, K. C. Tyagi, comments that "there is often a tendency in India to treat Muslims as *them* rather than us. And this tendency does have terrible manifestations. Even today, by and large, Muslims have not been admitted to what we call the Indian mainstream."

The emergence of nationalism(s) in India is actually a modern vehicle for many forces simultaneously at work: anticolonialist reactions, "patriotism" and nationalism, ethnic, class, and regional differences, and economic competition. The disturbing events of recent history in India demonstrate the potential ugliness of the forces of modern nationalism at work, even within a democratic order.

Nonetheless, the historical Muslim experience in India overwhelmingly indicates the fruitful coexistence in which both Muslim and Hindu profoundly enriched each other. The two cultures are now inextricably linked, cannot be spoken of as civilizational "borders," and have little option but to find some newer forms of coexistence in the Indian state to come. In this sense, Islam has indeed changed the course of history in India, but primarily through integration, assimilation, and fusion. Muslims are diverse, disparate, and scattered across India. Yet today, ironically, "Islam" has simply come to crystallize and embody the resentments that many Hindus feel over many other issues that have nothing to do with religion and everything to do with diverse communal struggles for power and influence. In this context Muslims are only one of many communal groups that compete on what can be a rough playing field. The role of Pakistan, caught in its own shaky national identity, troubled geopolitical fears, and involvement in Kashmir and Afghanistan, intensifies the problem. It would be a tragedy if in modern times, narrow-minded forces on all sides should take these deeply interwoven cultural strands and attempt to permanently rip them asunder.

It is reasonable to ask: If there had never been a British Raj, or any British control of India as an imperial colony, would there have been an eventual partition of India? If the Mughal Empire had gradually weakened in state after princely state over time in India, would Hindus and Muslims have eventually worked out some kind of messy organic solution to their relative interests and kept a concept of a united India as a common goal, albeit on a federal basis? Very possibly. It seems, furthermore, quite unlikely that the mechanism of a partition could ever have been conceived, much less executed by the Hindu and Muslim players themselves; it took major external imperial intervention and sweeping authority to make the entire operation possible. Maybe it is the British imperial control of India over several hundred years—far more than "Islam"—that has the most to answer for in contriving this ill-starred and perhaps unnecessary partition that solved nothing.

CHAPTER ELEVEN

Islam and China

Few in the West are aware of the close connections between Islam and China, yet China ranks high among countries containing large Muslim populations: some twenty million Muslims are scattered across the country—more than in most Arab countries. But there is a critical distinction to be drawn among them. About one half of China's Muslims are ethnically *Han Chinese*, with some admixture of Arab and Persian blood from the days of early Muslim settlers in China. They are referred to as *Hui*, or *Hui-Hui*. They speak only Chinese and follow a lifestyle similar to other Han Chinese, except for a few key cultural distinctions that arise from Islam. Over time, the Han and the Muslim elements have intermixed in fascinating ways and coexist fairly comfortably within broader Chinese culture. But the other half of China's Muslims are ethnically and linguistically quite distinct—primarily of Turkic origin. The Uyghurs living in far western China represent the largest Turkic group by far. Hui Muslims are basically well-integrated into Chinese life, whereas the Turkic Uyghurs are not. Chinese authorities treat the Uyghurs with suspicion and harshness, highlighting the essentially ethnic character of the problem, reinforced by Uyghur adherence to Islam.

The popular image of "propagation of Islam by the sword" is once again erroneous in the Chinese case. According to Muslim accounts, Islam reached China surprisingly early, in 651 CE, some eighteen years after the Prophet's death, brought by sea to Canton by an envoy of the Caliph 'Umar. There is a well-known saying of the Prophet, "Seek knowledge, even from China." According to Muslim tradition, the Tang Dynasty emperor ordered a mosque to be built in Canton, the first in China, which still stands today. The emperor believed Islam to be compatible with teachings of Confucianism and granted rights to Arab and Persian merchants to establish the first Muslim settlements in the area. Early Chinese encounters with Islam in Canton were therefore peaceful and productive, and Muslims were granted a place in Chinese society, where their mercantile skills and contacts were known from pre-Islamic Arab traders. China quickly recognized the great seafaring capabilities of the Muslims and the potential benefits to China in expanding its influence and reach. As a result, Muslims soon came to dominate the import/export industry of China by the time of the Song Dynasty (960–1279); the Director General of Shipping was an office consistently held by a Muslim.

But far away to the northwest borders of China, a very different geopolitical event occurred between China and Islam with profound long-term geopolitical consequences. There the expanding forces of the Tang Dynasty marched west down into Central Asia, where in 751 CE they encountered Arab forces of the Abbasid caliphate at Talas (in present-day Kyrgyzstan). The Arabs defeated the Chinese forces, an event that marked the beginning of the end of further Chinese expansion into Central Asia. Many see the battle of Talas as a decisive strategic and civilizational turning point: Central Asia did not fall to Chinese rule, and more important, the Turkic tribes of the region then increasingly turned to Islam, an event that indelibly marked their future in their centuries-long migrations, ultimately carrying their religion into the Byzantine world of the Mediterranean and Anatolia.

With time, Muslims grew more deeply engaged in the basic administration of the empire: by the Yüan (Mongol) Dynasty (1271–1368), the Mongols used Muslims to strengthen trade ties with the West. Mongol armies that had ranged as far to the West as Damascus rounded up hundreds of thousands of Arabs, Persians, and Central Asian Turks and sent them to China to help administer the empire—in finance and taxation, in calendar-making and astronomy, and in the building of the new capital at Beijing. This marked the first serious influx of Central Asian Turkic blood into China proper to complement the Arab and Persian ethnicity of the first Muslims. Muslims were appointed as administrators and to governorships, and many became fully absorbed into Chinese culture as Muslims. These helped make up the various blood strains of the Hui.

The Ming Dynasty (1368–1644) was a productive time for Muslims. After having been perceived primarily as outsiders of Arab and Persian trader stock, it was in this period that the Hui Muslims came to be more truly integrated into Chinese culture and adopted Chinese names. They established major centers of Muslim learning in Nanjing; Arabic and Persian were the two cultural languages for the study of Islam. Muslims increasingly intermarried with non-Muslim Chinese as well, thus losing their foreign status and becoming "indistinguishable" in appearance. Otherwise, the Hui have "no [distinctive] common language, no common territory, and no common economic life, though they are widely held to be genetically inclined toward skill at doing business in the marketplace." The only thing all Hui have in common is Islam and its culturally linked practices. And because of Islam's early presence in China, it has long been considered one of the official indigenous religions of the Chinese Empire, right until the present. With time, the Hui became more familiar and trusted by successive Chinese dynasties due to their fundamentally Han culture and greater integration into Chinese society, unlike the other Muslim minorities with distinctly different ethnicities, whose tendencies toward resistance against Hanization still persist today.

During the early fifteenth century, the most spectacular seafaring expeditions in Chinese history were undertaken by one Admiral Zheng He, a Chinese Muslim; he was dispatched by the emperor on a series of seven voyages across the length and breadth of the Indian Ocean, and brought back to China a vivid awareness of the extent of Muslim kingdoms and culture that existed to the west.

Cross-Cultural Influences

As in Russia and India, Islam in China reached some fascinating accommodations with ambient Chinese culture. And in China, as elsewhere in the world, periodic Islamic renewal movements cropped up, designed to scrub the faith, remove the accretions of non-Islamic thought and practice, and maintain a sharp focus on the essentials of Islam. Both of these contradictory trends—absorption of new ideas versus a rejection of innovation—affected Islam in China.

Fairly early on, Muslim thinkers in China were impressed with the huge body of Chinese philosophical thinking that was already in place upon Islam's arrival. As the historian Jonathan Lipman notes:

> The influence and permeation of Chinese Islam by Confucian thinking seems to have given late Ming and early Qing Islam, which was tending toward decline, a transfusion of fresh, new blood, a new vitality.... A group

of Sino-Islamicists sprang forth. They used Confucian language and Confucian ideas systematically to study, arrange, and summarize Islamic religious doctrine; they constructed a complete Chinese Islamic intellectual system, writing a set of Chinese-language Islamic works with a uniquely Chinese style. These works are called by the Muslims in China the Han Kitab — that is, the Chinese canon — and they have had a definite influence in Sino-Muslim society.

In China, mosques were all built in the style of Chinese traditional temples and pagodas. The Hui also created a unique Sino-Arabic script to render Chinese in Arabic script. Muslim scholars seeking some accommodation between Islamic and Chinese culture actually found their most accessible philosophical counterpart in Confucianism. One of China's most important Muslim scholars, Yusuf Ma Dexin, worked on establishing a synthesis between the two. Born in Yünnan province in the southwest, he made the *hajj* in 1841 and stayed in the Middle East for eight years, studying at al-Azhar in Cairo, and then traveling at length through the Ottoman Empire, including Jerusalem. He had an excellent knowledge of both Arabic and Persian, and was the first to translate the Qur'an into Chinese. He also brought back to China the latest currents of Islamic and political thought in the Middle East.

Muslim gravitation toward Confucianism might at first glance seem unusual, given the latter's essentially "secular" and ethical orientation, verging on philosophy rather than transcendental religious emphasis. Yet precisely because Confucianism primarily provides an ethical and moral framework, it was less challenging to Islam on a theological level. Confucianism is also the most "Chinese" of all religions in China, making it important for Muslims, under the watchful eyes of oppressive and suspicious Qing Dynasty officials, to convince the authorities of the compatibilities of Islam with Confucianism, demonstrating that it favored order, justice, good governance, and supported the Emperor.

Some Muslims believed they could enlist Confucianism as a gateway for spreading Islam among the Chinese. But full accommodation between the two religions was always a stretch, especially since the main body of Muslim belief extends well beyond the dispassionate, this-worldly, nontheistic moral precepts of Confucian thought. The powerful ethnocentricity of Chinese culture, furthermore, made difficult any acceptance of distant and exotic Mecca as the center of Islamic faith, while the miraculous elements and beliefs of all three Western revealed religions strained Chinese credulousness. Thus, Muslims had little success in acquiring new converts to Islam among Han Chinese. Buddhism was an even greater stretch for Muslims to identify with, being of Indian origin, nonnative to China, and too abstract, otherworldly, and nontheistic for Muslim sensibilities.

The Qing Dynasty (1644–1911)

The advent of the Qing Dynasty marked a sharp turning point for Muslims, perhaps the worst period for them in Chinese history until Mao's Cultural Revolution in the 1970s. Ethnically Manchu (Altaic) and not Han in origin, the Qing tended to be harsh, discriminatory, and xenophobic, and distrusted the Hui. The Qing forbade the building of any new mosques and banned pilgrimages to Mecca, immediately alienating Muslims. Discriminatory and declining Qing rule eventually led to two huge Muslim uprisings, the Panthay Rebellion (1855–1873) in Yünnan province in the southwest, and one in the northwest, the Dungan (Hui) Rebellion (1862–1877). In the course of the two rebellions, several million people died as a result of government policies sometimes bordering on genocide. Many Hui fled to Russian Central Asia during these bloody times where, known as Dungans, they still constitute a significant minority group with ties to China. Anti-Qing rebellion was hardly unique to the Muslims; there were increasing disorders, rebellions, and chaos all across China as the Qing Dynasty moved toward collapse. A key conclusion here, perhaps, is that as in Russia, Muslims have not seriously rebelled until presented with egregious conditions, such as represented by Qing Dynasty oppression, and later the Communist parties of both Russia and China.

———

SUFISM—that powerful Muslim force for facilitating interreligious contact via its emphasis on mysticism—entered China by way of Central Asia and points west in the Muslim world. A small but important number of Chinese Muslims had managed to travel to Egypt, the Arabian Peninsula, the Ottoman Empire, and elsewhere to study Islam at a time when the Middle East was itself generating renewal movements. These new ideas, called New Teachings, were brought back to China to confront the traditional, almost frozen forms of Islam there. The thrust of the New Teachings represented an intellectual renewal of contact between distant elements in the Muslim world, as new scholarly figures sought to bring Chinese Islam into closer conformity with thinking in the Muslim heartland.

But as China moved into the 1930s, leading Muslim scholars were still intent upon seeking synthesis of thought with Han Chinese culture and emphasis on modern education and science to strengthen the Muslim community. Many believed that only a strong, orderly, and well-administered China could provide the kind of cultural security Chinese Muslims sought. These efforts sought "to make Islam comprehensible, moral and effective within a Chinese political, intellectual, and cultural world without compromising its core principles."

But the Chinese Communist regime put an end to all that: it

harshly struck down all religions and traditional values, not just Islam, especially during the Cultural Revolution. Mosques were defaced, destroyed, or closed all over China, as were religious institutions of other faiths. But the Hui have made a comeback in post-communist China and are increasingly prominent everywhere. Hui and Central Asian Muslim culture have become a source of popular romanticism in Chinese epics—most recently in the popular film *Crouching Tiger, Hidden Dragon*—and influence Chinese costumes and music. Muslim restaurants, too, are commonplace in Chinese cities. They serve *halal* (similar to kosher) foods, as well as many delicious lamb specialties not normally part of more standard Chinese cuisine—reasons why they are frequented by non-Muslim Chinese as well. Hui are likely to play increasingly important roles in China's external relations, as "models of Chinese coexistence."

In 1995, an important colloquium—The International Seminar on Islam and Confucianism: A Civilizational Dialogue—was convened in Kuala Lumpur with scholars from around East Asia. The distinguished Malaysian statesman and Islamist thinker Anwar Ibrahim opened the meeting and observed that

> there are a number of striking similarities between Islam and Confucianism, both in ideals and historical experience, in their refusal to detach religion, ethics and morality from the public sphere. The Islamic argument against secularism, that is the separation of politics and other societal concerns from religion and morality, is not dissimilar to the Confucianist perspective presented by Professor Tu Wei-ming in his admirable book *Way, Learning and Politics*. A Muslim would have no difficulty identifying with the Confucian project to restore trust in government and to transform society into a moral community.

The Uyghurs

The story is entirely different when it comes to the other half of the Muslim population that is not ethnically Han at all, but primarily Turkic (along with a small group of Iranian-language Tajiks). Of these groups, the Uyghurs are overwhelmingly the largest, numbering some ten million people and living in Xinjiang province. As with Russian Muslims absorbed into an expanding Russian Empire, the Uyghurs came to be included in China primarily due to the expansion of the Chinese Empire. These Turkic and Tajik minorities live far from central China, in the western zones that border on Pakistan and Kazakstan and, historically speaking, were only relatively recently incorporated into the Chinese state. Uyghurs form an integral part of extended Central Asian Turkic culture and are closely related to other Turkic peoples in Central Asia, especially the Uzbeks, toward whom they had been oriented for most of history. These minorities therefore differ ethnically, culturally, and religiously from the Han, which makes for more powerfully distinct identities and intensifies potential resistance against the absorptive Han state.

Communist rule in China alienated many minorities in China, especially during the Cultural Revolution, when their cultures were ravaged. The Uyghurs have offered periodic armed resistance over many years to Chinese state policies that have crippled Uyghur autonomy and culture. The resistance, armed or peaceful, has been episodic and largely suppressed by police but has not disappeared as the Uyghurs continue to react strongly to Beijing's efforts to Sinicize them.

Their fear is hardly unfounded: as a means of exerting control over an "unruly" minority, Beijing has deliberately stimulated a massive flow of Han Chinese to migrate into Xinjiang province; these migrants are part of a relentless push to overwhelm the Uyghurs, who will eventually be swamped in a rising tide of Han settlers moving into the Uyghur homeland. Over time, ten million Uyghur will have little ability to preserve their identity and culture in the face of over 1.2 billion Han Chinese in China. At some point, Uyghur culture may become little more than a quaint tourist attraction and a museum piece from the past. And China was quick to take advantage of the Global War on Terror to proclaim that the Uyghur separatists are part of the same terrorism network that Washington is fighting.

It is evident that, as elsewhere in today's world, Beijing's problems are really not with Islam at all, but with ethnic minorities, especially when their unique ethnic identity is reinforced by a distinctive religion as well. We see this, for example, with the Muslim Uyghurs and Buddhist Tibetans and Mongols; this double distinction increases their determination to preserve their cultural existence under some form of autonomy.

Beijing knows that its own future power in Asia depends on close working relations with Muslim states and peoples, including the all-vital energy sector that lies primarily in Muslim hands from Xinjiang to the Caspian Sea. The chances are that the "bloody borders of Islam" is not at all an active working assumption for the leadership of Beijing, even as it seeks to crush sparks of Uyghur or Tibetan separatism, resistance, or violence. A tiny *jihadist* minority will probably seek to continue the struggle in Xinjiang, but with only minor and diminishing impact as China gradually and quietly extirpates the Uyghurs as a distinctive autonomous society.

In most of the Muslim world, China is seen as an important and welcome counterpoise to the unlimited exercise of American power in the Muslim world. Only in regions closer to China, as in Central Asia, does China present a more ambiguous picture to Muslims, who are familiar with Chinese expansionism in the past and its ability to permanently "absorb" (drown) other cultures through sheer demographic weight. But even here, China and

Russia each serve as counterweights to each other, giving Muslims slightly greater breathing space.

It is clear, then, that diverse ethnicity in China is the particular problem, not Islam. Problems with these ethnic groups would not have been greatly different even without Islam. Chinese Han Muslims are essentially integrated and creatively forge links between Muslim and Chinese cultures. Those Muslims who are ethnically very distinct are fighting an essentially ethnic war of separation, albeit bolstered by their religious differences with China as well.

PART THREE

THE PLACE OF ISLAM
IN THE MODERN WORLD

CHAPTER TWELVE

Colonialism, Nationalism, Islam, and the Independence Struggle

This is the brief sketch of a long and poignant trajectory for Muslims: Muslim glory, gradual Muslim decline, the rise of the West, the takeover of the Muslim world by Western imperial powers, the anticolonial struggle, and contemporary resentments against Western neo-imperial policies of control and interventionism. This story lies at the heart of the Muslim world's confrontation with the West and the United States today. An understanding of this trajectory is essential to grasping the turmoil and anger that emerges from the Muslim world. It is a history of dissatisfactions based on real, concrete, and negative series of events in the Middle East and the Muslim world; the factor of Islam provides focus, color, and vigor but is not especially central to its telling.

I say "Muslim world," but in reality, the problems are not limited to a world defined by Islam. These states are part of a broader swath of the developing world with similar struggles and resentments in Africa, Asia, and Latin America. The problems stemming from colonialism and imperialism would exist in equal measure without Islam. But the presence of a *worldwide, self-conscious Muslim culture* undeniably helps focus Muslim grievances more intensely than anywhere else. Furthermore, the psychology of resistance has eventually come to be framed in a Muslim cultural and historical context. The Chinese, for example, maintain equal sensitivities on issues of Western domination but frame it within their own particular cultural narration and historical context.

MUSLIMS HAVE LONG BEEN CONFIDENT about their role in history— the accomplishments of high Islamic civilization surely suggested that God was smiling on the Islamic project. The explosive early success of the new religion was astonishing; it spread across half of Asia and North Africa within a few decades of the Prophet's death, culminating in the establishment of brilliant, durable cultures and empires. For many centuries, Muslims led most of the world in the arts, sciences, philosophy, military skills, and technology, demonstrating to its followers that something was very *right* about this flourishing civilization.

The one region of the then known world in which Islam had limited impact or contact was Western Europe. It was only as Western Europe as a latecomer began to hit its stride, with the rapid rise of nation-states after the Reformation and the Age of Exploration, that the balance began to shift between Western and Eastern civilizations. Muslim cultures and states had begun to lose their creative élan and to move into decline.

Muslims still agonize over this vivid reversal of roles with Western Europe: Why did it happen, what went wrong, and how can Muslims recover their place in the sun? Was it because they lost their Islamic values? This was a period that saw the rise of European power to challenge and then even take over the entire Muslim world, ultimately sparking Muslim resistance against it. These experiences form the foundation of Muslim anti-imperial psychology today.

The vigor of civilizations reveals well-known patterns of rise and fall, a phenomenon that has affected Islamic civilization as well. Religious Muslims tend to agonize over a possible loss of moral direction in the decline of their civilization, but there are indeed other more objective reasons that must also be cited in the relative decline of the East and the rise of the West. These factors have little to do with Islam and a great deal to do with political and geopolitical changes in the world, as well as other objective external factors. In short, if Islam had not existed, it seems very likely the course of most of these events would not have been significantly different. We witness, for example, civilizational exhaustion in cases like China in the late nineteenth century as well.

Cultural and Intellectual Factors

In its time, Islam was perhaps the most significant early proto-globalization movement. Expanding over a far greater area than the Roman Empire, it came to link vast regions of the known world through a common Islamic culture, where Arabic and Persian served as the lingua francas. Yet it was the waning of this universalist spirit that led to localization and atrophy of what was once an open and searching intellectual society. And even then, a struggle had always existed between a narrower, more legalistic interpretation of the faith and a broader, more civilizational one.

The death of Islamic intellectual vigor and curiosity—an exhaustion of civilizational élan without dramatic new intellectual input—led to the decline of creative thinking in Islamic theology, philosophy, science, and technology. Ritual and narrow legalism came to triumph over thought and inquiry in what passed for the study of Islam. Thinking ossified, inhibiting even the kind of historical scrutiny of Islam's own texts and sources of authority that was possible in earlier centuries. This atrophy of Muslim intellectual vigor was well demonstrated in the collapse of Muslim science and, possibly more damaging, in a general passivity toward later scientific and technological development in the West — until that same technology landed on the Muslim doorstep and overwhelmed it. Even in the face of the West's challenge, most Muslim reformers looked at the West primarily as a warehouse of technological hardware, without grasping the need for the all-important cultural and intellectual software that made it all function.

Important external geopolitical factors played a major role in the decline of the Muslim world as well. The savage Mongol conquests erupting out of the Mongolian steppes in the thirteenth century obliterated the cream of the great Muslim urban centers — dozens of cities, along with their libraries, populations, and wealth — a blow from which they never fully recovered. Then the emergence of a Shi'ite state in Iran in the sixteenth century physically divided the Sunni Muslim world, complicating the once-ready communication and trade among Sunni Muslims across Eurasia. In a massive paradigm shift, with the rise of the new European nation-states and their maritime capabilities, trade between the Mediterranean and the Orient shifted away from land routes to the sea. Muslim kingdoms had long maintained a monopoly on overland trade, making it difficult for the West to participate directly in trans-Asian commerce. The appearance of the Black Death from Asia in the eastern Mediterranean in the early fourteenth century further dampened Western enthusiasm for the land route. Thus began a search for sea access to the East that would eliminate the hazards and difficulties of overland travel.

The development of new sea routes to the Orient was based on new maritime technologies. Western use of these technologies rode on the accomplishments of earlier centuries of Arab and Muslim seafaring skills, their broad exploration of the Indian Ocean, detailed map-making, use of the compass, and boat construction suitable for the open seas. These advanced maritime skills led to the momentous "discovery" of the New World. Europe's growing focus on the development of maritime trade across the Atlantic opened a new chapter in global history that immensely enriched Europe, spurred further European exploration of East Asia, and largely marginalized the role of Muslim seafarers who had once dominated Asian trade.

Important environmental changes powerfully affected the rise and fall of civilizations as well. Jared Diamond has suggested that the Fertile Crescent, long a cradle of civilization, essentially began to fail as deforestation, desiccation, and subsequent diminution of its natural and animal resources gradually caused the region to decline. For long periods after the fall of Rome, Western Europe had still contributed little to the overall development of world civilization until the late Middle Ages. Meanwhile, Europe's moderate climate, fertile land, and prolific flora and fauna, coupled with new civilizational energy, drove the eventual emergence of a new and powerful West European civilization, built on the successes and accomplishments of past Eastern societies whose environments had become far less productive.

Jeffrey Sachs, at the Harvard University Center for International Development, also points out the impact of climatic and ecological shifts: while Europe possessed a temperate climate, the Middle East was marked by growing aridity: "By 1900, at the final collapse of the Ottoman Empire, Europe had coal, hydropower, lumber, and iron ore. The Islamic countries had few stocks of these nineteenth-century necessities for industrialization. The oil fields were discovered and exploited only after the Europeans had seized colonial control." The urban record tells the story. In 800 CE, the Middle East and Western Europe both had roughly equal populations of around thirty million each. But the Middle East had thirteen cities with populations of over fifty thousand, while Europe had only one — Rome. By 1600, the balance had shifted dramatically.

European maritime exploration of the East and the New World laid the foundations for a long-term European presence along the seacoasts to Asia, where they first created entrepôts, then colonial outposts, and eventually colonial control and empires. Portugal, Spain, Holland, France, and England succeeded each other in establishing these outposts. While much of the eastern Mediterranean remained a Muslim lake, the Western imperial reach was opening an age of imperialism that would last many centuries. Europeans negotiated and fought with each other over rival claims, but, in the end, these imperial acquisitions took on de jure character—at least among themselves, even if not for their imperial subjects.

By the end of World War I, nearly the entire Muslim world had fallen under European imperial control—the inner desert fastnesses of Saudi Arabia and much of Afghanistan being the sole exceptions. And most European powers played in the overseas imperial game: Portugal, Spain, Holland, France, Britain, Germany, Belgium, and Italy. Although their imperial styles would differ considerably, all were resented and all were resisted by their colonized subjects.

It would be misleading, of course, to suggest that colonialism and imperialism are strictly Western phenomena, or constitute uniquely Western sins. After all, empires have long been part of the normal political order over most of the world, at various times. But several important features distinguish Western colonialism: first, it entailed *sea voyages* by Europeans over considerable distances to establish its imperial points of control abroad, which were inhabited by people ethnically and culturally utterly distinct. Europeans usually imported Christian missionaries into the areas they took over as part of the softening-up process. This mode of imperialism contrasts sharply with almost all non-European empires, which were land empires, hence *contiguous* empires, formed through gradual, incremental expansion. Expanding imperial land powers were well familiar with their newly acquired contiguous imperial regions and had often interacted with them in territorial give-and-take for centuries—sometimes as parts of cultural continuums.

Contiguous empires often extended only de facto political control. European imperialism tried to legalize these new forms of control through de jure imposition of legal, organic relationships between the imperial holdings and the metropole, and expected general European acknowledgment of the same; in some cases, such as Algeria and the Congo, France and Belgium formally annexed them. This imposed de jure control constituted a greater affront to local national sovereignty, as it seemingly received "legal" acknowledgment of the Western international order. While differing greatly in character, of course neither contiguous nor maritime imperial expansion is inherently any more virtuous.

Ultimately, the most destabilizing and thorny kind of imperialism entailed the actual settling of lands by foreigners—settler colonialism—who came in to live, take over land, and establish governmental rule over the native population, the net losers. These are the hardest kind of colonial situations to undo without real violence. Thus, we have witnessed huge tensions and bloodshed in such cases as South Africa, Southern Rhodesia (Zimbabwe), Portuguese Angola, Algeria, and with Palestinian lands settled by European Jews in Israel.

Colonial Impact on Muslim Societies

Imperial rule quickly distorted the natural development of the Muslim world, dismantling traditional structures of leadership and governance, destroying traditional institutions, and upsetting cultural patterns, while failing to encourage organic development of native alternatives. Imperialism represented the wholesale export of foreign cultural instruments and structures to be imposed upon the East. Such foreign bodies are not often successfully grafted onto the earlier civilization. Muslim societies today are still haunted by the specter of foreign domination, even if that domination no longer takes classic colonial shape.

The European imperial governing structures were designed to represent first and foremost the economic, political, and strategic interests of the metropole and not the structural needs of broad national development of the colony. Appointed native rulers had little independent authority and were in place to keep the lid on and preserve the metropole's interests.

Under colonial rule, the position of the 'ulama was sharply downgraded. Islamic institutions linked to governance, especially the legal system, were weakened, limited, or abolished. 'Ulama were generally relegated to relatively minor aspects of governance, such as personal and family law. But the removal of the 'ulama from the governing and legal process dealt a severe blow to the ability of Islamic institutions to evolve and modernize under contemporary conditions. Local traditions of rule were unable to evolve organically, and Islamic institutions, once removed from the processes of daily governance, tended to wither and atrophy and could no longer keep pace with the demands of developing societies. This left behind an entire class of traditional governance, which would prove a source of resentment in the future as it struggled to find a new power relationship within the country after independence.

The Algerian case was especially egregious in its cultural impact. Algeria was formally annexed to France, and its choice lands settled by tens of thousands of Europeans. A whole new francophone administrative and ruling elite of Algerians emerged with intimate ties to the colonial authorities. Their own worldview began to incorporate large elements of French culture, and they gradually grew alienated from the Arab roots of the country. This elite ultimately came to constitute a built-in social time bomb. In principle, such acculturation into more technically and administratively advanced French society could have benefited Algeria, but after a brutal eight-year armed struggle for independence, the Frankified elite found itself in a highly ambivalent situation: were they more French, or Algerian? A broader question arises: is it a service to a society to educate its elite in an entirely different language than the rest of the country's population? If a linguistic difference is perpetuated to create a permanent cultural gap between the elite and the rest of the population, it will produce serious political and social conflicts when new native elites arise who are educated in their native Arabic and confront the old francophone elite in a power struggle. Language, and even culture, then becomes a divisive rather than uniting element. These issues have not yet been resolved in the agony of contemporary Algerian politics.

It was primarily the Ottoman Empire that managed to *preserve* the core of its sovereignty in the face of European encroachments during the nineteenth century. Not surprisingly, this was also where the most searching debates about the relationship of religion to the state took place—in a natural process of evolution within the Turkish cultural tradition. This is why Turkish political institutions today, despite a few stumbles, are vastly more stable, more "organic," than almost anywhere else in the Muslim world.

Elsewhere, however, European colonial rule essentially suspended Islamic institutions from any possibility of organic evolution within developing societies. This is one key explanation for the sclerotic and atrophied nature of many Islamic institutions today, which end up playing an obstructive role in the political evolution of the state, and creating socially emotional contradictions between traditional and Western ways of conducting business. A strong argument can be made that prevention of the "normal" evolution of Islam within the state has created dangerous tensions across much of the Muslim world and provided grist for increased radicalism among Islamist movements.

The same applies to colonial education policy: Islamic schooling was largely sidelined, thereby eliminating normal organic societal pressures for evolutionary change in the system to meet modern challenges. Significantly, in the Russian Empire, the Western challenge to the Muslim populations of the Caucasus and Central Asia did spark strong native efforts at education reform through the so-called *Jadidist,* or renewal, movement. Schooling advanced within many reformist segments of the Ottoman Empire as well.

From Imperial Enterprise to Decolonization

For Muslims today, there are few issues more burning than freedom from intrusive and neo-imperial policies of the West. In the US, the term "neo-imperialism" has a sort of Marxist ring to it, causing it to be dismissed out of hand by many as ideological jargon. Others may be particularly offended by the term "American imperialism," although there are a wealth of books and studies on the phenomenon produced in the United States over the past few decades. The terms were, of course, heavily used in Marxist, Communist, and Third World rhetoric during the Cold War. Communist embrace of the term nonetheless does not invalidate it: the West for at least four centuries did indeed exercise dominant imperial power over the rest of the world with great profit and relative impunity. The United States today is, by its own reckoning, the overwhelmingly dominant power of the globe in nearly all spheres, with the determination to impose its will by one means or another. That phenomenon is called by many "hegemony," or imperial power. Some neoconservative thinkers even openly embrace the concept of American Empire. But whatever the name, it's the phenomenon that matters.

The term "imperialism" cannot be far off the mark: even after the end of the formal age of Western imperialism, new forms of imperialism were introduced in the modern era, especially in the Middle East, starting with the pliant rulers selected by the British to dominate the newly "independent" governments of most states; these rulers were expected to be responsive to Western needs and preferences, even in the absence of support from their own people. Revolutions in Iran, Iraq, Egypt, and Syria, among others, ensued when the tensions between pro-Western rulers and their publics reached the breaking point and military coups against them occurred—in Egypt, Algeria, Libya, Tunisia, Jordan, Syria, Iraq, and Yemen. Since then, a majority of leaders in the Arab world and elsewhere are supported in power by the West, are not elected, and pursue pro-Western policies unpopular with the local population.

Neo-imperialism remains strong in the Muslim world for two reasons: because so much of the Muslim world possesses huge geostrategic importance due to energy sources and transportation routes, and precisely because it remains the last area where weak and pliable authoritarianism is the rule. Even though direct forms of foreign rule have long since faded, modern mechanisms include large US economic subsidies—particularly in the case of Egypt—use of loan mechanisms controlled by the United States from the World Bank, military sales, diplomatic support, the presence of military bases, regular political intervention, manipulation of regional policies as pressure points, military threats, and near silence on violations of civil liberties and human rights in these states.

All of these policies are ultimately counterproductive in that they stir anger within the countries in question, weaken the prestige of their rulers, and stimulate local radicalism and violence. This kind of long-term political and economic interventionism has taken on rawer form in the Middle East than in almost any other part of the world; since the beginning of the Global War on Terror, it has extended and deepened its roots, causing emotions to boil over and making extrication difficult.

Anti-Imperial Rebellion

Rebellion and struggle in the Muslim world against foreign domination actually came surprisingly *late* in the history of the anticolonial movement. Looking back, it was the Americas that first rose against their European masters of Britain, Spain, and Portugal. But these rebellions did not represent the struggle of native populations against European colonial rule, but rather rebellion *by European colonials* themselves resisting the heavy-handed controls of their own metropoles—quite different from later anticolonial struggles elsewhere in the world.

The next key phase of anticolonial or self-determination movements actually emerged from a series of *Christian* revolts in the Balkans against the Muslim Ottoman Empire in the nineteenth century. A key source of their success lay with the support of European powers and Russia, which were ready to back Christian revolts in order to whittle down the power and size of the Ottoman state, subvert it, and gain new clients in the region. The Christian character of these rebellions stands in stark contrast to the basic loyalty of the Muslim populations under Ottoman rule, who still perceived themselves as part of a legitimate multinational Islamic empire—regardless of whatever particular grievances they had with specific local policies of the empire. As a result, Muslim rulers developed anxieties over the susceptibility of Christian minorities to rebellion, especially at the beck and call of Western states. Indeed, one hundred and fifty years ago, Muslim leaders could have spoken with some accuracy of "the bloody borders of *Christianity*" in stirring up rebellion against the Ottoman Empire. The Ottoman Empire did face local periodic rebellions by Muslims as well, but it was far more limited.

For most of the Arab world, the collapse of the Ottoman Empire at the end of World War I did not spell "independence" for them at all. In a cruel turn of events, immediately after the war, European powers quickly took over most of the Arab world as "mandates" and placed them under imperial domination. Thus, successful rebellion against European imperialism by Muslims mainly took place as late as the twentieth century. (One major exception was the extensive Muslim involvement in the Indian mutiny against British colonial rule in India in 1857, and Afghan routing of British imperial ventures there.) The first Muslim state to achieve some kind of independence was Afghanistan in 1919. Iraq was next, but achieved only nominal independence from Britain in 1932; the British continued to fully dominate the Iraqi government and its policies via indirect rule and an unpopular military presence there for twenty-six more years. Most other Muslim states only achieved limited or nominal forms of independence, usually under pliable Western-selected rulers, and only after World War II. The fact that so many Muslim states achieved independence so relatively late helps account for the raw emotions still linked with anti-imperialism among Muslims today; meanwhile, neo-imperial Western political interference is still ongoing in quite intensive ways.

The Struggle for Independence:
Islam? Or Nationalism?

Resistance against foreign domination is a basic instinct in all cultures. And the colonial powers dominating the Muslim world differed from their subjects not only ethnically, but also religiously: a colonizing Christian West over a conquered Muslim East—or over a Hindu India or a Confucian/Buddhist China. Thus, resistance to imperial power naturally stresses both ethnic as well as religious differences with the imperial foreigner. Why would religion *not* be used as an important fault line, and, additionally, as a way to "sanctify" the ethnic resistance struggle? And monotheistic religions, with theological certainty about their revealed character, may represent the most potent religious force to combine with nationalism.

Indeed, religion can sometimes be a more effective rallying force than mere ethnicity since it appeals to a higher power—at least for a certain interval, until the blood ties of ethnicity surpass it. Not surprisingly, then, Islam was regularly pressed into service in the anti-imperial struggle. But the issue was anticolonial resistance and not religious war. It was on a country-by-country ethnic basis rather than a cohesive transnational religious movement. Nor should we forget that the anticolonial resistance of Muslims was part of a broad, global, anticolonial movement that included Christians, Buddhists, Hindus, Confucianists, and others against European domination.

One of the outstanding sources of resistance to imperial power in the Muslim world came from Sufi groups. While Sufi brotherhoods are generally known for a more quietist and mystic approach to Islam, they traditionally rank among the best organized and most coherent groupings in society. They constitute ready-made organizations—social-based NGOs, if you will—for maintaining Islamic culture and practices under periods of extreme oppression and for fomenting resistance and guerrilla warfare against foreign occupation. The history of Sufi participation in dozens of liberation struggles is long and widespread across Asia, the Middle East, and Africa. Sufi groups were prominent in the anti-Soviet resistance, and later against the American occupation in Afghanistan and against US occupation forces in Iraq. But it would be a mistake to consider Islam as the *source* of the resistance; otherwise, we would have to believe that if these Muslims were not Muslim, they would not be rebelling against foreign domination.

Closer to home in the West, the entire Black Muslim movement in the US, beginning in the 1930s, reveals the deliberate use of religion to intensify existing social distinctions against the white oppressor. In the early twentieth century, black nationalist leaders in America, led by Elijah Muhammad and later Malcolm X, urged African-Americans to escape their "slave mentality" by adopting Islam, a religion allegedly closer to their African roots. African-Americans were already divided from the white population by *race;* Elijah Muhammad would now reinforce the struggle by seeking to promote distinctive *religious* identity as well.

Meanwhile, the West itself has never shrunk from employing anti-imperial Islamist movements to its own ends. During the Cold War, Washington viewed the Muslim peoples of the USSR as the "soft underbelly of Soviet power," potentially exploitable against Moscow. Washington, often in collusion with pro-US dictators, encouraged Islamists in many countries to struggle against local communist parties. The best-known case, of course, is US support for the *mujahideen* in Afghanistan—a group famously described by President Ronald Reagan as the "moral equivalent of America's Founding Fathers"—in the struggle against the Soviet occupation in the 1980s. In most cases, however, Muslims have not needed a lot of external support from outsiders to push back against outside imperial ventures.

Why the Expanding Role of Muslim Identity?

Every individual carries multiple identities: family, clan, region, ethnicity, nationality, religion, gender, language, class, income, profession, avocation. These various identities intertwine, come and go, operate during different phases of our daily life: family and clan are prominent during ritual ceremonies, celebrations, and support networks; political identity during elections; national identity during military service; religious identity during times of solemn passage-of-life ceremonies; professional identity during times of professional work and associations; gender identity in the presence of the opposite sex, and for females when facing

discrimination. Class solidarities can briefly overcome even ethnicity in periods of economic hardship and collective bargaining.
Differing circumstances evoke differing identity responses.

A Jew in liberal Berlin in 1920, if asked his or her identity,
might say, "German, professor of biology, socialist, Jew," in that
order. Fifteen years later, under Nazism, the Jewish identity would
take on the overwhelmingly urgent priority of a life-or-death character. An Iraqi Sunni in a Shi'ite Baghdad neighborhood during
the US occupation might find the Sunni identity to be a life-or-
death matter, while *Iraqi* identity mattered little. Religious identity
alone mattered in Bosnia in 2001, even where everyone's political
background and language were virtually identical; but the religious identity had not been very significant ten years earlier in
Tito's Yugoslavia.

At a time when the whole Muslim world is felt to be under
siege, the Muslim identity has often become paramount for most
Muslims. Muslims in Malaysia watch Palestinians being killed on
TV, Kashmiris watch Chechens, Nigerians watch Iraqis, Afghans
watch Somalis. Most other identities lose importance when communities are dominated by violence and the Global War on Terror. But this is not the normal state of affairs. The excessive
prominence of the Muslim identity over other elements of identity
primarily emerges in times of hardship. Islam then becomes an
expanded and international rallying cry. But, in fact, most struggles are local and ethnic. A key goal of Western policy must be to
allow these regions to calm down, allow life to return to a more
normal state, free of the provocative presence of foreign military
forces, which will allow the Muslim aspect of identity to subside to
its customary place as one of many competing characteristics of
an individual's life. During most times in their lives, Muslims have
many other things to think about than simply being Muslim.

When communities are obliged to protect themselves against
others, they seek to forge common ground against outsiders. This

is the context in which we have to view contemporary Islamic identity. Fifty years ago in the Middle East, nationalism loomed far larger than Islam as a rallying force. Yet today the implications of being Muslim may matter more on the global scale than at any other time in history. Muslims who seek to rally public support against external intervention will turn to whichever banner will unite more people most effectively.

When Arabs finally broke with the multiethnic Ottoman Empire at the end of World War I, Islam obviously played *no role* in the event; it was, after all, a Muslim versus Muslim struggle. When the conflict entailed Arab versus Turk, only ethnicity could serve as a rallying cry, not Islam. Ethnic nationalism achieved prominence in the Arab world, for example, under Egypt's Gamal Abdul Nasser in the 1950s and 1960s as the basis of resistance against European intervention and neo-imperialism. But in the face of the ultimate weaknesses of the Arab nationalist movement, nationalism became discredited as a force and the Islamic identity took its place — a stage that has not yet ended.

After watching the horrors of ethnically driven nationalism and war across the globe in the nineteenth and twentieth centuries, we might well ask whether ethnicity is, in fact, the most enlightened foundation for the creation of borders. Or is some sort of multiethnic order perhaps a "higher" form of social organization? Certainly the immigrant societies of the United States, Canada, Australia, and New Zealand have come to believe that multiethnic orders foster greater tolerance than ethnically based ones. But then, those immigrant states had few other options.

In the Muslim world, there is no conviction that ethnicity invariably provides the best basis for social and political organization. Islam itself instinctively abhors the forces of nationalism as narrow and divisive, even while acknowledging that differences are also enriching. "O humankind! We have created you male and female, and made you nations and tribes, that you may know one another" (Qur'an 49:13). From the perspective of Islam, it is better to aspire to unity under the banner of religion, since it will embrace a vastly broader swath of mankind, and no one is ever excluded from becoming a Muslim if he or she wishes. Thus, to seek solidarity within Islam is a higher concept than solidarity within a given ethnicity. And in terms of a rallying cry, Islam operates very effectively when it comes to a struggle against *non*-Muslims.

Many Islamists were therefore hostile to ideas of Arab nationalism, perceiving the very concept of "nationalism" to be a baleful and divisive Western creation. Indeed, their worst fears were fulfilled in the case of Turkey. The founder of the modern Turkish state, successor to the Ottoman Empire, Mustafa Kemal Atatürk, crushed nearly all independent instruments of Islamic power in the new Turkish nationalist state and adopted an unfriendly attitude toward Turkey's Muslim neighbors and toward Islam in general. Worst of all for devout Muslims, he abolished the very office of the caliphate, the nominal leader of Islam for all Sunni Muslims—tantamount to an Italian prime minister deciding impulsively to abolish the papacy. An Islamic world divided by nationalist differences is seen as impotent against an interventionist West.

In this sense, then, Western wars that are heavily perceived to be directed against Islam, as in the Global War on Terror, are guaranteed to inflate the role of Islam and to push Muslim solidarity to abnormal levels.

The Tragic Legacies of Imperialism for Muslims

The arbitrary redrawing of borders by the colonial powers, along lines designed to meet their specific national needs or rivalries with other colonial powers, was one of the most damaging aspects of colonial rule. Ethnic groups were often divided up, natural lines of political and social symbiosis were severed, arbitrary lines of new administration were established. Had Arabs been left to their own devices, there might be fewer Arab states in existence today: we might still see a historically familiar region such as Greater Syria, encompassing today's Syria, Lebanon, Jordan, and Palestine. Ruling these newly created artificial countries, especially after so-called independence, became much more problematic for Arab leaders. "Loyalty" to the newly created states was artificial, and border disputes were a natural outcome, as were ethnic struggles and interventions by divided peoples to reunite. Political development was to proceed primarily in accordance with the imperial needs of states often thousands of miles away.

Economic development was skewed to become complementary to that of the metropole, rather than meeting the needs of holistic economic development of the state itself. The metropoles undoubtedly did invest in the infrastructure in most of their colonies, but this was directed at serving the needs of the metropole; regional development was largely ignored. Railways in Africa, for example, ran from raw material resources to coastal entrepôts in Africa, but rarely linked one state with another. And in cultural terms, the metropole stamped each of these colonies with a new, arbitrary cultural character, favoring certain ethnic groups and languages over others, often in conformity with their pliability toward the metropole's policies. All of this left damaging political, economic, social, and psychological time bombs, which continue to explode and produce internal tensions that will take a long time to resolve.

Joseph Stiglitz, a chief economist of the World Bank and Nobel Prize winner, characterizes the problem:

> Colonialism left a mixed legacy in the developing world—but one clear result was the view among people there that they had been cruelly exploited.... The political independence that came to scores of colonies after World

War II did not put an end to economic colonialism. In some regions, such as Africa, the exploitation — the extraction of natural resources and the rape of the environment, all in return for a pittance — was obvious. Elsewhere it was more subtle. In many parts of the world, global institutions such as the International Monetary Fund and the World Bank came to be seen as instruments of post-colonial control. These institutions pushed market fundamentalism ("neoliberalism," it was often called), a notion idealized by Americans as "free and unfettered markets."...Free-market ideology turned out to be an excuse for new forms of exploitation.

Above all, the Muslim world's oil and energy resources have been a key driver for incessant Western intervention over ownership of the oil, control of the oil companies, pricing policies and shares of prices, political manipulation of leaders in order to obtain the best deals on oil, and political and armed intervention. The first democratically elected Prime Minister of Iran was overthrown by the United States and the United Kingdom in 1958 in order to prevent Iranian nationalization of oil. Oil politics remain a very dangerous high-risk game, played out among the great powers on Muslim world soil, and beyond.

Anti-Colonial Radicalism and Islam

Imperialism invariably engenders anti-imperialist reactions. Anti-imperial movements have embraced varying ideologies at different times to attain their ends. After World War II, it was leftist nationalist ideology that dominated the ideological scene in the Middle East. Nasser's nationalist message from Egypt still has a familiar ring: denunciation of Western intervention in the Middle East, a demand for Muslims to exercise sovereign control over their own energy resources, the elimination of Western military bases in the Middle East, and a call for a just solution to the running sore of the dispossessed Palestinians.

We forget that in the 1950s and 1960s, it was Arab *nationalism* that was viewed as the predominant threat to Western interests in the Middle East, stimulating the United States and Britain into covert operations to overthrow leaders in Iran and Syria and to manipulate the Egyptian political scene. (The United States disastrously continues to believe, into the twenty-first century, that it can ignore and override Arab, or other, nationalisms—which is what crises with Iraq and Syria have been all about.) And in an earlier time, as astonishing as it may seem today, the US and UK often identified the Islamists as the weapon with which to weaken Arab nationalist leadership and local Soviet interests.

The United States, in particular, never shrank from regular overthrow of unfriendly regimes by covert operations or outright military intervention in country after country, in order to maintain regimes favorable to it. The list is stunning: Korea (1950–1953), Iran (1953), Guatemala (1954), Costa Rica (1955), Syria (1957), Indonesia (1958), Dominican Republic (1960), Peru (1960), Ecuador (1960), Congo (1960), Vietnam (1961–1973), Cuba (1961), Brazil (1964), Chile (1972), Angola (1975), Nicaragua (1981), Lebanon (1982–1984), Grenada (1983), Panama (1989), Iraq/Gulf (1991), Somalia (1993), Bosnia (1994–1995), Kosovo (1999), Afghanistan (2001–to present) and Iraq (2003–to present).

Washington funded the Muslim Brotherhood opposition to Nasser in Egypt in the late 1950s and engaged the Saudis to do the same. It also worked with the Brotherhood to help overthrow a pro-Nasser regime in Yemen in 1962. Support may have extended to Indonesian Muslim movements as well. Israel itself played the same game: in the 1960s Israel released the Hamas leader Shaykh Ahmad Yassin from prison and funded Islamist Hamas as an instrument to play against the Arab nationalist Palestine

Liberation Organization (PLO) under the leadership of Yasir Arafat, in the foolish belief that the Islamists would be more manageable than the nationalists. Israel then returned in 2004 to assassinate Shaykh Yassin.

The United States bears some responsibility in artificially skewing the strength and role of differing ideological movements in the Muslim world, and has created legacies that have come back to haunt it. If Islam had not been available, Washington would have found other ideological forces to weaken or destroy radical nationalist movements of the period.

Arab nationalists were not alone in their resistance. An entire cohort of nationalist leaders emerged midcentury, creating in 1955 the Non-Aligned Movement (NAM), which positioned itself as a "third force" between the Soviet Union and Western camps during the Cold War. Its leaders galvanized the developing world in a call to stand up for sovereign rights against the neo-imperial Western forces that still sought strategic domination. Washington perceived the entire NAM as a threat, since the movement did indeed tilt toward the USSR against Western imperialism.

The platform of the Non-Aligned Movement, set forth in the Havana Declaration of 1979, called for preserving "the national independence, sovereignty, territorial integrity and security of non-aligned countries" in their "struggle against imperialism, colonialism, neo-colonialism, racism, Zionism, and all forms of foreign aggression, occupation, domination, interference or hegemony as well as against great power and bloc politics." Nearly *two-thirds* of the member countries of the United Nations became members of the NAM. From today's perspective, the language of this statement still rings true.

(Israelis, of course, had every reason to view the NAM as anti-Israel, and indeed it was. NAM opposition to Israel, however, was based not on anti-Semitism, but on opposition to an exclusivist Jewish nationalist ideology that supported the creation of a Zionist state designed only for Jews at the expense of three-quarters of a million Palestinian refugees who lost their homes and lands. For the Muslim world and many other Third World states, the strong backing of the creation of Israel by the West also raised fears that Israel was meant to be a creature of the West, deliberately implanted into the heart of the Middle East to dominate it. Subsequent events did little to overcome these suspicions.)

The Palestinian problem is a key case in demonstrating the irrelevance of Islam to the roots of the issue. Islam has nothing whatsoever to do with the creation of the Palestinian problem and the origins of the Arab-Israeli crisis. The Palestinian problem began with the immigration into Palestinian lands of Jews from Eastern Europe, slowly at first, later much more rapidly, with huge funding from Western Jewry, in the nineteenth and early twentieth centuries. The new Zionist movement emerged at a time of other exclusivist ethnonationalist movements in Europe such as those among Italians, Germans, Hungarians, Slavs, Turks, and others; Jews, furthermore, had every reason for seeking an exclusivist nationalist/religious movement in view of the longstanding discrimination against them in Europe and especially in Eastern Europe. Palestinians became increasingly worried about this huge influx of European settlers in their midst, however, as it became clear that Zionist ideology foresaw all of Palestine becoming the new Jewish homeland.

The crime of the Holocaust, which lay entirely on European shoulders, was the final push for Jews to go to Palestine, supported by guilty Europeans. Three-quarters of a million Palestinians were ultimately displaced in Israeli operations of ethnic cleansing and intimidation as the foundation of the new Jewish state was attained. Palestinians bitterly resent being asked to pay the price for European sins. If there had never been an Islam, Christian Palestinians would have no more happily lost their lands to Jews, or refrained from guerrilla actions to get them back. Indeed,

Palestinian Christians have been prominent among the guerrilla movements against Israel. Although this Palestinian-Jewish ethnic clash has eventually taken on religious overtones on both sides in recent years, Islam had nothing to do with its origins.

Indeed, Palestinian movements have passed through three distinct phases in their evolving ideological metamorphosis: an Arab nationalist phase, a Marxist-Leninist phase, and, finally, an Islamist phase. Yet each of them had as a goal the same independent Palestinian state. The Palestinian cause remained the same, but the ideological vehicle kept changing—shifting ideologies for permanent grievances.

All these events dramatically demonstrate the passions that lie behind the policies and sensitivities of the developing world's nations in their search for genuine sovereignty. The Muslim world is just one more part of that movement. And Islam functions as just one more vehicle, or banner, with which to oppose Western interventionism. If there were no Islam, the anti-imperial grievances would be no less, and the resistance no less; but the resistance movement might be deprived of the additional emotional and ideological power of Islam now coupled with nationalism.

As long as the invaders, occupiers, or oppressors are non-Muslim, Islam will invariably be invoked, along with nationalism, in the struggle against them.

CHAPTER THIRTEEN

War, Resistance, *Jihad*, and Terrorism

Probably no other region of the world has endured such intense and sustained intervention from the West than the Middle East. There are several major reasons: its immediate proximity to the West—a West that later developed powerful expansionist impulses; the attraction of the Middle East's huge energy resources and its related massive financial influence; and its strategic location for millennia as an East-West crossroads in international geopolitics. We saw in the last chapter the impact of colonialism, imperialism, and neo-imperialism over several centuries and the intensification of US interventionism in the present.

The cumulative anger, frustration, and radicalism that this history of intervention has produced are abundantly evident. The question perhaps is not how 9/11 could have happened, but instead, why didn't it happen sooner? As radical Middle East groups articulate their grievances in our globalized age, why should we be surprised that they ultimately carry their struggle to the heart of the West? It takes little brilliance, then, to have anticipated some kind of pushback, resistance, a sharp or even violent response to long-term Western actions. It is particularly disingenuous for the

West at this point to turn around and speculate on what is wrong with the Muslim world, or with Islam, that the West should be witnessing a violent response from the Muslim world. It borders on obtuseness or willful ignorance not to acknowledge any impact or role of its own policies over the last two centuries or more in stimulating the range of current responses from the Muslim world.

Nor should the use of violence be surprising. When situations deteriorate, is it moderates, or radicals, who tend to respond first? In this sense Usama bin Ladin is the canary in the cage of the Middle East mineshaft—his early violent actions suggest that conditions are going badly awry in the Middle East. If real radicals are taking up cudgels for the first time, how far behind are the more moderate forces, who share the same environment and misgivings? We already know that there is much tacit public sympathy, if not support, for bin Ladin in the Middle East, even while his methods are not fully condoned.

So it becomes analytically shaky to suggest that somehow Islam, *madrasas*, or radical ideology is the ultimate cause of the resistance. It is beyond doubt that religious or ideological factors play some role in helping crystallize and galvanize resistance and violent response, but they are not the actual *source* of the problem. Can we afford to confuse the vehicle for the problem? Or would we rather posit that the experiences of Muslims at the hands of the West over centuries wouldn't really have mattered all that much to its citizens if they hadn't happened to be Muslims?

Indeed, if Middle East resentments seek a vehicle by which to express them, why would they *not* settle upon religion, Islam? Religion and heresy are time-honored banners for the politics of resistance in the Middle East, going back to early Christianity, as we have already seen. Islam commands respect and authority, and provides a sense of righteousness to those who believe their cause is just—in this case, the self-defense of the nation or *umma* against outside intervention.

If not through Islam, how else might the Middle East formulate its resistance to the West? What would be the rallying cry? We have seen how Arab nationalism under Nasser's Egypt in the 1950s and 1960s was one such vehicle, but it was ultimately unsuccessful and a joint Anglo-French-Israeli military task force actually tried to overthrow him in the Suez crisis of 1956. Marxism-Leninism, too, enjoyed a heyday as an ideological vehicle but effected little change in the end. So Islamism, with its deep roots in the regional culture and the ability to stir up popular support in the name of the regional cause, is the most recent and most powerful ideological vehicle for action, at least for the foreseeable future.

When Russians object to the policies of the outside world against Russia, what is the vehicle of response to rally public support? When Stalin found himself under assault from the army of the Third Reich in World War II, he certainly knew that Marxism-Leninism could not stir the hearts of the people to resistance. He turned to Russian nationalism, and later, in desperation, ended up embracing the Orthodox Church itself as a rallying point, the symbol of Holy Mother Russia. The Japanese Empire prior to World War II sought a vehicle to gain Japanese public support for its expansionist and imperial policies in Asia; the sacred character of the Shinto religion and even forms of Buddhism were invoked to stir the Japanese soul. In Sri Lanka, the dominant Buddhist Sinhalese, in their struggle against the Hindu Tamil separatists, employed Buddhist monks to strengthen Sinhalese public support for the civil war. Hitler worked to gain church support for the German war effort. Even in the United States in times of war, most mainstream churches and clergy—Protestant, Catholic, and Jewish—are impressed into service to lend religious legitimacy to the national struggle.

In this context, then, it would seem exceptional if Islam would *not* be invoked in the struggle of Muslim peoples against Western

dominance—along with local nationalisms. These forces complement each other in the face of foreign threat.

Washington is understandably concerned that Islam is being
used as a powerful source of resistance and violent response to US
military actions. But could the United States realistically expect
the Middle East not to resist, to instead acquiesce to American
strategic goals? That is simply not going to happen; any expectation that it might suggests that policy makers are out of touch with
reality. (Empire is often out of touch with reality because it believes
it *creates* reality.) Thus, to examine the vehicle—in this case,
Islam—for flaws and problems, as if it were itself somehow the
source of the resistance problem, is to utterly miss the point. Or is
it a convenient way to deny the reality that others might have a
serious issue with what you are doing? This is again what the
Swiss scholar Tariq Ramadan calls "Islamizing the problem."

Robert Kaplan offers a slightly different take on this, arguing
that the Muslim component does bear some relevance to the issue.
His argument is worth hearing:

> The American ethnologist and orientalist Carleton Ste-
> vens Coon wrote in 1951 that Islam "has made possible the
> optimum survival and happiness of millions of human
> beings in an increasingly impoverished environment over
> a fourteen-hundred-year period." Beyond its stark, clearly
> articulated message, Islam's very militancy makes it attrac-
> tive to the downtrodden. It is the one religion that is pre-
> pared to fight. A political era driven by environmental
> stress, increased cultural sensitivity, unregulated urbaniza-
> tion, and refugee migrations is an era divinely created for
> the spread and intensification of Islam, already the world's
> fastest-growing religion. (Though Islam is spreading in
> West Africa, it is being hobbled by syncretization with ani-
> mism: this makes new converts less apt to become anti-

Western extremists, but it also makes for a weakened version of the faith, which is less effective as an antidote to crime.)

Kaplan's point indeed emphasizes that Islam is an effective rallying cry against foreign intervention. But even without Islam, we would expect violent reaction from most cultures under similarly stressful or violent conditions.

THE TELEVISION FOOTAGE of 9/11 produced iconic images for all time: the scale and daring of the operation, its ferocity, level of death, and the black smoke of destruction against a blue sky are riveting and shocking. But those images also tell different stories to different viewers.

For many Americans and some other Western viewers, the narrative is straightforward: the United States has been doing its best to try to preserve peace in the world, when it was savagely attacked out of the blue by fanatic killers. The event deserved swift punishment and the rooting out of all who might ever contemplate a similar act. Indeed, what is wrong with Muslim culture—some of them even allies—that it could produce such horrific actions? In short, history begins with 9/11.

But large numbers of others around the world, including some in the West itself, have come to read the events slightly differently. The attack was indeed shocking, outrageous, and a tragedy for the innocent civilians that died. But it should not have been a surprise. Given US policies in the Middle East and rising Muslim anger over such a long period of time over so many issues, it was inevitable that sooner or later some Muslims would strike back. History does not begin with 9/11, but has a very long prelude. The United States courts further such attacks as long as it maintains the same policies of global dominance and political and military

271

intervention, and builds reservoirs of anti-American feeling. As terrible as the events were, hopefully they may serve as a wake-up call to Washington to the seriousness of the situation and the need for reconsideration. This view is probably most common in the world anywhere outside the United States.

The Justness of the Cause

Most Muslims painfully acknowledge that their own societies are riddled with deep problems. But they also have little doubt about the justice of resisting Western dominance and even counterattacking if need be. Indeed, for a Muslim, or anyone else, to give one's life for a cause suggests that the cause is just and worthy. Yet this linkage of war and religion poses complex ethical problems in all major religious traditions. The Christian tradition of thinking about the moral foundations of war goes back at least to St. Augustine and poses a question that defies definitive response: what makes a war "just"? Traditional Western moral thinking about justice in war contained at least two distinct elements: the *reasons* for going to war, and the ethics of behavior *in* war. Classical Western thinking also sets forth various other criteria as well: on the *need* to go to war as opposed to *alternative* means for settlement of dispute; on the scope of war; the legitimacy of the authority that calls for war; the relative degree of justice of one's own cause; the proportionality of destruction to be inflicted; and the position of noncombatants, civilians, and civilian infrastructures in war.

To speak of ethics in war seems almost oxymoronic, when death and destruction lie at the heart of most military operations. And in absolute terms, of course, the taking of any life is immoral. But in war, ethical or moral principles are all relative: Whose justice? What kind of proportionality? How are limits set on inflicting civilian casualties? Who is right, and to what extent? Nearly all states in history that march off to war invariably claim—and generally believe—that justice is on their side in the face of an iniquitous enemy.

In democratic societies, the dilemma often grows: were the state to acknowledge any notions of moral ambiguity in the course of conflict, it would invite disaffection among its own troops and population and undermine the proclaimed absolute justice of the cause and its implementation. Hence the need to demonize the enemy and paint the struggle in black-and-white moral terms. Modern communication complicates the problem further when the course of a war can be viewed on television and the Internet from multiple perspectives. The administration of George W. Bush managed to impose serious (self)censorship upon American media in covering the bloody details of the Iraq War. Indeed, to Washington one of the great outrages of the Arab satellite station *al-Jazeera* was its regular, on-site, and graphic portrayal of the impact that bombing and combat were having on real people on the ground in real neighborhoods. Pictures of American dead, sometimes even civilian casualties, are often termed "obscene" in American media, partly in order to prevent them from being witnessed. And the acts that produced the pictures are likewise obscene. War is most easily fought when its human consequences remain distant, invisible, abstract.

Jihad

Theories of *jihad* and the extensive literature around it are the functional equivalent of Christian "just war" theory; the concept is designed to define and limit the actions of Muslims in war. *Jihad* is probably the most controversial and emotive word that the West associates with Islam today; not a day goes by in the media when the word is not invoked, either by *jihadis* themselves or critics of Islam. Many observers are impatient with examinations on the origins and use of the word, feeling it represents

273

little more than rationalization of the horrific character of the *jihadi* challenge to Western power, to peace and stability.

In the Qur'an and the Hadith, *jihad* has many meanings. The basic root of the word *jihad* in Arabic means "effort" or "struggle." It is widely used to refer to the struggle of the individual to live a virtuous life, to uphold religious values in one's personal life, to help propagate Islam through personal effort by way of personal example and promoting the Faith. In that context the word *jihad* for Muslims retains quite positive religious connotations of personal devotion toward betterment. It is also routinely used in colloquial Arabic simply to mean "I'll make an effort, do my best." That is the "great *jihad*," or personal *jihad*, as defined by the Prophet.

"Lesser *jihad*," as defined originally by the Prophet, came to refer to military efforts in a context of military struggle in which the key obligations were defense and preservation of Islam and the *umma*. Since the fledgling Muslim community in Medina was under siege from pagan forces from Mecca over repeated years of battle, the defense of the community was central to many Qur'anic revelations and personal concerns of the Prophet. But as the early Muslim community stabilized, it moved into a phase of military expansion. As Islam spread, it encountered other states and empires with which it fought for control over vast regions.

Islamic jurisprudence set forth lengthy rulings on rules of conduct in war, including the fact that women and children could not be targeted, that proportionality of force must be used, that civilian structures should not be gratuitously destroyed, that *jihad* must be declared by a legitimate ruler or head of state, and that warfare outside of the rules of *jihad* is not legitimate. The Prophet is on record for ordering his soldiers to "avoid harming women, children, the elderly, or people at temples and monasteries." The 'ulama in the Middle Ages, for example, debated whether it would be lawful to use catapults against enemy fortresses. Quite a few 'ulama found them unlawful, because such imprecise weapons could harm civilians as well as soldiers.

Just as Christian doctrines of morality in warfare have been abused on the ground, so, too, have Islamic precepts. "Collateral damage," a terrifying clinical euphemism designed to distance us from the human dimension of civilian deaths, has been routinely adopted in the United States. And of course, during World War II, the firebombing of Hamburg and Dresden, and the first use of nuclear weapons in history against Hiroshima and Nagasaki, were directed almost exclusively against civilian populations in a demonstration of "shock and awe."

As von Clausewitz pointed out, war is fueled by emotion, which always outruns intent. Once the conflict begins, hatred is ratcheted up on both sides, atrocity generates counteratrocity in an endless upward spiral of mindless violence.

Jihad in its more modern usage has been applied to many quite secular tasks, just as the term "crusade" in English is casually applied to fighting crime or a campaign against drugs. The Hindu leader Mahatma Gandhi's anti-British struggle was referred to as *jihad* in Arabic, as was the secularist President Habib Bourgiba's campaign for national economic development in Tunisia. *Jihad* has been applied by some women to the struggle for women's liberation or by others to a struggle for a just moral and social order. But the term has primarily been applied to those engaged in both defense of Muslim lands against the West and offensive operations against numerous Western states, especially those involved in military operations in the Muslim world. Indeed, some Wahhabis and zealous Salafis even invoke the term, erroneously, to justify fighting against Shi'a.

Over time, defense and offense became increasingly conflated, and the concept of *jihad* began to be used extensively to refer to warfare in Muslim military campaigns. Muslim states often warred with other Muslim states, in which the spread of Islam was obviously quite irrelevant to the struggle. Indeed the "Mahdi," the rebel leader in nineteenth-century Sudan, called his rebellion against the Ottoman Empire a *jihad,* and he called for the death of all Turks. The Wahhabis declared *jihad* against virtually all non-Wahhabi Muslims. So the term has been used and abused heavily over the centuries, and has come into its own again today in the resistance against the Western forces in the Muslim world.

Some extreme radical groups have now appropriated the Qur'anic concept even for war against their own domestic political opponents within the Muslim world. Some radicals declare *jihad* to be the "sixth pillar" of Islam alongside the traditional five (prayer, almsgiving, pilgrimage, and so on). Whatever the name, it is important to note that international law does justify armed resistance by a people against invading or occupying foreign military forces.

The concept of *jihad* has now achieved a perfect symbiosis with Western interventionism: they have both created a self-reinforcing two-way belligerence, a kind of codependency of violence, each justifying the other. Furthermore, the study of *jihad* has become a cottage industry in the United States, largely dominated by committed partisans on both sides, who passionately debate the nature of the problem. The bulk of these studies seek out various pathologies of Middle Eastern and Muslim cultures, and Islam itself, to justify the struggles; *jihad* becomes a key source of the "problem" rather than the symptom or expression.

There is no question that extreme radical and violent groups have abused the term *jihad,* along with their extreme interpretations of Islam, to promote hatred of the West in times of conflict. We will discuss elements of that later. But is it credible to believe that if the concept of *jihad* did not exist, that the Muslim world would not then be carrying out guerrilla warfare against the West? After all, the US attack against Saddam Hussein was a purely secular affair and the earliest signs of resistance were from Ba'thist and nationalist forces who had nothing to do with Islam or *jihad*. Yet *jihad* later became central to most of the response of the Iraqi opposition to the US war and occupation. Here again, we confuse the Islamic vehicle for the source of the problem.

Just Authority and Usama bin Ladin

The question of *jihad* emerged again with the stationing of American troops in Saudi Arabia during the first Gulf War to liberate Kuwait. Classical Islamic law devotes great consideration to the legality of a Muslim ruler cooperating with *non-Muslims* to kill other Muslims. Any such cooperation is limited to some quite specific situations and requires narrow treaty terms; in the case of Saudi Arabia, the Saudi ʿulama finally agreed to permit US forces on Saudi soil on a strictly temporary basis for the purposes of defending the kingdom against possible invasion by Iraq, with the understanding that these troops would depart once the conflict was over. In any event, US troops did not depart at the end of the war, which the ʿulama saw as a violation of the agreement, but most dared not raise the issue against the Saudi state. Usama bin Ladin and large numbers of clerics and citizens did raise it, however, and the issue occupied a significant part of one of bin Ladin's early denunciations of US military policies in the region. As he stated in an interview with Robert Fisk of the *Guardian* in 1996:

> When the American troops entered Saudi Arabia, the land of the two holy places [Mecca and Medina], there was a strong protest from the ʿ*ulama* [religious authorities] and from students of the *Shariʾa* law all over the country against the interference of American troops....
>
> ...The ordinary man knows that his country is the largest oil producer in the world, yet at the same time he is suffering from taxes and bad services. Now the people understand the speeches of the ʿ*ulama* in the mosques—that

our country has become an American colony. They act decisively with every action to kick the Americans out of Saudi Arabia....

Ultimately, all Muslims will unite in the fight against America....I believe that sooner or later the Americans will leave Saudi Arabia and that the war declared by America against the Saudi people means war against all Muslims everywhere. Resistance against America will spread in many, many places in Muslim countries.

We do not have to accept bin Ladin's interpretation of events to realize he was making a credible legal case to the Saudi public and other Muslims against the legitimacy of foreign troops on Saudi soil. But this is how bin Ladin began to build his larger case, starting with the US military presence in Saudi Arabia, and then proceeding to broaden the scope of his attacks. His case obviously achieved huge prominence in the Muslim world after 9/11 and the resulting Global War on Terror, which strengthened the desire among the disillusioned and the zealots to turn to terrorism and suicide bombing. There is little of Islam in here except the rhetoric, while there is a great deal of geopolitics and nationalistic perception of the Saudi-Muslim interest.

But that is the language of al-Qa'ida, an extremist *jihadi* organization, whose religious credentials lack the authority of established institutions. Look at a totally mainstream religious institution, the Islamic Research Academy at Al-Azhar University in Cairo—as establishment as it can get. On the eve of the US attack on Iraq on March 11, 2003, it issued a statement that has the weight of a *fatwa:* it

called upon Muslims to unify their efforts and join forces in facing this illegitimate and aggressive war...represented by the military troops armed with the most powerful and dangerous weapons of destruction.... Our Arab and Islamic *ummah* (nation) and even our religious belief (Islam) are undoubtedly the main goal of these military troops, whose targets will be millions of the members of our *ummah* as well as our belief, sacred places and all sources of power and wealth that Arabs and Muslims possess. The first stage to achieve these goals is to attack Iraq and occupy its land and seize its abundant reserve of oil wealth.... The Academy hails and backs the resolution of the Islamic Summit, which rejected an attack on Iraq and stressed the necessity of resorting to peaceful means in solving the crisis.... In light of all the current events, most people think that attacking Iraq is inevitable. According to Islamic Shari'ah, jihad becomes an individual duty (*fard 'ayn*) upon all Muslims if the enemy occupies a Muslim land. Our Arab and Muslim *ummah* will face a new inhumane campaign that aims to deprive us of our land, belief, honor, and dignity.... The Academy calls upon all Arabs and Muslims not to surrender to prospective attacks, as Allah has guaranteed to render His religion victorious.

In November 2004, twenty-six highly prominent Saudi religious scholars and professors at Saudi universities issued a *fatwa* denouncing the war in Iraq. After discussing the need to first search for peace, their statement said:

> There is no doubt that *jihad* against the occupiers is a requirement for every able person. It is a defensive *jihad* that falls under the category of fighting the aggressor. In this case the conditions are different than initiating *jihad* and pursuing it. You don't have to have a general leadership. You should have that only when it is feasible (Fear Allah as much as you can). Without a doubt the occupiers

are aggressors and all divine laws permit fighting them until they leave humiliated, God willing. Additionally, all man made laws recognize the right of nations to resist. The original permission for *jihad* was granted for this reason, when Allah said "Permission to fight is given to those who are fighting because they have been wronged, and surely, Allah will grant them victory" [Al-Hajj, Verse 39]. Allah has decreed that fighting one another is natural where it guarantees the protection of life or when it upholds justice and the power of the Shari'ah. So resistance is not only a legitimate right, but a religious duty that obliges the Iraqi people to defend themselves and defend their honor, land, oil, their present and their future against this colonial coalition as they once before resisted their British occupiers.

Even the cautious and conservative Shi'ite Ayatollah Sistani in Iraq has issued rulings that it is legal to fight American troops in Iraq in self-defense. These are but a handful of the multiple rulings and *fatwas* that have emerged in the context of this war, setting forth careful legal briefs on the permissible Islamic conditions for *jihad* and war. Resistance against an invader anywhere is natural; providing legal Islamic justification further bolsters the case.

Motivations for Terrorism

Acts of terrorism and suicide operations have now entered into the Western vocabulary of Muslim actions in the context of war. The United States had, of course, encountered Japanese kamikaze missions in World War II against its battleships. But it is a truism that terrorism is the weapon of the weak; as Shaykh Ahmad Yassin of Hamas once commented, if the Palestinians had had fighter aircraft and high-altitude bombers, those would be the weapons of choice. British troops in North America during the Revolutionary War accused American irregular forces of illegal actions when they engaged in guerrilla operations rather than frontally face crack British military formations. And so the United States today seeks to confine war to standard military operations in which it obviously enjoys the overwhelming advantage; it simultaneously condemns those irregular operations that play to Muslim strength as being immoral or cowardly. (And although one may accuse suicide bombers of many sins, cowardice hardly seems one.)

Does the problem reside primarily with Islam? Or are there political and social origins of these issues that require more complex policy analysis and treatment? Clearly this book argues that the problem is not basically "Islam," but the legacy of geopolitical and social issues that affect Muslims, who are indeed adopting weapons of the weak. Terrorist operations have a long and venerable history in different places and times, but in the last century, some of the more dramatic cases of such operations have included the Vietcong, the Basque ETA, Shining Path in Peru, PKK (a Kurdish organization in Turkey), MJK (an Iranian group operating against the Islamic Republic), Tamil Tigers in Sri Lanka, Sikhs in India, the Communist Party in India, Naxalites in India, the IRA in Ireland, Kach in Israel, Red Brigades, Aum Shinrikyo, FARC in Columbia, and so on. In recent decades, however, the number of Muslim organizations on the list has increased dramatically with the new confrontations with the West.

———

WHAT DO WE DIE FOR? Do the particular circumstances of death lend it greater meaning? To die for others—for the family, the clan, the tribe, the nation—or to die for one's own God: these are events that over history are treated with the utmost sanctity, honor, and communal solidarity. Death, especially violent death, demands meaning. Survivors and those left behind crave solace and explanation, some meaning or purpose from the phenomenon of unnatural and premature death. And what of the act of killing itself? Under what circumstances is killing justified? Answers to these profound ethical and moral issues are generated anew in each era in new situations on both sides of conflicts. They are often framed in the highest and most exalted moral terms available—the religious beliefs of the culture.

Motivations will be argued for a long time. There is no doubt that Middle East societies are less developed in many respects. Education levels, living standards, and job opportunities are often low for the great majority of its citizens, aside from a few oil elites and the tiny rich Gulf State populations. Prospects for the future are perceived as limited. There is a higher proportion of bad governance compared to most of the world, except Africa. The major fact, however, is that nearly all of these conditions have existed in the Middle East for a long time, and Islam has been around for fifteen hundred years. Yet the massive increase in violence, terrorism, and suicide bombings is very *recent* and directly linked with a period of highly invasive European and US policies in the Middle East. Even if, as some argue, the very culture of the Muslim world itself is somehow predisposed to violence more than other societies—a questionable proposition—we are still left with the need to explain the huge surge in violence in the Middle East under *recent* conditions.

Sadly, we have all become so accustomed, in the last decade or so, to a world of violence, terrorism, and suicide bombing that we have come to feel that this is the routine method of Muslim warfare. But, quite to the contrary, they represent new factors on the strategic scene. It is now hard to recall that some two and a half decades ago such events were highly unusual. Suicide bombing was almost unheard of in the Muslim world in the 1950s to the 1970s, even at the height of the revolutionary fervor of Arab nationalism and the disastrous defeat of the Arabs in the 1967 war with Israel. Palestinians committed terrorist acts against Israel, but they were not suicide missions. It was the Shi'a of Lebanon who first began to successfully employ suicide bombings in Lebanon, with devastating effect against American targets—the US embassy and the US Marine barracks in the early 1980s. But it was the Hindu Tamil Tigers in Sri Lanka who were the first to operationalize regular use of the suicide vest in the 1980s, with one of the highest rates of suicide operations in that era. Since that time, the frequency of suicide bombing in the Middle East has grown dramatically, peaking since the US occupation of Iraq and Afghanistan.

In 2007, the year with the highest rate to date, there were 658 suicide attacks, including 542 in US-occupied Afghanistan and Iraq, according to US government figures. This is more than double the number of attacks in any of the past twenty-five years. Furthermore, more than four-fifths of all those suicide bombings occurred only in the last seven years, and the practice is now spreading around the globe. The *Washington Post* notes that "Since 1983 bombers in more than 50 groups from Argentina to Algeria, Croatia to China, and India to Indonesia have adapted car bombs to make explosive belts, vests, toys, motorcycles, bikes, boats, backpacks and false-pregnancy stomachs.... Of 1,840 incidents in the past 25 years, *more than 86 percent have occurred since 2001*, and the highest annual numbers have occurred in the past four years."

Theories abound about the reasons for the huge increase in suicide bombing; most theories advance one or another ideological view of the nature of the struggle. Some analysts believe that religious motivations are paramount: the desire to defend the *umma* and the Muslim world, to sacrifice oneself for Islam, and to achieve paradise. Others suggest various personal pathologies as lying behind a willingness to commit suicide, suggesting that the actor is irrational. Yet others suggest that economic and social desperation triggers such an abnormal act. Robert A. Pape at the University of Chicago argues that most such actions come in direct response to foreign occupation and the desire to rid the country of the invader. Yet others, such as Marc Sageman in a variation on that idea, agree that nationalist and cultural outrage is a driver, but that the actual commitment to undertake an operation at the personal level is also driven by the powerful impact of group-think—a group of friends or members of a neighborhood community who jointly decide to volunteer together to fight and die for the cause.

Motivations matter because they suggest the antidote. The United States has tried to get into the business of interpreting the Qur'an to "prove" to insurgents that their actions are wrong in religious terms, indeed are "anti-Islamic." Washington has convened numerous Muslim clerics to denounce terrorism in the name of Islam. And large numbers do. Regrettably, however, a solution to the problem does not lie simply in exposing radicals to the "correct interpretation" of Islam. It is, furthermore, unlikely that any Islamic authority can readily be invoked capable of stilling violent guerrilla action against detested policies, or invading American armies and occupation forces. Saudi or Egyptian senior 'ulama have issued repeated statements and *fatwas* denouncing the violence of al-Qa'ida and other groups. And there are some jail cell "conversions" by prisoners who have been "led to see the error of their ways" and to renounce their previous violent affiliations.

It is possible that over time some radicals have been persuaded by clerics to see the error of their radicalism. But prisons also represent more persuasive venues for such conversions, raising doubt about the ultimate seriousness of prisoners' change of heart. In the case of Saudi Arabia or Egypt, most senior 'ulama are perceived as being in the pocket of the regime, serving the regime's understandable anxiety about radical ideologies. Thus, the number of truly credible moderate clerics who can actually change minds among radical youth is limited.

Most youth are radicalized by the situation on the ground:

foreign occupation; killings of large numbers of civilians by American, Western, or Israeli military forces; a sense of humiliation and defeat; a thirst for revenge, sometimes for people killed within their own family. These are very concrete and practical issues, quite unrelated to Islamic theology. If a horrific experience is not lived firsthand, it is witnessed on television. A radicalized individual will not likely be deterred from taking up violence simply because he heard a sermon that says Islam does not support suicide bombing or the killing of civilians. An individual bent on revenge and retribution for the real or imagined assault against family, community, and religion will seek the blood of the enemy. He will likely shop around among theological opinions until he finds the one that gives license and authority to his murderous anger. The rage comes first, the theological justification is an afterthought, a moral reinforcement to support an act already determined upon. In this sense, it is very hard to simply find some persuasive phrase in the Qur'an that will suddenly clarify minds, melt the anger, and quell resentment. The gut precedes the mind. Furthermore, texts in most religions contain intemperate phrases that can be drawn out of context to support violent action, regardless of what the overall thrust of the religion is.

Brainwashing by Muslim authorities does not necessarily change views either. Shi'ites in Saudi Arabia are forced in schools to use textbooks that demean Shi'ism. Yet Shi'ites from the area say that their children know to laugh off these messages in school. Similarly, in totalitarian societies like the Soviet Union, large numbers of the population knew that the propaganda distributed by government media was false, and fairly systematically discounted these ideas in their own minds, even while paying lip service to them in public. In short, just because school texts or the information systems make certain claims does not mean that the messages are accepted in skeptical societies.

Many moderate Muslims do not accept the theological

interpretations and justifications offered by al-Qa'ida for many of their bloody acts. But they do accept that times are perilous for the Muslim world and that mere surrender to the West is not an option either. They may abhor the action, but also find it the only available response, the "weapon of the weak." Muslim societies may deeply regret such actions and fear involvement by their sons and daughters in it, but also find it "understandable" that these things should be happening under current conditions, and hence hard to personally condemn those who take violent action in response to events. Societal acquiescence to such violent response is at least as important a factor in the perpetuation of terrorist acts as the existence of violent individuals themselves.

Societies defend themselves. At one level, it's that simple. The Bush administration claimed it was just trying to defend itself, to "kill the terrorists in Iraq before they get to the US." But the scene of almost all the battles, wars, and power games is taking place on *Muslim* soil under assault from outside forces, and has been for a very long time; the argument about defense is really more relevant to Muslims than to the United States, whose forces project global reach.

Religion will always be invoked wherever it can to galvanize the public and to justify major campaigns, battles, and wars, especially in monotheistic cultures. But the causes, campaigns, battles, and wars are not about religion. Take away the religion, and there are still causes, campaigns, battles, and wars.

CHAPTER FOURTEEN

What to Do? Toward a New Policy with the Muslim World

Defining Terrorism in the Real World

No one can ever bring terrorism to an end on this earth. It is one of the many—and one of the more vicious—forms of politics by other means. But it can be controlled and limited. Unfortunately, current US policies are not going to do that; in fact, they have exacerbated the problem. The first mistake is US government use of a legalistic and self-serving definition for terrorism that does not address the real-world problem. Admittedly, the problem of gaining international consensus on defining terrorism has long been thorny. Governments in effect end up saying that "terrorism is what I say it is," that is, a subjective, self-serving definition to meet the needs of the moment. The 2004 definition offered by the US Department of Defense is particularly slanted: "The calculated use of *unlawful violence* or threat of unlawful violence to inculcate fear; intended to coerce or to intimidate governments or societies in the pursuit of goals that are generally political, religious, or ideological."

The political hooker in this statement is the phrase "use of *unlawful* violence." No definition is offered for the term "unlawful," but it appears to mean "not sanctioned by government." Yet

isn't this precisely what political struggles usually revolve around—
the exact definition of lawful? Modern Western political thinkers
tend to define the *state* as possessing the sole legitimate monopoly
on the use of violence. Thus "state" = "lawful." That equation
may be appropriate in most Western democracies where governments rule by consent, but it is a far shakier argument in authoritarian states that exclude and persecute political opposition and
where change often never comes about except through some kind
of "unlawful" activity. Such governments seek to ensure that all
opposition is "unlawful." And such activity is often countered by
what, in effect, are forms of state terrorism directed against a significant group of its own citizens.

The events of 9/11 and the Global War on Terror hugely
empowered all states facing any kind of domestic insurgency,
enabling them to brand their opponents with the charge of "terrorism." "Terrorism" is, of course, the clinching argument; once
it is invoked, no political approach or negotiation is required, and
the state has full moral authority to apply maximum violence to
wipe out the opposition. Regimes all over the world found a wind-
fall in joining Bush's Global War on Terror, placing themselves in
the camp of the morally righteous against the forces of evil, with
whom there could be no compromise. Michael Walzer deftly sum-
marizes the problem: "First oppression is made into an excuse for
terrorism, and then terrorism is made into an excuse for oppression. The first is the excuse of the far left; the second is the excuse
of the neoconservative right."

Everyone would agree that political violence in any society is
undesirable. Terrorism is a form of political violence. But in much
of the world, political violence is routinely exercised by repressive
regimes themselves against their domestic opponents. Illegitimate
regimes will inevitably be faced with political violence. That is the
basis for the language in the American Declaration of Independence:

Governments are instituted among Men, deriving their just powers from the consent of the governed.... That whenever any Form of Government becomes destructive of these ends, it is the Right of the People to alter or to abolish it...when a long train of abuses and usurpations...evinces a design to reduce them under absolute Despotism, it is their right, it is their duty, to throw off such Government, and to provide new Guards for their future security.

In the contemporary Muslim world—and we are not just talking about Muslims here, but about the entire developing world—there are at least three conditions under which the use of political violence becomes arguable: overthrow of despotic regimes, struggle for national liberation, and armed resistance against foreign occupation.

1. *Overthrow of despotic regimes:* The Muslim world has a high proportion of despotic regimes, many supported by the West for decades. They are skilled at suppressing political opposition through multiple means, including violence and imprisonment. Does political violence against the regime constitute terrorism, thereby justifying its total suppression? If the state is oppressive, how justified is armed struggle and rebellion? Regrettably few states produce Mahatma Gandhis or Nelson Mandelas.

2. *The struggle for national liberation:* For historical reasons, including imperial redrawing of colonial borders in Africa and Eurasia, hundreds of ethnic groups find themselves divided by artificial borders, or included within a state culturally alien to them, which is often suppressive of their identity and cultural rights, and they were never consulted about incorporation within these states. These ethnic groups include Chechens; Kashmiris; Uyghurs

and Tibetans in China; Sri Lankan Tamils; Palestinians; Sikhs in India; Kurds in Turkey, Iran, and Iraq; Moros in the Philippines; Bengalis in Pakistan (pre-Bangladesh); Igbos in Nigeria; Eritreans in Ethiopia (before achieving independence); Albanian Kosovars in Serbia—the list is long. These communities can be either ethnic or religious.

History reveals how many states now accepted as fully legitimate have been born out of "unlawful violence," usually against anticolonial or anti-imperialist struggle: Turkey, Israel, China, Mexico, Algeria, Indonesia, Greece, Bulgaria, Cuba, Vietnam, Kenya, South Africa, and the United States, just to name a few major ones. If the criterion of the Pentagon today had been applied to the "unlawful violence" practiced by American revolutionaries in 1776 against the perceived legitimacy of British rule, we would not have an American Republic. We should not forget the terrorist origins of leaders like Jomo Kenyatta in Kenya, Menachem Begin in Israel, or Nelson Mandela in South Africa, all of whom came to be viewed as serious and respected statesmen after their victories.

American policies in the modern era have pretty consistently been toward *support of the status quo and the state,* including even state repression to preserve the status quo—albeit with occasional transient twinges of conscience. The major exception is when the state facing separatist insurgency is hostile to Washington, in which case issues of principle break down: US policy then demonstrates greater sympathy or support for the separatists: Kurds in Saddam's Iraq; Baluch in Iran; Ukrainians, Latvians, and others in the USSR; Tibetans in Mao's China, and so on.

3. *Armed resistance against foreign occupation:* Most recently, resistance against the US invasion of Iraq, Afghanistan, and Somalia. Yet terrorist resistance against the Red Army in Afghanistan in the 1980s was enthusiastically supported by Washington. Do not occupied peoples in war have the right of armed resistance? States at war, even democratic ones, generally refuse to deal openly with such questions about what constitutes acceptable violence. They will prefer to bend universal definitions to the immediate need of the state to justify their acts. In its own eyes, the state is always right, the state is always moral.

Questions of proportionality of response lie also within classic arguments for just war. When several soldiers are killed by terrorists, for example, can a response entailing one hundred times the deaths be considered morally legitimate? What of the informal Israeli support for the tactic of "one hundred eyes for an eye," as a form of deterrence? Or the morality of "shock and awe"? Of regime change by military invasion? Or the bombing of civilian populations? Here, we are caught again on the slippery slope of relativism and subjectivity: is it licit to drop bombs from fifty thousand feet in the effort to kill terrorists—with predictable widespread deaths of innocents—but immoral for a single suicide bomber to kill the enemy from five feet in the struggle for national liberation, also killing innocents? No doubt some acts of terrorism are quite indiscriminate and specifically designed to spread fear and demoralization; but what then of Dresden, Hiroshima, or Nagasaki, in which the major purpose of the exercise was to terrify and demoralize—in modern parlance, to create "shock and awe" to win the conflict? All of these questions are directly relevant to multiple crises in the Muslim world—and outside. There is nothing at all "Muslim" about these situations—except that Islamic solidarity may well strengthen the will to resist.

Despite these questions, it would be wrong to simply define away the existence of terrorism through facile and slippery definitions of relative justice. Terrorism does exist and is a scourge upon society. People who commit terrorist acts are often brutal and psychotic, on the fringes of society, engaged in criminal activities, or powerfully driven ideological zealots. But not all, by any means. Severe conditions such as oppression and war elicit a violent response from undesirable social elements, as well as from many other citizens. The definition chosen for terrorism must be consistently applied. Washington's self-serving and selective use of the term casts doubt over its legal, analytic, and persuasive validity and largely undermines its case in the eyes of the world, not to mention in the Muslim world.

Nor should lack of consensus on definitions create paralysis of will. What is essential is policy acknowledgment of international norms—how most of the rest of the world regards these issues. In Iraq, the reality was that vast portions of the world did not see these issues as Washington saw them, or as the narrow spectrum of US mainstream news coverage reported—or ignored—them. Failure to acknowledge regional realities and treat existing grievances will guarantee the certain failure of President Obama's policies as surely as under the Bush administration. Most Muslims fighting in the name of nationalist grievances, like other nationalists, must not be treated as "terrorists" but as political opponents whose needs require some kind of political treatment or negotiation. Insurgency may be "illegal," but it is the essence of human response to unjust conditions.

Nearly everyone agrees that the killing of another human being is morally wrong. Yet within that framework, Western law draws careful distinctions among first-degree, second-degree, and third-degree murder, manslaughter, and negligent homicide; it also condemns certain killers to death, others not. Policy must distinguish among a variety of gradations in the sphere of political violence and terrorism as well. Nearly all statesmen would acknowledge distinctions between (a) Hamas, which employs guerrilla and terrorist tactics within the narrow geographical limits of occupied territory of Palestine and Israel, or (b) Iraqis and Pashtuns fighting American military occupation on their own soil, or (c) groups like al-Qa'ida, which confront the West in its totality, as did the Red Brigades, Baader Meinhof group, or Aum Shinrikyo.

"Negotiating" with Terrorists

In viewing terrorist movements around the world, the Bush administration rejected distinctions among terrorist groups — there is no such thing as a "good" terrorist. But for all their inveighing against terrorism in principle, statesmen do end up regularly negotiating with many terrorist groups — precisely because they grasp that negotiations might eventually bring about a resolution. The British did end up talking to the IRA; considerable numbers of Israelis believe that they must talk with Hamas. (Remember when Israel, on principle, refused to talk to the terrorist PLO?) Many Americans believe we must talk to Hamas and Hizballah, or elements of the Ba'thists in Iraq, or the Taliban in Afghanistan, for example, because they are perceived as "rational" groups with domestic, finite political goals.

"Rational" political groups engaged in political violence usually do possess specific, finite, concrete goals. They have offices that can be visited, possess programs, pamphlets, promotional materials and articles in their lobbies, are led by identifiable figures who can be interviewed and who speak publicly. We understand their goals and perceive them as rational, even if we oppose them for political reasons. Some evoke sympathy in our eyes, others rebuke. To label them all strictly as "terrorists" is analytically crude and counterproductive. Authorities endlessly repeat they "will *never* negotiate" with terrorists—until they do; we "will *never* recognize…"—until we do. Often these supposed principled positions on terrorism end up being little more than negotiating postures on the way to a more serious negotiated settlement.

The statement that "one man's terrorist is another man's freedom fighter" is facile, yet very close to the truth. It is an argument that infuriates most governments because it creates "moral equivalency" between warring parties—a concept hated by both sides. The nub of the problem is that what we recognize as "resistance" eventually is a *political call,* depending on whether one favors the authority or the resisters. Major governments around the world talk about principle, but end up choosing their definitions of who is a "terrorist" in accordance with their own transient interests. If we are hung up on the idea that all these movements are driven by some implacable radical Islamic agenda, then we will never find ways to reduce the problem. Nearly all of the movements have nonreligious, ultimately negotiable goals.

How Terrorism Ends

One of the most comprehensive and interesting statistical analyses on terrorists conducted in recent years is the 2008 RAND report "How Terrorist Groups End." The RAND group examined 648 movements that operated from 1968 to 2008; the key finding was that "transition to the political process is the most common way in which terrorist groups ended." In brief:

- The largest group, 43 percent of terrorist groups, ended through *transition into the political process,* in other words, through compromise. The RAND study also determined that "the possibility of a political solution is inversely linked to the breadth of terrorist goals." In other words, the more *finite, practical, and local* the grievances and goals, the greater the likelihood of their being accommodated.

- In the 40 percent of cases in which the terrorist organization was not able or willing to make the transition to political accommodation, it was *policing, rather than military action* that was by far the most effective means of neutralizing the group. Police and intelligence organizations are far more capable of understanding, penetrating, and neutralizing such groups than the indiscriminate blunt instrument of military means.

- In 10 percent of the cases, the terrorist groups came to an end because their goals were achieved. In only 7 percent of cases was military action effective in terminating the activities of terrorist groups.

- "Religious terrorist groups take longer to eliminate than other groups." On the other hand, "Religious groups rarely achieve their objectives." The report also states: "Size is also a significant determinant of a group's fate. Big groups of more than 10,000 members have been victorious more than 25 percent of the time, while victory is rare when groups are smaller than 1,000 members."

- "When a *terrorist* group becomes involved in an *insurgency,* it does not end easily. Nearly 50 percent of the time, groups ended by negotiating a settlement with the government; 25 percent of the time, they achieved victory; and 19 percent of the time, military forces defeated them." This speaks to the situation in Iraq and Afghanistan.

The simultaneous existence of "global" movements mixed in among "pragmatic" ones, as we see in Iraq and Afghanistan, likely reinforces the overall radicalization of the public, including moderates. Similarly, political settlement with "pragmatic" terrorist groups greatly reduces the charged political atmosphere, and the local public then becomes less accommodating to groups like al-Qa'ida, who then are seen fighting for a cause no longer truly relevant to the local public interest.

Policy Response

In the end, terrorism cannot be separated from the conditions, concerns, and distress of people in the Middle East. We all know that terrorism is the tool of the weak. But Muslim recourse to terrorism, however unacceptable, does not delegitimize their grievances either. For the al-Qa'ida hijackers, Islam functioned as a magnifying glass in the sun, collecting these widespread, shared common grievances and focusing them into an intense ray, a moment of clarity of action against the long-standing source of foreign intrusion. The grievances preexisted the attacks and still largely exist.

As we noted, history did not begin with 9/11. The past several decades have demonstrated an accelerating American effort to bend the Muslim will to US goals; not only has the effort failed and solved no problems, it has vastly heightened the intensity of fervor against the United States across the Muslim world and has cost the country dearly.

Terrorism in the Middle East and elsewhere can eventually be greatly reduced, but only as the *conditions that promote it recede*. Ever greater efforts by US armies to hunt down and kill the existing radicals only produce new, more motivated generations of radicals. Military action may organizationally weaken them, but their numbers are quickly bolstered by shock troops of a Muslim foreign legion traveling from conflict zone to conflict zone, or cause the population to turn to violence against their own authoritarian regimes—often American-supported. It does not take that many insurgents or terrorists to tie countries and armies up in knots. Forty-plus years of ongoing Israeli occupation in Palestine vividly demonstrates this kind of failure; Israel has only achieved the creation of an iconic resistance with region-wide, almost global reverberations.

Ultimately, the burden of ending terrorism falls upon Muslim populations themselves. But for this to happen, there must first be an end to the conditions that foster this radicalism and that generate widespread anti-Americanism. In bluntest terms, that means no more foreign boots on the ground in Muslim countries, and no more foreign military attacks by foreign soldiers—images that remain daily fare on all the television screens of the world, except in America itself. Muslim societies must be given a chance to calm down and return to a state of normalcy. Second, only Muslims themselves can begin to change thinking in their own societies to truly fight terrorism. Indeed, it is probable that moderate *Islamists* are the ones best equipped to intellectually and physically disarm the radicals, to delegitimize whatever legitimacy they have sought in invoking Islam—even for non-Islamic causes. They perhaps can delegitimize the Islamic foundation for the use of terror, but not the practical grounds that spur it. It is not because the Islamists are religious that their voice is strong, but because they are the sole remaining political faction at this point in modern Muslim history that enjoys much legitimacy and respect. And realistically, credible Muslim leaders are not going to push for moderation as long as existing conditions make it difficult to argue for it. Present conditions will not last forever. But in the meantime, the very presence of foreign armies actually undercuts the authority of moderates, whose views cannot prevail under radicalized circumstances.

"Zero tolerance for terrorism" is another slogan that needs to disappear. It is an empty phrase, demagogic and utopian in character, just as "zero tolerance for crime" has no functional meaning in contemporary society.

It does not take immense insight to suggest that Muslims are no more likely to welcome heavy-handed foreign intervention in their societies than American society would. It does not take special insight to conclude that stopping the activities causing these violent responses from Muslim societies might be a reasonable policy alternative to the present disastrous American course. At this stage, things have deteriorated so far that terrorism against the United States will not even come to an end abruptly upon the departure of US troops from the region. But it will be the first critical and indispensable step in winding it down. A military withdrawal will seriously undercut a key justification for the existence of radical movements like al-Qa'ida. Within individual Muslim countries, where once their presence may have been justified as a means to fight the foreign invader, they will no longer be welcome. The space for terrorism will rapidly shrink under new strategic circumstances when Muslim populations themselves will no longer need or accept outside warriors visiting violence upon them. We must not Islamize this problem if we are to grasp its practical, concrete nature. Regrettably, Washington has been slow to abandon its determination to exert US strategic dominance over the Muslim world, and globally—a key source of the problem.

President Obama's change of style and direction in Washington and his openness to new approaches have commanded much attention in the Muslim world. It is apparent to all that he understands the feelings and motivations of the Muslim world and other developing nations. He is aware of the important role of dignity and respect in communications, replacing bluster, swagger, and force. But whether he can turn a policy supertanker around is another question, and so far it looks like the task may be beyond his powers. Most Muslims are heartened by Obama, but they want to see real change, new realities on the ground. US military forces, nonetheless, are still expanding their overseas reach with military solutions to political, cultural, and economic problems.

What to Do?

―――――――

THROUGH GLOBAL DEVELOPMENTS over the past half century, Islam has become the most politically self-conscious culture in the world today. Nonetheless, I have tried to portray Islamic civilization in a broader context of world events, from historical times to the present; it should by now be clear how so many of the events that we associate with Islam are actually political and social impulses shared by most other cultures as well. For some readers, this kind of explanation may seem to constitute an apologia for Islam— seemingly "excusing" Islam. But this book is not about narrating the glories or the failings of Islamic civilization. I do not attempt to create a balance sheet of all that is good and bad on both sides. The goal is rather to make Muslim impulses, emotions, and choices clear and comprehensible to non-Muslims—to outline the reasons and conditions that make so many Muslims feel and act the way they do. That is the key to finding solutions, not ignoring the issues or fighting the problem. Feelings, in any case, are not homogeneous across the Muslim world. But the worse the conditions, the greater the degree of consensus that emerges.

Awareness of the dynamics that drive other societies might have helped to avoid the decades-long series of predictable American crises and confrontations with Iraqis, Palestinians, Afghans, Pashtuns, Somalis—or with other nationalist movements in other countries like China, Vietnam, Venezuela, or even Russia today. Such insights would have permitted us to see the inexorable buildup of pressure that eventually burst forth on 9/11. Certainly those policy makers that reject this kind of an understanding of Muslim societies, and who prefer their own self-serving version of "why they hate us," have pursued demonstrably failing policies at a huge cost to everyone—producing the greatest mess in the history of American dealings with the Muslim world.

Grand Strategy

In keeping with the title of this book, *Washington should act as if Islam did not exist in formulating its policies in the Middle East.* The vast majority of issues in the region can be dealt with and resolved without recourse to Islam as an explanation or operating factor. Indeed, viewing Islam as an explanation *obfuscates* a clear vision of the issues. Islam, particularly in its more extreme ideological form, can complicate, even exacerbate, but not create such problems. The issues and problems, instead, spring from quite specific, concrete regional political, economic, and social challenges—including inadequate education—that transcend religion, however wrapped in Islamic (cultural) rhetoric they may be.

To view the problems as linked to Islam suggests we should devote time and energy to examining religion and seek to change religion and its understanding in ways we find desirable for our interests. But any "American version of Islam" is destined for rejection. Indeed, the term "American Islam" was coined first in the Iranian revolution, a biting reference to an Islam devoted strictly to personal piety, that conveniently stays out of politics and does not address the burning political issues of the day—in short, that does not make geopolitical waves. Focus upon Islam, furthermore, conveniently shifts the problem to the "Other" and entails no serious examination of our own policy failures. This is not to say there are not serious problems in the Middle East and the developing world that require treatment. There very much are. Indeed, just as we cannot "blame Islam" for everything, so we cannot "blame the West" for everything. But focusing upon specific issues, their causes, and potential solutions is the most reliable way forward.

In order to reduce the present confrontation between the Muslim world and the United States, the following specific steps need to be taken:

- Western military and political intervention in the Muslim world—all highly provocative to Muslims—must cease so that the area can begin to calm. That means withdrawal of all US and Western forces from Muslim soil.
- Efforts to identify and stymie terrorist acts must be carried out through intelligence and police work; capture of terrorists should be the prerogative of international organizations or local countries, and not by the United States operating on an illegal extraterritorial extension of its sovereign rights to capture and assassinate individuals at will.
- The United States must withdraw its special support from pro-American dictators that discredit the US, give the lie to US-stated commitments to democracy, and only lead to the buildup of more explosive political environments and anti-American resentments.
- Democratization must be allowed to proceed in the Muslim world, but Washington must not be the vehicle for its implantation. Ideally, Washington should keep its hands off the process so as not to tarnish it, as has been the case in the past, through association with US self-interest. Past selective and instrumental use of democratization by Washington for pursuit of US strategic goals has discredited the very concept of its democratization programs.
- The United States must accept that under democratic processes Islamist parties *will* be legitimately elected in early elections in most Muslim countries. The good news is that Islamists will be quickly discredited in a year or so if they cannot deliver to the public what they promised, or what the public expects. That means treatment of urgent economic and social problems and not empty anti-imperial rhetoric.

- An early solution to the Palestinian problem must be found. It is perceived across the Muslim world as the single most egregious case of foreign imperialism, which has displaced local people and cast them into desperate living conditions in refugee camps, imposed second-class citizenship upon them in Israel, or pushed them into exile — for more than sixty years. Palestinian suffering has grown, accompanied by a radicalization that has spread beyond Palestine. The crisis demands a quick solution, the general outlines of which are well known to all parties. The Israeli colonization efforts in Palestinian territories must end and be reversed.
- If only a tenth of the potentially one trillion plus dollars squandered by Washington on Middle East wars, which have sown death and destruction with little to show for it, could be devoted to building schools, universities, hospitals, clinics, and training institutes, the region would be transformed, the US image would soar, and huge regional progress could be made in living conditions.
- Enlightened US policies could soon bring an end to international and transnational sources of violence and radicalism; domestic sources of violence in individual countries require separate analysis and treatment in accordance with local conditions, and, in any case, pose a lesser immediate problem.
- Only Muslims (i.e., locals) in the end will be able to find solutions to dealing with Islamic (i.e., local) radicalism.

But the contemporary expression of Islam, for a variety of complex historical factors, is now often dispirited and unfocused, fighting its own demons, caught up in its own postcolonial mess, struggling toward its own reformation and reestablishment of its dignity and independence — all in the face of huge military, political, and cultural onslaught from the West. Islam's roots and vision are deep and broad; an intellectual renaissance can emerge if it is not obstructed by brutal international geopolitical forces contesting for power, oil, and bases in its midst.

It is a culture of profound intellectual, spiritual, cultural, and social thought. But it is also a culture currently rubbed raw, best not gratuitously provoked at this sensitive stage in its development and when it feels under existential threat. Such assaults against it only heighten its most atavistic and narrow aspects, sideline impulses for reform and moderation, and cause Muslims to circle the wagons.

The West must rise to this challenge—but the West is, in fact, quite schizophrenic in its own behavior. Domestically the West has the best record in the world today for democratic process, economic well-being, education, protection of human and minority rights, and a rich panoply of public watchdogs and institutions to guard those rights. These qualities are admired in the Muslim world. On the other hand, the power of the West at the *international* level has for many years flagrantly abused human rights, individual liberties, and right to life in its foreign policies and in its conduct of imperial or military campaigns—all in the name of ideals such as anticommunism, "democratization," preservation of "American leadership," and protection against terrorism. These qualities are detested in the Muslim world. Muslims have suffered more at the receiving end of such military campaigns than they have ever gained from US policies. The West, and especially the all-powerful United States, has a long way to go to bring its national ideals to bear in its conduct of policy overseas.

The abuses that have rankled the developing world have happened not because the West is somehow evil; the West has simply possessed the power *to do* all those things to others on a global scale. I would be no more happy to see an unchecked concentration of global power in the hands of others, either: France, the

UK, Germany, China, Russia, or whoever. The fact is the United States now does possess dominant global power. But monopolies of power are never healthy in any context. We have domestic checks and balances in our Constitution, antimonopoly laws to keep any corporation, however excellent, from crushing all competition. Similarly, we shouldn't want to see power monopolized on the international level either—it's not good for anybody.

Islam and statecraft are likely to be linked in some way for some period of time to come. For Muslims, it is a reassurance that values in politics are not ignored in what has often been a cynical power game. Nor will religion disappear as a force in international relations anywhere, for better or for worse. It seems to be part of a human philosophical yearning of the heart to break free into transcendent realms. But religion linked to statecraft tends to be a poor combination. It is not a new revelation to note that power and *any* ideology tend to corrupt each other. If there was no Islam, there would certainly be other religions around playing similar roles under similar conditions. With no religions at all, we would still readily find or create other ideologies to justify the same acts. Thus, a world without Islam does not markedly change the nature of things.

If we think religion has been a negative force in modern world history, consider the alternative. Religion couldn't have done worse than the history of savage *secular* violence and unprecedented butchery that dominated the history of the West in the twentieth century, marked by two world wars, fascism, nazism, and communism—none of which had anything to do with religion. Secular extremism has only offered us worse. The real problem lies in the nature of human aspirations, good and bad. We in the West will be on a sounder path if we can de-Islamize our perceptions of regional issues and view them simply as universal human social and political problems for which we, too, share some responsibility.

Acknowledgments

This book reflects ideas and insights I have gained over long years, from many hundreds of people, Westerners and Muslims. I can't begin to sort out who has helped influence me on these themes over the years.

I would like to acknowledge here, however, the very direct help and comments on this manuscript from a number of people, in particular Daniel Bogert-O'Brien, Russell Brant, George Fowler, Andre Gierolymatos, Dimitrios Krallis, and Glenn Perry. I fear I have neglected to mention many others who have passed along thoughts to me here and there or who have provided useful debate on some of the ideas in the book. Any errors are, of course, my own.

I wish to thank my thoughtful and supportive editor at Little, Brown, Junie Dahn — always a pleasure to deal with — and editor in chief, Geoff Shandler, for having originally encouraged me to write a book on this topic.

Notes

This is a book about ideas and alternative ways of thinking about them; I have not attempted to "prove" or to document an alternative history, but rather to look at familiar events and to explore their motivating factors quite apart from religion.

The arguments in this book are based on my own thinking about the history of the Middle East and Islamic Asia over a very long period of time. I have been a student of the Middle East ever since early youth, when my imagination was captured by pictures, books, music, and films of the region. I have read innumerable books on the region, and I have lived, worked, and studied in many different Middle Eastern countries for over a decade and a half.

I have turned to mainstream reference sources primarily for dates, for refining my memory, and for additional details pertinent to this alternative reading of East-West conflict, which diminishes the centrality of religion per se — as opposed to so many other formative factors in history. In this case, the *Encyclopædia Britannica*, the *Encyclopedia of Islam*, and the ever-sharpening online resource Wikipedia have been helpful in establishing some general details of events.

Chapter One: Islam and the Abrahamic Faiths

Ira M. Lapidus's fine study *A History of Islamic Societies* (Cambridge: Cambridge University Press, 1988) is a valuable resource on many aspects of broader Islamic history, including the early Islamic conquests.

Good general books on the life of the Prophet Muhammad are Maxime Rodinson's *Muhammad: Prophet of Islam* (London: I. B. Taurus, 2002) and Karen Armstrong's *Muhammad: A Biography of the Prophet* (New York: HarperOne, 1993).

There are diverse positions about the role of Jesus in history among Jewish scholars. For the section on Jewish perspectives on Jesus, I drew from Rabbi Shraga Simmons's article, "Why Jews Don't Believe in Jesus," which can be found at http://www.aish.com/jewishissues/jewishsociety/Why_Jews_Dont_Believe_In_Jesus.asp.

The Maimonides quote is from Abraham S. Halkin, ed., and Boaz Cohen, trans., *Moses Maimonides' Epistle to Yemen: The Arabic Original and the Three Hebrew Versions* (New York: American Academy for Jewish Research, 1952), iii–iv.

Chapter Two: Power, Heresy, and the Evolution of Christianity

University of North Carolina at Chapel Hill scholar Bart D. Ehrman's *Lost Christianities: The Battles for Scripture and the Faiths We Never Knew* (New York: Oxford University Press, 2003) is a fascinating and groundbreaking study of the problems of early documents in the evolution of Christianity.

For a discussion of texts that did or did not make it into the formal Christian canon, see http://gbgm-umc.org/umw/Bible/noncanon.html.

For the discussion on Marcionism, I drew from http://www.earlychurch.org.uk/article_marcion.html.

Chapter Three: Byzantium versus Rome

Orthodox Christianity and Eastern Europe, a volume edited by Jonathan Sutton and Wil van den Bercken, features invaluable information on the culture of Eastern Orthodoxy. Particularly noteworthy is the paper by Vasilios N. Makrides and Dirk Uffelman, "Studying Eastern Orthodox Anti-Westernism: The Need for a Comparative Research Agenda." It is available online at http://www.unierfurt.de/orthodoxes_christentum/worddocs/makridesleeds1.doc.

Chapter Four: Islam Meets Eastern Christianity

This chapter draws from well-established events and the time lines of the region widely available in many books. The striking quote on Syrian antipathy to the West is from Arthur Vööbus's article "The Monophysite Church in Syria and Mesopotamia," *Church History* 42, no. 1 (March 1973): 17–26. See also analysis by Andrew James in the discussion section of the Wikipedia article on Monophytism.

The quote on the siege of Damascus is from the work of Ahmad Ibn Yahya Al-Balazuri, a ninth-century classical Arab historian.

The quotes from Ira Lapidus on Muslim conquests are from his *History of Islamic Societies* (Cambridge: Cambridge University Press, 1988), 41–43, 53.

Merlin Swartz's assertion on Jewish attitudes in the Byzantine Empire is drawn from his article "The Position of Jews in Arab Lands Following the Rise of Islam," *The Muslim World* 60, no. 1 (January 1970): 6–24.

Arnold J. Toynbee's quote on the use of force in the propagation of Islam is from his magisterial *Study of History* (abridgement of vols. I–VI), D. C. Somervell, ed. (New York: Oxford University Press, 1987), 488.

Richard Bulliet discusses this process of conversion to Islam in *Conversion to Islam in the Medieval Period: An Essay in Quantitative History* (Cambridge: Harvard University Press, 1979).

Chapter Five: The Great Crusades (1095–1272)

The classic study of the Crusades remains Stephen Runciman's *History of the Crusades* (Cambridge: Cambridge University Press, 1951–54).

Five versions of Urban II's speech can be found at Fordham University's *Medieval Sourcebook*, http://www.fordham.edu/halsall/source/urban2-5vers.html.

The quote on cannibalism is from *The Crusades Encyclopedia* article, "Cannibalism During the Crusades." You can find it at http://www.crusades-encyclopedia.com/cannibalism.html.

The story of Umar and the Jewish temple is drawn from Ben Abrahamson and Joseph Katz's "The Persian Conquest of Jerusalem in 614 CE Compared with Islamic Conquest of 638 CE: Its Messianic Nature and the Role of the Jewish Exilarch," which can be found at http://www.eretzyisroel.org/~jkatz/The%20Persian%20conquest%20of

%20Jerusalem%20in%20614CE%20compared%20with%20Islamic%20conquest%20of%20638CE.pdf.

The Catholic Encyclopedia entry on the Crusades can be found at http://www.newadvent.org/cathen/04543c.htm.

The quote from Spiros Vryonis describing the attack on Constantinople is from *Byzantium and Europe* (New York: Harcourt, Brace & World, 1967), 152.

The statement from Pope Innocent III is quoted in Victoria Clark's *Why Angels Fall: A Journey Through Orthodox Europe from Byzantium to Kosovo* (New York: St. Martin's Press, 2000), 27.

The assertion about the transformation of the east Baltic world is taken from the Wikipedia article on the Northern Crusades.

The characterization of Muslim views of Franks is drawn from Carole Hillenbrand and Thomas Madden's "Why the Crusades Still Matter," *National Catholic Reporter,* February 24, 2006.

Chapter Six: Shared Echoes

I am indebted to Russell F. Brant for the insight on the "intimate linkage between religion and state power" in Christian history that historically exceeds that of Islam.

I used the History Learning Site as a resource for much of the basic Calvin information.

The statement about human weakness is taken from a Wikipedia article on the Great Apostasy.

Chapter Seven: The "Third Rome" and Russia

Numerous legendary accounts exist of Russia's choice of Orthodox Christianity, including the well-known maxim that "drinking is the joy of the Rus; we cannot live without it."

Philotheus's letter is quoted in Theodore Pulcini's "Russian Orthodoxy and Western Christianity," *Russia and Western Civilization* (New York: M. E. Sharpe, 2003), 89. Pulcin's article cites Nicolas Zernov's *The Russians and Their Church* (Crestwood, NY: St. Vladimir's Seminary Press, 1978), 49.

Eric Ormsby reviewed Andrew Wheatcroft's *The Enemy at the Gate: Hapsburgs, Ottomans, and the Battle for Europe, New York Times,* June 15, 2009, BR22.

For the section on Russian philosophy and culture and anti-Westernism, I again relied on Vasilios N. Makrides and Dirk Uffelman's "Studying Eastern Orthodox Anti-Westernism: The Need for a Comparative Research Agenda." It is available online at http://www.unierfurt.de/orthodoxes_christentum/worddocs/makridesleeds1.doc.

The extract on evangelism in Russia and the Orthodox Church's 1,005-year-old traditions are from Patricia Lefevere's "Tide of Evangelism May Swamp Religious Freedoms—Russia," *National Catholic Reporter*, June 18, 1993.

The passage featuring the words of Valery Ganichev is drawn from Olga Kostromina and Yelena Dorofeyeva's "World Council of Russian People Denounces Sects, Immorality," *Itar-Tass* via COMTEX, December 13, 2001.

Chapter Eight: Russia and Islam

The extract focusing on Makarii's influence is drawn from Matthew P. Romaniello's "Mission Delayed: The Russian Orthodox Church after the Conquest of Kazan," *Church History*, September 1, 2007. See http://goliath.ecnext.com/coms2/summary_0199-7006685_ITM.

The quotes about Moscow's desire to "transform religious authority" and how Russia came to play the role of "defender of the state" are from Robert D. Crews's *For Prophet and Tsar: Islam and Empire in Russia and Central Asia* (Cambridge: Harvard University Press, 2006), 2. The observations that the Russian state claimed its authority was "grounded in religion" and based on a "shared moral universe" are drawn from pages 7–8 of the same source.

Some of the background information on Jadidism is from Daniel Kimmage's "Central Asia: Jadidism—Old Tradition of Renewal," *Radio Free Europe/Radio Liberty*, August 9, 2005. You can read the article at http://www.rferl.org/content/article/1060543.html.

Gaspirali is quoted in Şener Aktürk's "Identity Crisis: Russia's Muslims in the Debate over Russian Identity vis-à-vis Europe," *International Affairs Journal*, UC Davis, December 31, 2005. The italics are mine.

Much of the information on Russian politics as they relate to Russian Muslims is drawn from Shireen T. Hunter's *Islam in Russia: The Politics of Identity and Security* (Armonk, NY: M. E. Sharpe, 2004), 15–21.

Information about Sultan-Galiev can be found in Maxime Rodinson and Richard Price's article "Sultan Galiev—A Forgotten Precursor: Socialism and the National Question," October 2004, which can be found at http://www.europe-solidaire.org/spip.php?article3638.

The long quote from Sultan-Galiev is from Mirsäyet Soltanğäliev, quoted from I. G. Gizzatullin, D. R. Sharafutdinov (compilers), *Mirsaid Sultan-Galiev. Stat'i, Vystupleniya, Dokumenty* (Kazan': Tatarskoe Knizhskoe Izdatel'stvo, 1992), 52. Cited by Wikipedia.

The quote from Dmitry Shlapentokh is from his article "Islam and Orthodox Russia: From Eurasianism to Islamism," *Communist and Post-Communist Studies* 41 (2008). The italics are mine.

Chapter Nine: Muslims in the West

Tariq Ramadan's quote is from "Europe and Its Muslims: Building a Common Future," Lectures in Japan by Tariq Ramadan, July 12, 2007. See http://www.tariqramadan.com/spip.php?article1049 for more information.

The statistics and information on European Muslim populations are from Jocelyne Cesari's "Immigration and Integration," *Islam-on-Line,* May 1, 2006. See http://www.islamonline.net/servlet/Satellite?c=Article_C&cid=1162385926736&pagename=Zone-English-Euro_Muslims%2FEMELayout.

The quote highlighting the 2004 Dutch parliamentary report is from Liz Fekete's "Anti-Muslim Racism and the European Security State, Race and Class," *Race and Class* 46.1 (2004), quoted in Cesari's article.

Eric L. Goldstein's quote is from his book *The Price of Whiteness: Jews, Race, and American Identity* (Princeton: Princeton University Press, 2006), 14.

The quotes on the alliance between the Left and Islam and Amir Taheri are from "Electing a New People: The Leftist-Islamic Alliance," *Dhimmi Watch,* May 30, 2006. See http://jihadwatch.org/dhimmiwatch/archives/011610.php.

Much of the information on first-generation Muslims is drawn from Amin Nasser's "Muslims Are Trying to Integrate," Islam-on-Line. See http://www.islamonline.net/servlet/Satellite?c=Article_C&cid=1165994195133&pagename=Zone-English-Euro_Muslims%2FEME Layout.

The information on French Muslims and Catholic schools is drawn from Katrin Bennhold's "French Muslims Find Haven in Catholic Schools," *New York Times*, September 30, 2008.

Tariq Ramadan's statements on integration are drawn from "Europe and Its Muslims: Building a Common Future," Lectures in Japan by Tariq Ramadan, July 12, 2007. See http://www.tariqramadan.com/spip.php?article1049 for more information.

The quote from Rod Parsley is from David Corn's "McCain's Spiritual Guide: Destroy Islam," *Mother Jones*, March 12, 2008.

The quote from Franklin Graham is from http://cbs11tv.com/watercooler/Franklin.Graham.Islam.2.265296.html.

The comments by Sheikh Omar Bakri Muhammad and Dyab Abu Jahjah are from David Pryce-Jones's "The Islamization of Europe?" *Commentary*, December 31, 2004.

Cardinal Jean-Louis Tauran's quote is from Tom Heneghan's "Muslim Return God to Europe, Catholic Prelate Says," *Reuters*, November 29, 2008.

The extract on the 2006 rioting in Paris is from the International Crisis Group's "France and Its Muslims: Riots, Jihadism and Depoliticization," July 2, 2006. See http://www.islamonline.net/servlet/Satellite?c=Article_C&cid=1162385923118&pagename=Zone-English-Euro_Muslims%2FEMELayout.

The extract by the UK Muslim convert is from Shaikh Abdal-Hakim Murad's "Tradition or Extradition," Islam Online. See http://www.islamonline.net/servlet/Satellite?c=Article_C&cid=1158658504101&pagename=Zone-English-Living_Shariah%2FLSELayout.

The question-and-response extract can be found at http://www.islamonline.net/servlet/Satellite?cid=1213871143613&pagename=IslamOnline-English-Ask_Scholar%2FFatwaE%2FFatwaEAskTheScholar.

The quote by William Dalrymple can be found in *Emel*, November 2007, 27.

Chapter Ten: Islam and India

Stephen P. Cohen's quote is from his *India: Emerging Power* (Washington, DC: Brookings, 2001), 11–12.

The al-Biruni quote on Hinduism and monotheism is from W. Montgomery Watt's article "Biruni and the Study of Non-Islamic Religions," http://www.fravahr.org/spip.php?article31.

Saeed Naqvi's *Reflections of an Indian Muslim* (New Delhi: Har-Anand Publications, 1993), 23–27, was a great resource in researching Indian Muslims.

Sunil Khilnani's *The Idea of India* (New York: Farrar, Straus & Giroux, 1997), 161–165, informed my sections on partition.

Information on the Gujarat anti-Muslim riots was drawn from Luke Harding's "Gujarat's Muslim Heritage Smashed in Riots," *The Guardian,* June 29, 2002.

The Library of Congress country study on India is James Heitzman and Robert L. Worden's *India: A Country Study* (Washington: Government Printing Office for the Library of Congress, 1995).

The extract on the likelihood of Indian Muslims' being the victims of violence and various statistics on the discrepancies between Hindus and Muslims are from Alex Perry's "India's Great Divide," *Time,* August 4, 2003.

Chapter Eleven: Islam and China

Basic volumes on Muslims and Islam in China include:

Michael Dillon, *China's Muslim Hui Community, Migration, Settlement and Sects* (Richmond, Surrey, UK: Curzon Press, 1999).

Dru C. Gladney, *Dislocating China: Muslims, Minorities, and Other Subaltern Subjects* (Chicago: University of Chicago Press, 2004).

Jonathan N. Lipman, *Familiar Strangers: A History of Muslims in Northwest China* (Seattle: University of Washington Press, 1997).

James A. Millward, *Eurasian Crossroads: A History of Xinjiang* (London: C. Hurst, 2007).

S. Frederick Starr, ed., *Xinjiang: China's Muslim Borderland* (London: M. E. Sharpe, 2004).

Some of the information on the Hui, including the quote on their lack of common language, common territory, and common economic life, is from "Jonathan Lipman on Chinese Muslims," on Wang Daiyu's *Islam in China* website, November 4, 2007. See http://islaminchina.wordpress.com/2007/11/04/jonathan-lipman-on-chinese-muslims/.

The section on Zheng He is informed by Richard Gunde's "Zheng He's Voyages of Discovery," UCLA International Institute, April 20, 2004. See http://www.international.ucla.edu/article.asp?parentid =10387, and Jonathan N. Lipman's *Familiar Strangers: A History of Muslims in Northwest China* (Seattle: University of Washington Press, 1997), 43.

The extract on the influence of Confucianism on Chinese Islam is from Jonathan N. Lipman's *Familiar Strangers: A History of Muslims in Northwest China* (Seattle: University of Washington Press, 1997), 72. Quoting from Feng Jinyuan, *Cong Zhongguo*, 280.

The biographical information on Yusuf Ma Dexin is from the Wikipedia article of the same name.

The quote about the desire of Islamic scholars to make Islam "comprehensible, moral and effective" is from Jonathan N. Lipman's *Familiar Strangers: A History of Muslims in Northwest China* (Seattle: University of Washington Press, 1997), 211.

The text of Ibrahim Anwar's 1995 speech can be seen at http://ikdasar.tripod.com/anwar/95-08.htm.

Chapter Twelve: Colonialism, Nationalism, Islam, and the Independence Struggle

A few of the early paragraphs of this chapter are borrowed from my earlier work: Graham E. Fuller, *The Future of Political Islam* (New York: Palgrave, 2003), 5–7.

The section on environmental changes is drawn from Jared Diamond's *Guns, Germs and Steel: The Fate of Nations* (New York: Norton, 1997), 409–411, and Jeffrey Sachs's "Islam's Geopolitics as a Morality Tale," *The Financial Times*, October 28, 2001.

The Joseph Stiglitz extract is from "Wall Street's Toxic Message," *Vanity Fair*, July 2009.

Chapter Thirteen: War, Resistance, *Jihad,* and Terrorism

The Robert Kaplan quote is from his article "The Coming Anarchy," *The Atlantic*, February 1994.

The section on just war is informed by Garry Wills, "What Is a Just War?" a book review of Michael Walzer's *Arguing about War* in *The New York Review of Books* 51, no. 18 (November 18, 2004).

The section on rules of conduct in war is informed by John L. Esposito, "Jihad: Holy or Unholy War," in *Understanding Jihad, Deconstructing Jihadism,* Esposito and Glenn, eds. (Washington, DC: Center for Muslim-Christian Understanding, 2007).

Robert Fisk's interview with Usama bin Ladin can be read at http://www.robert-fisk.com/fisk_interview3.htm.

The Islamic Research Academy's statement is here: http://www.islamonline.net/servlet/Satellite?pagename=IslamOnline-English-Ask_Scholar/FatwaE/FatwaE&cid=1119503546644.

The *fatwa* of the twenty-six Saudi scholars is here: http://www.globalterroralert.com/saudifatwairaq.pdf.

Some of the statistics on suicide bombings are from Robin Wright's "Since 2001, a Dramatic Increase in Suicide Bombings," *Washington Post,* April 18, 2008.

Chapter Fourteen: What to Do?

The Department of Defense's definition of "terrorism" comes from Department of Defense Dictionary of Military Terms as amended 17 March 2009, http://www.dtic.mil/doctrine/jel/doddict/data/t/7591.html. The italics are mine.

Walzer's quote is from Garry Wills, "What Is a Just War?" a book review of Michael Walzer's *Arguing about War* in *The New York Review of Books* 51, no. 18 (November 18, 2004).

Seth G. Jones, Martin C. Libicki, *How Terrorist Groups End,* RAND Report (Santa Monica, 2006).

Index

Havana Declaration, 264
heresies: Arianism, 55–56; and Byzantine
Empire, 53, 116; Calvinism as, 126;
Docetism, 57; Ebionism, 56;
Eutychianism, 56–57; and evolution of
religion, 36; Marcionism, 53–54;
Monophysitism, 56, 80, 82–83;
Monotheletism, 57; and nature of Jesus,
30–31, 45–46, 48, 54–58, 62;
Pelagianism, 57; and political power,
23, 38–40, 46, 50, 57–58; and
Reformation, 137; and scripture, 49;
and state/religion affiliation, 38,
45–46, 50, 52; and Syrian Christianity,
80; as vehicle for local resistance, 92
Hijaz, 24
Hillenbrand, Carole, 114–15
Hinduism, 13–14, 22, 36, 39, 42, 211–28
Hindu nationalism, 42, 223
Hindu Tamils, 42
History of God (Armstrong), 35
Hizballah, 59, 293
Holland, 187, 198, 248
Holocaust, 33, 204, 265
Holy Lands: and Byzantine Empire, 68; and
Crusades, 95, 98–99, 102–03, 107, 109,
112, 123; and Eastern Orthodoxy, 74;
and Russia, 172
Holy Roman Empire, 68
"How Terrorist Groups End" (RAND),
294–95
Hui Chinese, 229, 231–34, 236
Huntington, Samuel, 13, 61, 84, 139, 141–42
Hussein, Saddam, 276

Ibrahim, Anwar, 236
iconoclasm, 72
identity: and culture, 66, 68; and ethnicity,
89, 143, 171, 182, 238, 289; Iraqi, 258;
Jewish, 194, 258; and multiculturalism,
189, 209; multiple identifications, 199,
257–58; Pakistani, 228; and religion,
37, 63, 75, 171, 257–58; Russian, 153,
158–59, 166–67, 169, 171, 175–77,
183–84; Sunni, 258; Uyghur, 238. *See
also* Muslim identity
immigration, 172, 189–95, 191, 197–99
imperialism: American, 252; and anti-
Americanism, 145, 156; British, 173,
180, 220–21, 228, 248, 253, 255; and
Crusades, 115; and Eurasianism, 184;
European, 180, 248, 255; and Islamists,

257; Japanese, 269; legacy of, 260–62;
Middle East struggles with, 14; Muslim
opposition to, 257, 266; Muslim support
enlisted for, 172–73, 178; neo-
imperialism, 184, 243, 252–53, 255, 259,
264, 267; and Ottoman Empire, 152–53;
and Palestinian problem, 302; and
political violence, 289–90; and religion
versus ethnicity, 256; and Russia, 164,
168–69, 178–81, 183; Western, 156, 164,
178–81, 183, 243, 248, 252–53, 255, 264,
303. *See also* colonialism
inclusivity, 43–44
India: and Afghanistan, 214, 223, 228; and
Alexander the Great, 63; and anti-
Westernism, 146; and Britain, 178,
211–12, 218, 220–22, 228, 255, 275; and
Buddhism, 22; Hindu-Islam
relationship, 13–14, 211–28; and
Pakistan, 211–12, 218, 221–23, 225, 228;
and violence, 42, 221, 223–24, 226–27
Innocent III, Pope, 104, 105–06
Innocent IV, Pope, 156
insurgency, 288, 290, 292, 295
International Crisis Group, 205–06
International Monetary Fund, 262
International Seminar on Islam and
Confucianism, 236
Iran, 41, 59, 63, 79, 93, 122, 133, 186
Iraq: and Alexandria, 63; and divided ethnic
groups, 289; and independence, 255;
and nationalism, 263, 299; and
radicalization, 295; and revolution, 253;
and Syria, 79; and terrorist insurgency,
295; US war on, 187–88, 256, 258, 263,
273, 276–80, 283, 285, 291–93
Irene, Empress, 67–68
Islam: as Abrahamic faith, 21–22; alliance
with the Left, 195–96; and American
Muslim social responsibilities, 207–08;
American version of, 300; and anti-
imperialism/colonialism, 243–44,
250–51, 256, 257, 266, 280; and anti-
Westernism, 30, 59–60, 62, 75–76, 93,
94, 143–46; and Buddhism, 234; and
caste system, 218–19; as cause of
East-West confrontations, 4–5, 7–8,
10–11, 300; characterized as infidels,
95, 97–98, 108, 110, 142; and China,
229–36, 238–39; and Christian
heresies, 48, 53; and clerical influence
on radicalism, 284–85; and compulsion